# THE "SUMMA THEOLOGICA"

# THE
# "SUMMA THEOLOGICA"

OF

# ST. THOMAS AQUINAS

PART II.

(*SECOND PART*)

LITERALLY TRANSLATED BY

## FATHERS OF THE ENGLISH DOMINICAN PROVINCE

SECOND NUMBER

(QQ. XLVII.—LXXIX.)

LONDON

BURNS OATES & WASHBOURNE LTD.

PUBLISHERS TO THE HOLY SEE

1929

Nihil Obstat.

FR. INNOCENTIUS APAP, O.P., S.T.M.,
CENSOR THEOL.

Imprimatur.

EDUS. CANONICUS SURMONT,
VICARIUS GENERALIS.

WESTMONASTERII.

---

APPROBATIO ORDINIS.

Nihil Obstat.

FR. VINCENTIUS McNABB, O.P., S.T.M.
FR. ÆLREDUS WHITACRE, O.P., S.T.L.

Re-Imprimatur.

FR. BEDA JARRETT, O.P., S.T.L., M.A.
PRIOR PROVINCIALIS ANGLIÆ.

LONDINI,
die 28 Maii, 1929.

*Made and Printed in Great Britain*

# CONTENTS

## TREATISE ON PRUDENCE AND JUSTICE

### PRUDENCE

#### 1. PRUDENCE AND ITS PARTS

#### 2. THE VICES OPPOSED TO PRUDENCE

### JUSTICE

#### 1. JUSTICE IN ITSELF

# CONTENTS

# THE "SUMMA THEOLOGICA"

## SECOND PART OF THE SECOND PART.

### QUESTION XLVII.

### OF PRUDENCE, CONSIDERED IN ITSELF.

*(In Sixteen Articles.)*

AFTER treating of the theological virtues, we must in due sequence consider the cardinal virtues. In the first place we shall consider prudence in itself; secondly, its parts; thirdly, the corresponding gift; fourthly, the contrary vices; fifthly, the precepts concerning prudence.

Under the first head there are sixteen points of inquiry: (1) Whether prudence is in the will or in the reason? (2) If in the reason, whether it is only in the practical, or also in the speculative reason? (3) Whether it takes cognizance of singulars? (4) Whether it is a virtue? (5) Whether it is a special virtue? (6) Whether it appoints the end to the moral virtues? (7) Whether it fixes the mean in the moral virtues? (8) Whether its proper act is command? (9) Whether solicitude or watchfulness belongs to prudence? (10) Whether prudence extends to the governing of many? (11) Whether the prudence which regards private good is the same in species as that which regards the common good? (12) Whether prudence is in subjects, or only in their rulers? (13) Whether prudence is in the wicked? (14) Whether prudence is in all good men? (15) Whether prudence is in us naturally? (16) Whether prudence is lost by forgetfulness?

## FIRST ARTICLE.

### WHETHER PRUDENCE IS IN THE COGNITIVE OR IN THE APPETITIVE FACULTY?

*We proceed thus to the First Article :—*

*Objection* 1. It would seem that prudence is not in the cognitive but in the appetitive faculty. For Augustine says (*De Morib. Eccl.* xv.): *Prudence is love choosing wisely between the things that help and those that hinder.* Now love is not in the cognitive, but in the appetitive faculty. Therefore prudence is in the appetitive faculty.

*Obj.* 2. Further, As appears from the foregoing definition it belongs to prudence *to choose wisely.* But choice is an act of the appetitive faculty, as stated above (I.-II., Q. XIII., A. 1). Therefore prudence is not in the cognitive but in the appetitive faculty.

*Obj.* 3. Further, The Philosopher says (*Ethic.* vi. 5) that *in art it is better to err voluntarily than involuntarily, whereas in the case of prudence, as of the virtues, it is worse.* Now the moral virtues, of which he is treating there, are in the appetitive faculty, whereas art is in the reason. Therefore prudence is in the appetitive rather than in the rational faculty.

*On the contrary,* Augustine says (*QQ. LXXXIII., qu.* 61): *Prudence is the knowledge of what to seek and what to avoid.*

*I answer that,* As Isidore says (*Etym.* x.): *A prudent man is one who sees as it were from afar, for his sight is keen, and he foresees the event of uncertainties.* Now sight belongs not to the appetitive but to the cognitive faculty. Wherefore it is manifest that prudence belongs directly to the cognitive, and not to the sensitive faculty, because by the latter we know nothing but what is within reach and offers itself to the senses: while to obtain knowledge of the future from knowledge of the present or past, which pertains to prudence, belongs properly to the reason, because this is done by a process of comparison. It follows therefore that prudence, properly speaking, is in the reason.

*Reply Obj.* 1. As stated above (P.I., Q. LXXXII., A. 4) the will moves all the faculties to their acts. Now the first act of the appetitive faculty is love, as stated above (I.-II., Q. XXV., AA. 1, 2). Accordingly prudence is said to be love, not indeed essentially, but in so far as love moves to the act of prudence. Wherefore Augustine goes on to say that *prudence is love discerning aright that which helps from that which hinders us in tending to God.* Now love is said to discern because it moves the reason to discern.

*Reply Obj.* 2. The prudent man considers things afar off, in so far as they tend to be a help or a hindrance to that which has to be done at the present time. Hence it is clear that those things which prudence considers stand in relation to this other, as in relation to the end. Now of those things that are directed to the end there is counsel in the reason, and choice in the appetite, of which two, counsel belongs more properly to prudence, since the Philosopher states (*Ethic.* vi. 5, 7, 9) that a prudent man *takes good counsel.* But as choice presupposes counsel, since it is *the desire for what has been already counselled (Ethic.* iii. 2), it follows that choice can also be ascribed to prudence indirectly, in so far, to wit, as prudence directs the choice by means of counsel.

*Reply Obj.* 3. The worth of prudence consists not in thought merely, but in its application to action, which is the end of the practical reason. Wherefore if any defect occur in this, it is most contrary to prudence, since, the end being of most import in everything, it follows that a defect which touches the end is the worst of all. Hence the Philosopher goes on to say (*ibid.*) that prudence *is something more than a merely rational habit,* such as art is, since, as stated above (I.-II., Q. LVII., A. 4) it includes application to action, which application is an act of the will.

## Second Article.

### WHETHER PRUDENCE BELONGS TO THE PRACTICAL REASON ALONE, OR ALSO TO THE SPECULATIVE REASON ?

*We proceed thus to the Second Article :—*

*Objection* 1. It would seem that prudence belongs not only to the practical, but also to the speculative reason. For it is written (Prov. x. 23): *Wisdom is prudence to a man.* Now wisdom consists chiefly in contemplation. Therefore prudence does also.

*Obj.* 2. Further, Ambrose says (*De Offic.* i. 24): *Prudence is concerned with the quest of truth, and fills us with the desire of fuller knowledge.* Now this belongs to the speculative reason. Therefore prudence resides also in the speculative reason.

*Obj.* 3. Further, The Philosopher assigns art and prudence to the same part of the soul (*Ethic.* vi. 1). Now art may be not only practical but also speculative, as in the case of the liberal arts. Therefore prudence also is both practical and speculative.

*On the contrary,* The Philosopher says (*Ethic.* vi. 5) that prudence is right reason applied to action. Now this belongs to none but the practical reason. Therefore prudence is in the practical reason only.

*I answer that,* According to the Philosopher (*Ethic.* vi. 5) *a prudent man is one who is capable of taking good counsel.* Now counsel is about things that we have to do in relation to some end: and the reason that deals with things to be done for an end is the practical reason. Hence it is evident that prudence resides only in the practical reason.

*Reply Obj.* 1. As stated above (Q. XLV., AA. 1, 3), wisdom considers the absolutely highest cause: so that the consideration of the highest cause in any particular genus belongs to wisdom in that genus. Now in the genus of human acts the highest cause is the common end of all human life, and it is this end that prudence intends. For the Philosopher says (*Ethic.* vi. 5) that just as he who reasons well for the realization of a particular end, such as victory, is said to be prudent, not absolutely, but in a particular genus, namely warfare, so he that reasons well with regard to right conduct as a whole, is said to be prudent absolutely. Wherefore it is clear that prudence is wisdom about human affairs: but not wisdom absolutely, because it is not about the absolutely highest cause, for it is about human good, and this is not the best thing of all. And so it is stated significantly that *prudence is wisdom for man*, but not wisdom absolutely.

*Reply Obj.* 2. Ambrose, and Tully also (*De Invent.* ii. 53) take the word prudence in a broad sense for any human knowledge, whether speculative or practical. And yet it may also be replied that the act itself of the speculative reason, in so far as it is voluntary, is a matter of choice and counsel as to its exercise; and consequently comes under the direction of prudence. On the other hand, as regards its specification in relation to its object which is the *necessary true*, it comes under neither counsel nor prudence.

*Reply Obj.* 3. Every application of right reason in the work of production belongs to art: but to prudence belongs only the application of right reason in matters of counsel, which are those wherein there is no fixed way of obtaining the end, as stated in *Ethic.* iii. 3. Since then, the speculative reason makes things such as syllogisms, propositions and the like, wherein the process follows certain and fixed rules, consequently in respect of such things it is possible to have the essentials of art, but not of prudence; and so we find such a thing as a speculative art, but not a speculative prudence.

### Third Article.

#### WHETHER PRUDENCE TAKES COGNIZANCE OF SINGULARS ?

*We proceed thus to the Third Article :—*

*Objection* 1. It would seem that prudence does not take cognizance of singulars. For prudence is in the reason, as stated above (AA. 1, 2). But *reason deals with universals,* according to *Phys.* i. 5. Therefore prudence does not take cognizance except of universals.

*Obj.* 2. Further, Singulars are infinite in number. But the reason cannot comprehend an infinite number of things. Therefore prudence which is right reason, is not about singulars.

*Obj.* 3. Further, Particulars are known by the senses. But prudence is not in a sense, for many persons who have keen outward senses are devoid of prudence. Therefore prudence does not take cognizance of singulars.

*On the contrary,* The Philosopher says (*Ethic.* vi. 7) that *prudence does not deal with universals only, but needs to take cognizance of singulars also.*

*I answer that,* As stated above (A. 1, *ad* 3), to prudence belongs not only the consideration of the reason, but also the application to action, which is the end of the practical reason. But no man can conveniently apply one thing to another, unless he knows both the thing to be applied, and the thing to which it has to be applied. Now actions are in singular matters: and so it is necessary for the prudent man to know both the universal principles of reason, and the singulars about which actions are concerned.

*Reply Obj.* 1. Reason first and chiefly is concerned with universals, and yet it is able to apply universal rules to particular cases: hence the conclusions of syllogisms are not only universal, but also particular, because the intellect by a kind of reflexion extends to matter, as stated in *De Amina* iii.

*Reply Obj.* 2. It is because the infinite number of singulars cannot be comprehended by human reason, that *our counsels are uncertain* (Wis. ix. 14). Nevertheless experience reduces the infinity of singulars to a certain finite number which occur as a general rule, and the knowledge of these suffices for human prudence.

*Reply Obj.* 3. As the Philosopher says (*Ethic.* vi. 8), prudence does not reside in the external senses whereby we know sensible objects, but in the interior sense, which is perfected by memory and experience so as to judge promptly of particular cases. This does not mean however that prudence is in the interior sense as in its principle subject, for it is chiefly in the reason, yet by a kind of application it extends to this sense.

## FOURTH ARTICLE.
### WHETHER PRUDENCE IS A VIRTUE ?

*We proceed thus to the Fourth Article :—*

*Objection* 1. It would seem that prudence is not a virtue. For Augustine says (*De Lib. Arb.* i. 13) that *prudence is the science of what to desire and what to avoid.* Now science is condivided with virtue, as appears in the *Predicaments* (vi.). Therefore prudence is not a virtue.

*Obj.* 2. Further, There is no virtue of a virtue: but *there is a virtue of art,* as the Philosopher states (*Ethic.* vi. 5): wherefore art is not a virtue. Now there is prudence in art, for it is written (2 Paralip. ii. 14) concerning Hiram, that he knew *to grave all sort of graving, and to devise ingeniously (prudenter) all that there may be need of in the work.* Therefore prudence is not a virtue.

*Obj.* 3. Further, No virtue can be immoderate. But prudence is immoderate, else it would be useless to say (Prov. xxiii. 4): *Set bounds to thy prudence.* Therefore prudence is not a virtue.

*On the contrary,* Gregory states (*Moral.* ii. 49) that prudence, temperance, fortitude and justice are four virtues.

*I answer that,* As stated above (I.-II., Q. LV., A. 3: Q. LVI., A. 1) when we were treating of virtues in general, *virtue is that which makes its possessor good, and his work good likewise.* Now good may be understood in a twofold sense: first, materially, for the thing that is good, secondly, formally, under the aspect of good. Good, under the aspect of good, is the object of the appetitive power. Hence if any habits rectify the consideration of reason, without regarding the rectitude of the appetite, they have less of the nature of a virtue, since they direct man to good materially, that is to say, to the thing which is good, but without considering it under the aspect of good. On the other hand those virtues which regard the rectitude of the appetite, have more of the nature of virtue, because they consider the good not only materially, but also formally, in other words, they consider that which is good under the aspect of good.

Now it belongs to prudence, as stated above (A. 1, *ad* 3, A. 3) to apply right reason to action, and this is not done without a right appetite. Hence prudence has the nature of virtue not only as the other intellectual virtues have it, but also as the moral virtues have it, among which virtues it is enumerated.

*Reply Obj.* 1. Augustine there takes science in the broad sense for any kind of right reason.

*Reply Obj.* 2. The Philosopher says that there is a virtue of art, because art does not require rectitude of the appetite; wherefore in order that a man may make right use of his art, he needs to have a virtue which will rectify his appetite. Prudence however has nothing to do with the matter of art, because art is both directed to a particular end, and has fixed means of obtaining that end. And yet, by a kind of comparison, a man may be said to act prudently in matters of art. Moreover in certain arts, on account of the uncertainty of the means for obtaining the end, there is need for counsel, as for instance in the arts of medicine and navigation, as stated in *Ethic.* iii. 3.

*Reply Obj.* 3. This saying of the wise man does not mean that prudence itself should be moderate, but that moderation must be imposed on other things according to prudence.

## FIFTH ARTICLE.
### WHETHER PRUDENCE IS A SPECIAL VIRTUE ?

*We proceed thus to the Fifth Article:*—

*Objection* 1. It would seem that prudence is not a special virtue. For no special virtue is included in the definition of virtue in general, since virtue is defined (*Ethic.* ii. 6) *an elective habit that follows a mean appointed by reason in relation to ourselves, even as a wise man decides.* Now right reason is reason in accordance with prudence, as stated in *Ethic.* **vi.** 13. Therefore prudence is not a special virtue.

*Obj.* 2. Further, The Philosopher says (*Ethic.* vi. 13) that *the effect of moral virtue is right action as regards the end, and that of prudence, right action as regards the means.* Now in every virtue certain things have to be done as means to the end. Therefore prudence is in every virtue, and consequently is not a special virtue.

*Obj.* 3. Further, A special virtue has a special object. But prudence has not a special object, for it is right reason *applied to action* (*Ethic.* vi. 5); and all works of virtue are actions. Therefore prudence is not a special virtue.

*On the contrary,* It is distinct from and numbered among the other virtues, for it is written (Wis. viii. 7): *She teacheth temperance and prudence, justice and fortitude.*

*I answer that,* Since acts and habits take their species from their objects, as shown above (I.-II., Q. I., A. 3: Q. XVIII., A. 2: Q. LIV., A. 2), any habit that has a corresponding special object, distinct from other objects, must needs be a special habit, and if it be a good habit, it must be a special virtue. Now an object is called special, not merely according to the consideration of its matter, but rather according to its formal aspect, as explained above (I.-II., Q. LIV., A. 2, *ad* 1). Because one and the same thing is the subject matter of the acts of different habits, and also of different powers, according to its different formal aspects. Now a yet greater difference of object is requisite for a difference of powers than for a difference of habits, since several habits are found in the same power, as stated above (I.-II., Q. LIV., A. 1). Consequently any difference in the aspect of an object, that requires a difference of powers, will *a fortiori* require a difference of habits.

Accordingly we must say that since prudence is in the reason, as stated above (A. 2), it is differentiated from the other intellectual virtues by a material difference of objects. *Wisdom, knowledge* and *understanding* are about necessary things, whereas *art* and *prudence* are about contingent things, art being concerned with *things made*, that is, with things produced in external matter, such as a house, a knife and so forth; and prudence, being concerned with *things done*, that is, with things that have their being in the doer himself, as stated above (I.-II., Q. LVII., A. 4). On the other hand prudence is differentiated from the moral virtues according to a formal aspect distinctive of powers, *i.e.*, the intellective power, wherein is prudence, and the appetitive power, wherein is moral virtue. Hence it is evident that prudence is a special virtue, distinct from all other virtues.

*Reply Obj.* 1. This is not a definition of virtue in general, but of moral virtue, the definition of which fittingly includes an intellectual virtue, viz. prudence, which has the same matter in common with moral virtue; because, just as the subject of moral virtue is something that partakes of reason, so moral virtue has the aspect of virtue, in so far as it partakes of intellectual virtue.

*Reply Obj.* 2. This argument proves that prudence helps all the virtues, and works in all of them; but this does not suffice to prove that it is not a special virtue; for nothing prevents a certain genus from containing a species which is operative in every other species of that same genus, even as the sun has an influence over all bodies.

*Reply Obj.* 3. Things done are indeed the matter of prudence, in so far as they are the object of reason, that is, considered as true: but they are the matter of the moral virtues, in so far as they are the object of the appetitive power, that is, considered as good.

## SIXTH ARTICLE.

### WHETHER PRUDENCE APPOINTS THE END TO MORAL VIRTUES ?

*We proceed thus to the Sixth Article :—*

*Objection* 1. It would seem that prudence appoints the end to moral virtues. Since prudence is in the reason, while moral virtue is in the appetite, it seems that prudence stands in relation to moral virtue, as reason to the appetite. Now reason appoints the end to the appetitive power. Therefore prudence appoints the end to the moral virtues.

*Obj.* 2. Further, Man surpasses irrational beings by his reason, but he has other things in common with them. Accordingly the other parts of man are in relation to his reason, what man is in relation to irrational creatures. Now man is the end of irrational creatures, according to *Polit.* i. 3. Therefore all the other parts of man are directed to reason as to their end. But prudence is *right reason applied to action*, as stated above (A. 2). Therefore all actions are directed to prudence as their end. Therefore prudence appoints the end to all moral virtues.

*Obj.* 3. Further, It belongs to the virtue, art, or power that is concerned about the end, to command the virtues or arts that are concerned about the means. Now prudence disposes of the other moral virtues, and commands them. Therefore it appoints their end to them.

*On the contrary,* The Philosopher says (*Ethic.* vi. 12) that *moral virtue ensures the rectitude of the intention of the end, while prudence ensures the rectitude of the means.* Therefore it does not belong to prudence to appoint the end to moral virtues, but only to regulate the means.

*I answer that,* The end of moral virtues is human good. Now the good of the human soul is to be in accord with reason, as Dionysius declares (*Div. Nom.* iv.). Wherefore the ends of moral virtue must of necessity pre-exist in the reason.

Now, just as, in the speculative reason, there are certain things naturally known, about which is *understanding*, and certain things of which we obtain knowledge through them, viz., conclusions, about which is *science*, so in the practical reason, certain things pre-exist, as naturally known principles, and such are the ends of the moral virtues, since the end is in practical matters what principles are in speculative matters, as stated above (Q. XXIII., A. 7, *ad* 2: I.-II., Q. XIII., A. 3); while certain things are in the practical reason by way of conclusions, and such are the means

which we gather from the ends themselves. About these
is prudence, which applies universal principles to the
particular conclusions of practical matters. Consequently
it does not belong to prudence to appoint the end to moral
virtues, but only to regulate the means.

*Reply Obj*. 1. Natural reason known by the name of
*synderesis* appoints the end to moral virtues, as stated above
(P. I., Q. LXXIX., A. 12): but prudence does not do this
for the reason given above.

This suffices for the *Reply* to the *Second Objection*.

*Reply Obj*. 3. The end concerns the moral virtues, not
as though they appointed the end, but because they tend
to the end which is appointed by natural reason. In this
they are helped by prudence, which prepares the way
for them, by disposing the means. Hence it follows that
prudence is more excellent than the moral virtues, and
moves them: yet *synderesis* moves prudence, just as the
understanding of principles moves science.

### Seventh Article.

#### WHETHER IT BELONGS TO PRUDENCE TO FIND THE MEAN IN MORAL VIRTUES?

*We proceed thus to the Seventh Article:—*

*Objection* 1. It would seem that it does not belong to
prudence to find the mean in moral virtues. For the achieve-
ment of the mean is the end of moral virtues. But prudence
does not appoint the end to moral virtues, as shown above
(A. 6). Therefore it does not find the mean in them.

*Obj*. 2. Further, That which of itself has being, would
seem to have no cause, but its very being is its cause, since
a thing is said to have being by reason of its cause. Now
*to follow the mean* belongs to moral virtue by reason of itself,
as part of its definition, as shown above (A. 5, *obj*. 1). Therefore prudence does not cause the mean in moral virtues.

*Obj*. 3. Further, Prudence works after the manner of
reason. But moral virtue tends to the mean after the
manner of nature, because, as Tully states (*De Invent*.

*Rhet.* ii. 53), *virtue is a habit like a second nature in accord with reason.* Therefore prudence does not appoint the mean to moral virtues.

*On the contrary*, In the foregoing definition of moral virtue (A. 5, *obj.* 1) it is stated that it *follows a mean appointed by reason . . . even as a wise man decides.*

*I answer that*, The proper end of each moral virtue consists precisely in conformity with right reason. For temperance intends that man should not stray from reason for the sake of his concupiscences; fortitude, that he should not stray from the right judgment of reason through fear or daring. Moreover this end is appointed to man according to natural reason, since natural reason dictates to each one that he should act according to reason.

But it belongs to the ruling of prudence to decide in what manner and by what means man shall obtain the mean of reason in his deeds. For though the attainment of the mean is the end of a moral virtue, yet this mean is found by the right disposition of these things that are directed to the end.

This suffices for the *Reply* to the *First Objection*.

*Reply Obj.* 2. Just as a natural agent makes form to be in matter, yet does not make that which is essential to the form to belong to it, so too, prudence appoints the mean in passions and operations, and yet does not make the searching of the mean to belong to virtue.

*Reply Obj.* 3. Moral virtue after the manner of nature intends to attain the mean. Since, however, the mean as such is not found in all matters after the same manner, it follows that the inclination of nature which ever works in the same manner, does not suffice for this purpose, and so the ruling of prudence is required.

## EIGHTH ARTICLE.

### WHETHER COMMAND IS THE CHIEF ACT OF PRUDENCE ?

*We proceed thus to the Eighth Article:—*

*Objection* 1. It would seem that command is not the chief act of prudence. For command regards the good to be ensued.   Now Augustine (*De Trin.* xiv. 9) states that it is an act of prudence *to avoid ambushes*.   Therefore command is not the chief act of prudence.

*Obj.* 2. Further, The Philosopher says (*Ethic.* vi. 5) that *the prudent man takes good counsel*.   Now *to take counsel* and *to command* seem to be different acts, as appears from what has been said above (I.-II., Q. LVII., A. 6).   Therefore command is not the chief act of prudence.

*Obj.* 3. Further, It seems to belong to the will to command and to rule, since the will has the end for its object, and moves the other powers of the soul.   Now prudence is not in the will, but in the reason.   Therefore command is not an act of prudence.

*On the contrary*, The Philosopher says (*Ethic.* vi. 10) that *prudence commands*.

*I answer that*, Prudence is *right reason applied to action*, as stated above (A. 2).   Hence that which is the chief act of reason in regard to action must needs be the chief act of prudence.   Now there are three such acts.   The first is *to take counsel*, which belongs to discovery, for counsel is an act of inquiry, as stated above (I.-II., Q. XIV., A. 1). The second act is *to judge of what one has discovered*, and this is an act of the speculative reason.   But the practical reason, which is directed to action, goes further, and its third act is *to command*, which act consists in applying to action the things counselled and judged.   And since this act approaches nearer to the end of the practical reason, it follows that it is the chief act of the practical reason, and consequently of prudence.

In confirmation of this we find that the perfection of art consists in judging and not in commanding: wherefore he who sins voluntarily against his craft is reputed a better craftsman than he who does so involuntarily, because the former seems to do so from right judgment, and the latter from a defective judgment.   On the other hand it is the reverse in prudence, as stated in *Ethic.* vi. 5, for it is more imprudent to sin voluntarily,—since this is to be lacking in the chief act of prudence, viz. command,—than to sin involuntarily.

*Reply Obj.* 1. The act of command extends both to the ensuing of good and to the avoidance of evil. Nevertheless Augustine ascribes *the avoidance of ambushes* to prudence, not as its chief act, but as an act of prudence that does not continue in heaven.

*Reply Obj.* 2. Good counsel is required in order that the good things discovered may be applied to action: wherefore command belongs to prudence which takes good counsel.

*Reply Obj.* 3. Simply to move belongs to the will; but command denotes motion together with a kind of ordering, wherefore it is an act of the reason, as stated above (I.-II., Q. XVII., A. 1).

## NINTH ARTICLE.

### WHETHER SOLICITUDE BELONGS TO PRUDENCE?

*We proceed thus to the Ninth Article:—*

*Objection* 1. It would seem that solicitude does not belong to prudence. For solicitude implies disquiet, wherefore Isidore says (*Etym.* x.) that *a solicitous man is a restless man.* Now motion belongs chiefly to the appetitive power: wherefore solicitude does also. But prudence is not in the appetitive power, but in the reason, as stated above (A. 1). Therefore solicitude does not belong to prudence.

*Obj.* 2. Further, The certainty of truth seems opposed to solicitude, wherefore it is related (1 Kings ix. 20) that Samuel said to Saul: *As for the asses which were lost three days ago, be not solicitous, because they are found.* Now the certainty of truth belongs to prudence, since it is an intellectual virtue. Therefore solicitude is in opposition to prudence rather than belonging to it.

*Obj.* 3. Further, The Philosopher says (*Ethic.* iv. 3) the *magnanimous man is slow and leisurely.* Now slowness is contrary to solicitude. Since then prudence is not opposed to magnanimity, for *good is not opposed to good,* as stated in the *Predicaments* (viii.), it would seem that solicitude does not belong to prudence.

*On the contrary*, It is written (1 Pet. iv. 7): *Be prudent. . . . and watch in prayers*. But watchfulness is the same as solicitude. Therefore solicitude belongs to prudence.

*I answer that*, According to Isidore (*Etym.* x.), a man is said to be solicitous through being shrewd (*solers*) and alert (*citus*), in so far as a man through a certain shrewdness of mind is on the alert to do whatever has to be done. Now this belongs to prudence, whose chief act is a command about what has been already counselled and judged in matters of action. Hence the Philosopher says (*Ethic.* vi. 9) that *one should be quick in carrying out the counsel taken, but slow in taking counsel*. Hence it is that solicitude belongs properly to prudence, and for this reason Augustine says (*De Morib. Eccl.* xxiv.) that *prudence keeps most careful watch and ward, lest by degrees we be deceived unawares by evil counsel*.

*Reply Obj*. 1. Movement belongs to the appetitive power as to the principle of movement, in accordance however, with the direction and command of reason, wherein solicitude consists.

*Reply Obj*. 2. According to the Philosopher (*Ethic.* i. 3), *equal certainty should not be sought in all things, but in each matter according to its proper mode*. And since the matter of prudence is the contingent singulars about which are human actions, the certainty of prudence cannot be so great as to be devoid of all solicitude.

*Reply Obj*. 3. The magnanimous man is said to be *slow and leisurely* not because he is solicitous about nothing, but because he is not over solicitous about many things, and is trustful in matters where he ought to have trust, and is not over solicitous about them: for over much fear and distrust are the cause of over solicitude, since fear makes us take counsel, as stated above (I.-II., Q. XLIV., A. 2) when we were treating of the passion of fear.

## TENTH ARTICLE.

### WHETHER PRUDENCE EXTENDS TO THE GOVERNING OF MANY?

*We proceed thus to the Tenth Article :—*

*Objection* 1. It would seem that prudence does not extend to the governing of many, but only to the government of oneself. For the Philosopher says (*Ethic.* v. 1) that virtue directed to the common good is justice. But prudence differs from justice. Therefore prudence is not directed to the common good.

*Obj.* 2. Further, He seems to be prudent, who seeks and does good for himself. Now those who seek the common good often neglect their own. Therefore they are not prudent.

*Obj.* 3. Further, Prudence is specifically distinct from temperance and fortitude. But temperance and fortitude seem to be related only to a man's own good. Therefore the same applies to prudence.

*On the contrary*, Our Lord said (Matth. xxiv. 45): *Who, thinkest thou, is a faithful and prudent* (Douay, *wise*) *servant whom his lord hath appointed over his family?*

*I answer that*, According to the Philosopher (*Ethic.* vi. 8) some have held that prudence does not extend to the common good, but only to the good of the individual, and this because they thought that man is not bound to seek other than his own good.

But this opinion is opposed to charity, which *seeketh not her own* (1 Cor. xiii. 5): wherefore the Apostle says of himself (*ibid.* x. 33): *Not seeking that which is profitable to myself, but to many, that they may be saved.* Moreover it is contrary to right reason, which judges the common good to be better than the good of the individual.

Accordingly, since it belongs to prudence rightly to counsel, judge, and command concerning the means of obtaining a due end, it is evident that prudence regards not only the private good of the individual, but also the common good of the multitude.

*Reply Obj.* 1. The Philosopher is speaking there of moral virtue. Now just as every moral virtue that is directed to the common good is called *legal* justice, so the prudence that is directed to the common good is called *political* prudence, for the latter stands in the same relation to legal justice, as prudence simply so called to moral virtue.

*Reply Obj.* 2. He that seeks the good of the many, seeks in consequence his own good, for two reasons. First, because the individual good is impossible without the common good of the family, state, or kingdom. Hence Valerius Maximus says* of the ancient Romans that *they would rather be poor in a rich empire than rich in a poor empire*. Secondly, because, since man is a part of the home and state, he must needs consider what is good for him by being prudent about the good of the many. For the good disposition of parts depends on their relation to the whole; thus Augustine says (*Conf.* iii. 8) that *any part which does not harmonize with its whole, is offensive.*

*Reply Obj.* 3. Even temperance and fortitude can be directed to the common good, hence there are precepts of law concerning them as stated in *Ethic.* v. 1: more so, however, prudence and justice, since these belong to the rational faculty which directly regards the universal, just as the sensitive part regards singulars.

### ELEVENTH ARTICLE.

#### WHETHER PRUDENCE ABOUT ONE'S OWN GOOD IS SPECIFICALLY THE SAME AS THAT WHICH EXTENDS TO THE COMMON GOOD ?

*We proceed thus to the Eleventh Article:—*

*Objection* 1. It seems that prudence about one's own good is the same specifically as that which extends to the common good. For the Philosopher says (*Ethic.* vi. 8) that *political prudence, and prudence are the same habit, yet their essence is not the same.*

* *Fact. et Dict. Memor.* iv. 6.

*Obj.* 2. Further, The Philosopher says (*Polit.* iii. 2) that *virtue is the same in a good man and in a good ruler.* Now political prudence is chiefly in the ruler, in whom it is architectonic, as it were. Since then prudence is a virtue of a good man, it seems that prudence and political prudence are the same habit.

*Obj.* 3. Further, A habit is not diversified in species or essence by things which are subordinate to one another. But the particular good, which belongs to prudence simply so called, is subordinate to the common good, which belongs to political prudence. Therefore prudence and political prudence differ neither specifically nor essentially.

*On the contrary, Political prudence,* which is directed to the common good of the state, *domestic economy* which is of such things as relate to the common good of the household or family, and ' *monastic* ' *economy* which is concerned with things affecting the good of one person, are all distinct sciences. Therefore in like manner there are different kinds of prudence, corresponding to the above differences of matter.

*I answer that,* As stated above (A. 5: Q. LIV., A. 2, *ad* 1), the species of habits differ according to the difference of object considered in its formal aspect. Now the formal aspect of all things directed to the end, is taken from the end itself, as shown above (I.-II., *Prolog.*: Q. CII., A. 1), wherefore the species of habits differ by their relation to different ends. Again the individual good, the good of the family, and the good of the city and kingdom are different ends. Wherefore there must needs be different species of prudence corresponding to these different ends, so that one is *prudence* simply so called, which is directed to one's own good, another, *domestic prudence* which is directed to the common good of the home, and a third, *political prudence,* which is directed to the common good of the state or kingdom.

*Reply Obj.* 1. The Philosopher means, not that political prudence is substantially the same habit as any kind of prudence, but that it is the same as the prudence which is directed to the common good. This is called *prudence* in respect of the common notion of prudence, *i.e.*, as being right reason applied to action, while it is called *political*, as being directed to the common good.

*Reply Obj.* 2. As the Philosopher declares (*ibid.*), *it belongs to a good man to be able to rule well and to obey well*, wherefore the virtue of a good man includes also that of a good ruler. Yet the virtue of the ruler and of the subject differ specifically, even as the virtue of a man and of a woman, as stated by the same authority (*ibid.*).

*Reply Obj.* 3. Even different ends, one of which is subordinate to the other, diversify the species of a habit; thus for instance, habits directed to riding, soldiering, and civic life, differ specifically although their ends are subordinate to one another. In like manner, though the good of the individual is subordinate to the good of the many, that does not prevent this difference from making the habits differ specifically; but it follows that the habit which is directed to the last end is above the other habits and commands them.

## TWELFTH ARTICLE.

### WHETHER PRUDENCE IS IN SUBJECTS, OR ONLY IN THEIR RULERS ?

*We proceed thus to the Twelfth Article:—*

*Objection* 1. It would seem that prudence is not in subjects but only in their rulers. For the Philosopher says (*Polit.* iii. 2) that *prudence alone is the virtue proper to a ruler, while other virtues are common to subjects and rulers, and the prudence of the subject is not a virtue but a true opinion*.

*Obj.* 2. Further, It is stated in *Polit.* i. 5 that *a slave is not competent to take counsel*. But prudence makes a man take good counsel (*Ethic.* vi. 5). Therefore prudence is not befitting slaves or subjects.

*Obj.* 3. Further, Prudence exercises command, as stated above (A. 8). But command is not in the competency of slaves or subjects but only of rulers. Therefore prudence is not in subjects but only in rulers.

*On the contrary*, The Philosopher says (*Ethic.* vi. 8) that there are two kinds of political prudence, one of which is *legislative* and belongs to rulers, while the other *retains the common name political*, and is about *individual actions*. Now it belongs also to subjects to perform these individual actions. Therefore prudence is not only in rulers but also in subjects.

*I answer that*, Prudence is in the reason. Now ruling and governing belong properly to the reason; and therefore it is proper to a man to reason and be prudent in so far as he has a share in ruling and governing. But it is evident that the subject as subject, and the slave as slave, are not competent to rule and govern, but rather to be ruled and governed. Therefore prudence is not the virtue of a slave as slave, nor of a subject as subject.

Since, however, every man, for as much as he is rational, has a share in ruling according to the judgment of reason, he is proportionately competent to have prudence. Wherefore it is manifest that prudence is in the ruler *after the manner of a mastercraft* (*Ethic.* vi. 8), but in the subjects, *after the manner of a handicraft*.

*Reply Obj.* 1. The saying of the Philosopher is to be understood strictly, namely, that prudence is not the virtue of a subject as such.

*Reply Obj.* 2. A slave is not capable of taking counsel, in so far as he is a slave (for thus he is the instrument of his master), but he does take counsel in so far as he is a rational animal.

*Reply Obj.* 3. By prudence a man commands not only others, but also himself, in so far as the reason is said to command the lower powers.

### THIRTEENTH ARTICLE.

#### WHETHER PRUDENCE CAN BE IN SINNERS?

*We proceed thus to the Thirteenth Article:—*

*Objection* 1. It would seem that there can be prudence in sinners. For our Lord said (Luke xvi. 8): *The children of this world are more prudent* (Douay, *wiser*) *in their genera-tion than the children of light.*  Now the children of this world are sinners.  Therefore there can be prudence in sinners.

*Obj.* 2. Further, Faith is a more excellent virtue than prudence.  But there can be faith in sinners.  Therefore there can be prudence also.

*Obj.* 3. Further, According to *Ethic.* vi. 7, *we say that to be of good counsel is the work of the prudent man especially.* Now many sinners can take good counsel.  Therefore sinners can have prudence.

*On the contrary,* The Philosopher declares (*Ethic.* vi. 12) that *it is impossible for a man to be prudent unless he be good.* Now no sinner is a good man.  Therefore no sinner is prudent.

*I answer that,* Prudence is threefold.  There is a false prudence, which takes its name from its likeness to true prudence.  For since a prudent man is one who disposes well of the things that have to be done for a good end, who-ever disposes well of such things as are fitting for an evil end, has false prudence, in so far as that which he takes for an end, is good, not in truth but in appearance.  Thus a man is called *a good robber*, and in this way we may speak of *a prudent robber*, by way of similarity, because he devises fitting ways of committing robbery.  This is the prudence of which the Apostle says (Rom. viii. 6): *The prudence* (Douay, *wisdom*) *of the flesh is death,* because, to wit, it places its ultimate end in the pleasures of the flesh.

The second prudence is indeed true prudence, because it devises fitting ways of obtaining a good end; and yet it is imperfect, from a twofold source.  First, because the good which it takes for an end, is not the common end of all human life, but of some particular affair; thus when a man devises fitting ways of conducting business or of sailing a ship, he is called a prudent business-man, or a prudent sailor:—secondly, because he fails in the chief act of pru-dence, as when a man takes counsel aright, and forms a good judgment, even about things concerning life as a whole, but fails to make an effective command.

The third prudence is both true and perfect, for it takes counsel, judges and commands aright in respect of the good end of man's whole life: and this alone is prudence simply so-called, and cannot be in sinners, whereas the first prudence is in sinners alone, while imperfect prudence is common to good and wicked men, especially that which is imperfect through being directed to a particular end, since that which is imperfect on account of a failing in the chief act, is only in the wicked.

*Reply Obj.* 1. This saying of our Lord is to be understood of the first prudence, wherefore it is not said that they are prudent absolutely, but that they are prudent *in their generation.*

*Reply Obj.* 2. The nature of faith consists not in conformity with the appetite for certain right actions, but in knowledge alone. On the other hand prudence implies a relation to a right appetite. First because its principles are the ends in matters of action; and of such ends one forms a right estimate through the habits of moral virtue, which rectify the appetite: wherefore without the moral virtues there is no prudence, as shown above (I.-II., Q. LVIII., A. 5); secondly because prudence commands right actions, which does not happen unless the appetite be right. Wherefore though faith on account of its object is more excellent than prudence, yet prudence, by its very nature, is more opposed to sin, which arises from a disorder of the appetite.

*Reply Obj.* 3. Sinners can take good counsel for an evil end, or for some particular good, but they do not perfectly take good counsel for the end of their whole life, since they do not carry that counsel into effect. Hence they lack prudence which is directed to the good only; and yet in them, according to the Philosopher (*Ethic.* vi. 12) there is *cleverness,**
*i.e.*, natural diligence which may be directed to both good and evil; or *cunning,*† which is directed only to evil, and which we have stated above, to be *false prudence* or *prudence of the flesh.*

* δεινότικη. † πανουργία.

## Fourteenth Article.

### WHETHER PRUDENCE IS IN ALL WHO HAVE GRACE?

*We proceed thus to the Fourteenth Article:—*

*Objection* 1. It would seem that prudence is not in all who have grace. Prudence requires diligence, that one may foresee aright what has to be done. But many who have grace have not this diligence. Therefore not all who have grace have prudence.

*Obj.* 2. Further, A prudent man is one who takes good counsel, as stated above (A. 8, *obj.* 2: A. 13, *obj.* 3). Yet many have grace who do not take good counsel, and need to be guided by the counsel of others. Therefore not all who have grace, have prudence.

*Obj.* 3. Further, The Philosopher says (*Top.* iii. 2) that *young people are not obviously prudent.* Yet many young people have grace. Therefore prudence is not to be found in all who have grace.

*On the contrary,* No man has grace unless he be virtuous. Now no man can be virtuous without prudence, for Gregory says (*Moral.* ii. 46) that *the other virtues cannot be virtues at all unless they effect prudently what they desire to accomplish.* Therefore all who have grace have prudence.

*I answer that,* The virtues must needs be connected together, so that whoever has one has all, as stated above (I.-II., Q. LXV., A. 1). Now whoever has grace has charity, so that he must needs have all the other virtues, and hence, since prudence is a virtue, as shown above (A. 4), he must, of necessity, have prudence also.

*Reply Obj.* 1. Diligence is twofold: one is merely sufficient with regard to things necessary for salvation; and such diligence is given to all who have grace, whom *His unction teacheth of all things* (1 Jo. ii. 27). There is also another diligence which is more than sufficient, whereby a man is able to make provision both for himself and for others, not only in matters necessary for salvation, but also in all things relating to human life; and such diligence as this is not in all who have grace.

*Reply Obj.* 2. Those who require to be guided by the counsel of others, are able, if they have grace, to take counsel for themselves in this point at least, that they require the counsel of others and can discern good from evil counsel.

*Reply Obj.* 3. Acquired prudence is caused by the exercise of acts, wherefore *its acquisition demands experience and time* (*Ethic.* ii. 1), hence it cannot be in the young, neither in habit nor in act. On the other hand gratuitous prudence is caused by divine infusion. Wherefore, in children who have been baptized but have not come to the use of reason, there is prudence as to habit but not as to act, even as in idiots; whereas in those who have come to the use of reason, it is also as to act, with regard to things necessary for salvation. This by practice merits increase, until it becomes perfect, even as the other virtues. Hence the Apostle says (Heb. v. 14) that *strong meat is for the perfect, for them who by custom have their senses exercised to the discerning of good and evil.*

### Fifteenth Article.

#### WHETHER PRUDENCE IS IN US BY NATURE?

*We proceed thus to the Fifteenth Article:—*

*Objection* 1. It would seem that prudence is in us by nature. The Philosopher says (*Ethic.* vi. 11) that things connected with prudence *seem to be natural*, namely *synesis*, *gnome** and the like, but not those which are connected with speculative wisdom. Now things belonging to the same genus have the same kind of origin. Therefore prudence also is in us from nature.

*Obj.* 2. Further, The changes of age are according to nature. Now prudence results from age, according to Job xii. 12: *In the ancient is wisdom, and in length of days prudence.* Therefore prudence is natural.

*Obj.* 3. Further, Prudence is more consistent with human nature than with that of dumb animals. Now there are instances of a certain natural prudence in dumb animals,

* σύνεσις and γνώμη, *cf.* I.-II., Q. LVII., A. 6. See footnote *infra*, p. 53.

according to the Philosopher (*De Hist. Anim.* viii. 1).
Therefore prudence is natural.

*On the contrary*, The Philosopher says (*Ethic.* ii. 1) that
*intellectual virtue is both originated and fostered by teaching ;
it therefore demands experience and time.*  Now prudence is
an intellectual virtue, as stated above (A. 4).  Therefore
prudence is in us, not by nature, but by teaching and
experience.

*I answer that*, As shown above (A. 3), prudence includes
knowledge both of universals, and of the singular matters
of action to which prudence applies the universal principles.
Accordingly, as regards the knowledge of universals, the
same is to be said of prudence as of speculative science,
because the primary universal principles of either are known
naturally, as shown above (A. 6): except that the common
principles of prudence are more connatural to man; for as
the Philosopher remarks (*Ethic.* x. 7) *the life which is according
to the speculative reason is better than that which is according
to man:* whereas the secondary universal principles, whether
of the speculative or of the practical reason, are not in-
herited from nature, but are acquired by discovery through
experience, or through teaching.

On the other hand, as regards the knowledge of particulars
which are the matter of action, we must make a further
distinction, because this matter of action is either an end
or the means to an end.  Now the right ends of human
life are fixed; wherefore there can be a natural inclination
in respect of these ends; thus it has been stated above
(I.-II., QQ. LI., A. 1; LXIII., A. 1) that some, from a
natural inclination, have certain virtues whereby they are
inclined to right ends; and consequently they also have
naturally a right judgment about suchlike ends.

But the means to the end, in human concerns, far from
being fixed, are of manifold variety according to the variety
of persons and affairs.  Wherefore since the inclination of
nature is ever to something fixed, the knowledge of those
means cannot be in man naturally, although, by reason of
his natural disposition, one man has a greater aptitude than

another in discerning them, just as it happens with regard to the conclusions of speculative sciences. Since then prudence is not about the ends, but about the means, as stated above (A. 6; I.-II., Q. LVII., A. 5), it follows that prudence is not from nature.

*Reply Obj.* 1. The Philosopher is speaking there of things relating to prudence, in so far as they are directed to ends. Wherefore he had said before (vi. 5, 11) that *they are the principles of the οὗ ἕνεκα,** namely, the end; and so he does not mention εὐβουλία among them, because it takes counsel about the means.

*Reply Obj.* 2. Prudence is rather in the old, not only because their natural disposition calms the movement of the sensitive passions, but also because of their long experience.

*Reply Obj.* 3. Even in dumb animals there are fixed ways of obtaining an end, wherefore we observe that all the animals of a same species act in like manner. But this is impossible in man, on account of his reason, which takes cognizance of universals, and consequently extends to an infinity of singulars.

## SIXTEENTH ARTICLE.

### WHETHER PRUDENCE CAN BE LOST THROUGH FORGETFULNESS ?

*We proceed thus to the Sixteenth Article :—*

*Objection* 1. It would seem that prudence can be lost through forgetfulness. For since science is about necessary things, it is more certain than prudence which is about contingent matters of action. But science is lost by forgetfulness. Much more therefore is prudence.

*Obj.* 2. Further, As the Philosopher says (*Ethic.* ii. 3) *the same things, but by a contrary process, engender and corrupt virtue.* Now the engendering of prudence requires experience which is made up *of many memories,* as he states at the beginning of his *Metaphysics* (i. 1). Therefore since forgetfulness is contrary to memory, it seems that prudence can be lost through forgetfulness.

* Literally *for the sake of which* (are the means).

*Obj.* 3. Further, There is no prudence without knowledge of universals. But knowledge of universals can be lost through forgetfulness. Therefore prudence can also.

*On the contrary,* The Philosopher says (*Ethic.* vi. 5) that *forgetfulness is possible to art but not to prudence.*

*I answer that,* Forgetfulness regards knowledge only, wherefore one can forget art and science, so as to lose them altogether, because they belong to the reason. But prudence consists not in knowledge alone, but also in an act of the appetite, because as stated above (A. 8), its principal act is one of command, whereby a man applies the knowledge he has, to the purpose of appetition and operation. Hence prudence is not taken away directly by forgetfulness, but rather is corrupted by the passions. For the Philosopher says (*Ethic.* vi. 5) that *pleasure and sorrow pervert the estimate of prudence:* wherefore it is written (Dan xiii. 56): *Beauty hath deceived thee, and lust hath subverted thy heart,* and (Exod. xxiii. 8): *Neither shalt thou take bribes which blind even the prudent* (Douay, *wise*).

Nevertheless forgetfulness may hinder prudence, in so far as the latter's command depends on knowledge which may be forgotten.

*Reply Obj.* 1. Science is in the reason only: hence the comparison fails, as stated above.*

*Reply Obj.* 2. The experience required by prudence results not from memory alone, but also from the practice of commanding aright.

*Reply Obj.* 3. Prudence consists chiefly, not in the knowledge of universals, but in applying them to action, as stated above (A. 3). Wherefore forgetting the knowledge of universals does not destroy the principal part of prudence, but hinders it somewhat, as stated above.

* Cf. I-II., Q. LIII., A. 1.

# QUESTION XLVIII.

## OF THE PARTS OF PRUDENCE

*(In one Article.)*

WE must now consider the parts of prudence, under which head there are four points of inquiry: (1) Which are the parts of prudence ? (2) Of its integral parts: (3) Of its subjective parts: (4) Of its potential parts.

### ARTICLE.

#### WHETHER THREE PARTS OF PRUDENCE ARE FITTINGLY ASSIGNED ?

*We proceed thus to the Article :—*

*Objection* 1. It would seem that the parts of prudence are assigned unfittingly. Tully *(De Invent. Rhet.* ii. 53) assigns three parts of prudence, namely, *memory, understanding* and *foresight.* Macrobius *(In Somn. Scip.* i.) following the opinion of Plotinus ascribes to prudence six parts, namely, *reasoning, understanding, circumspection, foresight, docility* and *caution.* Aristotle says *(Ethic.* vi. 9, 10, 11) that *good counsel, synesis* and *gnome* belong to prudence. Again under the head of prudence he mentions *conjecture, shrewdness, sense* and *understanding.* And another Greek philosopher* says that ten things are connected with prudence, namely, *good counsel, shrewdness, foresight, reignativa,† military, political* and *domestic prudence, dialectics, rhetoric* and *physics.* Therefore it seems that one or the other enumeration is either excessive or deficient.

*Obj.* 2. Further, Prudence is specifically distinct from

---

\* Andronicus; *cf.* Q. LXXX., *obj.* 4. † *Regnativa.*

science. But politics, economics, logic, rhetoric, physics are sciences. Therefore they are not parts of prudence.

*Obj.* 3. Further, The parts do not exceed the whole. Now the intellective memory or intelligence, reason, sense and docility, belong not only to prudence but also to all the cognitive habits. Therefore they should not be set down as parts of prudence.

*Obj.* 4. Further, Just as counselling, judging and commanding are acts of the practical reason, so also is using, as stated above (I.-II., Q. XVI., A. 1). Therefore, just as *eubulia* which refers to counsel, is connected with prudence, and *synesis* and *gnome* which refer to judgment, so also ought something to have been assigned corresponding to use.

*Obj.* 5. Further, Solicitude pertains to prudence, as stated above (Q. XLVII., A. 9). Therefore solicitude also should have been mentioned among the parts of prudence.

*I answer that,* Parts are of three kinds, namely, *integral,* as wall, roof, and foundation are parts of a house; *subjective,* as ox and lion are parts of animal; and *potential,* as the nutritive and sensitive powers are parts of the soul. Accordingly, parts can be assigned to a virtue in three ways. First, in likeness to integral parts, so that the things which need to concur for the perfect act of a virtue, are called the parts of that virtue. In this way, out of all the things mentioned above, eight may be taken as parts of prudence, namely, the six assigned by Macrobius; with the addition of a seventh, viz., *memory* mentioned by Tully; and εὐστοχία or *shrewdness* mentioned by Aristotle. For the *sense* of prudence is also called *understanding :* wherefore the Philosopher says (*Ethic.* vi. 11): *Of such things one needs to have the sense, and this is understanding.* Of these eight, five belong to prudence as a cognitive virtue, namely, *memory, reasoning, understanding, docility* and *shrewdness :* while the three others belong thereto, as commanding and applying knowledge to action, namely, *foresight, circumspection* and *caution.* The reason of their difference is seen from the fact that three things may be observed in reference to knowledge. In the first place, knowledge itself, which, if it be of the past, is called *memory*, if of the present, whether contingent or necessary, is called *understanding* or *intelligence*. Secondly, the acquiring of knowledge, which is caused either by teaching, to which pertains *docility*, or by discovery, and to this belongs εὐστοχία—i.e., *a happy conjecture*, of which *shrewdness* is a part, which is a *quick conjecture of the middle term*, as stated in *Poster.* i. 9. Thirdly, the use of knowledge, in as much as we proceed from things known to knowledge or judgment of other things, and this belongs to *reasoning*. And the reason, in order to command aright, requires to have three conditions. First, to order that which is befitting the end, and this belongs to *foresight*; secondly, to attend to the circumstances of the matter in hand, and this belongs to *circumspection*; thirdly, to avoid obstacles, and this belongs to *caution*.

The subjective parts of a virtue are its various species. In this way the parts of prudence, if we take them properly, are the prudence whereby a man rules himself, and the prudence whereby a man governs a multitude, which differ specifically as stated above (Q. XLVII., A. 11). Again, the prudence whereby a multitude is governed, is divided into various species according to the various kinds of multitude. There is the multitude which is united together for some particular purpose; thus an army is gathered together to fight, and the prudence that governs this is called *military*. There is also the multitude that is united together for the whole of life; such is the multitude of a home or family, and this is ruled by *domestic prudence*: and such again is the multitude of a city or kingdom, the ruling principle of which is *reignative prudence* in the ruler, and *political prudence*, simply so called, in the subjects.

If, however, prudence be taken in a wide sense, as including also speculative knowledge, as stated above (Q. XLVII., A. 2, *ad* 2) then its parts include *dialectics*, *rhetoric* and *physics*, according to three methods of prudence in the sciences. The first of these is the attaining of science by demonstration, which belongs to *physics* (if physics be understood to comprise all demonstrative sciences). The second method is to arrive at an opinion through probable premisses, and this belongs to *dialectics*.   The third method is to employ conjectures in order to induce a certain suspicion, or to persuade somewhat, and this belongs to *rhetoric*.   It may be said, however, that these three belong also to prudence properly so called, since it argues sometimes from necessary premisses, sometimes from probabilities, and sometimes from conjectures.

The potential parts of a virtue are the virtues connected with it, which are directed to certain secondary acts or matters, not having, as it were, the whole power of the principal virtue.   In this way the parts of prudence are *good counsel*, which concerns counsel, *synesis*, which concerns judgment in matters of ordinary occurrence, and *gnome*, which concerns judgment in matters of exception to the law: while *prudence* is about the chief act—viz., that of commanding.

*Reply Obj.* 1. The various enumerations differ, either because different kinds of parts are assigned, or because that which is mentioned in one enumeration includes several mentioned in another enumeration.   Thus Tully includes *caution* and *circumspection* under *foresight*, and *reasoning*, *docility* and *shrewdness* under *understanding*.

*Reply Obj.* 2. Here domestic and civic prudence are not to be taken as sciences, but as kinds of prudence.   As to the other three, the reply may be gathered from what has been said.

*Reply Obj.* 3. All these things are reckoned parts of prudence, not by taking them altogether, but in so far as they are connected with things pertaining to prudence.

*Reply Obj.* 4. Right command and right use always go together, because the reason's command is followed by obedience on the part of the lower powers, which pertain to use.

*Reply Obj.* 5. Solicitude is included under foresight.

# QUESTION XLIX.

## OF EACH QUASI-INTEGRAL PART OF PRUDENCE.

### (*In Eight Articles.*)

WE must now consider each quasi-integral part of prudence, and under this head there are eight points of inquiry: (1) Memory: (2) Understanding or intelligence: (3) Docility: (4) Shrewdness: (5) Reason: (6) Foresight: (7) Circumspection: (8) Caution.

## FIRST ARTICLE.

### WHETHER MEMORY IS A PART OF PRUDENCE?

*We proceed thus to the First Article :—*

*Objection* 1. It would seem that memory is not a part of prudence. For memory, as the Philosopher proves (*De Memor. et Remin.* i.), is in the sensitive part of the soul: whereas prudence is in the rational part (*Ethic.* vi. 5). Therefore memory is not a part of prudence.

*Obj.* 2. Further, Prudence is acquired and perfected by experience, whereas memory is in us from nature. Therefore memory is not a part of prudence.

*Obj.* 3. Further, Memory regards the past, whereas prudence regards future matters of action, about which counsel is concerned, as stated in *Ethic.* vi. 2, 7. Therefore memory is not a part of prudence.

*On the contrary*, Tully (*De Invent. Rhet.* ii. 53) places memory among the parts of prudence.

*I answer that*, Prudence regards contingent matters of action, as stated above (Q. XLVII., A. 5). Now in suchlike matters a man can be directed, not by those things that are

33

3

simply and necessarily true, but by those which occur in the majority of cases: because principles must be proportionate to their conclusions, and *like must be concluded from like* (*Ethic.* vi.).* But we need experience to discover what is true in the majority of cases: wherefore the Philosopher says (*Ethic.* ii. I) that *intellectual virtue is engendered and fostered by experience and time.* Now experience is the result of many memories as stated in *Metaph.* i. I, and therefore prudence requires the memory of many things. Hence memory is fittingly accounted a part of prudence.

*Reply Obj.* I. As stated above (Q. XLVII., AA. 3, 6), prudence applies universal knowledge to particulars which are objects of sense: hence many things belonging to the sensitive faculties are requisite for prudence, and memory is one of them.

*Reply Obj.* 2. Just as aptitude for prudence is in our nature, while its perfection comes through practice or grace, so too, as Tully says in his *Rhetoric,*† memory not only arises from nature, but is also aided by art and diligence. There are four things whereby a man perfects his memory. First, when a man wishes to remember a thing, he should take some suitable yet somewhat unwonted illustration of it, since the unwonted strikes us more, and so makes a greater and stronger impression on the mind; and this explains why we remember better what we saw when we were children. Now the reason for the necessity of finding these illustrations or images, is that simple and spiritual impressions easily slip from the mind, unless they be tied as it were to some corporeal image, because human knowledge has a greater hold on sensible objects. For this reason memory is assigned to the sensitive part of the soul. Secondly, whatever a man wishes to retain in his memory he must carefully consider and set in order, so that he may pass easily from one memory to another. Hence the Philosopher says (*De Mem. et Rem.* ii.): *Sometimes a place brings memories back to us : the reason being that we pass quickly from the one to the other.* Thirdly, we must be anxious and earnest about the things we wish to remember, because the

* *Anal. Post.* i. 32.        † *Ad Herenn. de Arte Rhet.* iii. 16, 24.

more a thing is impressed on the mind, the less it is liable to slip out of it. Wherefore Tully says in his *Rhetoric** that *anxiety preserves the figures of images entire.* Fourthly, we should often reflect on the things we wish to remember. Hence the Philosopher says (*De Memoria* i.) that *reflexion preserves memories,* because as he remarks (*ibid.* ii.) *custom is a second nature :* wherefore when we reflect on a thing frequently, we quickly call it to mind, through passing from one thing to another by a kind of natural order.

*Reply Obj.* 3. It behoves us to argue, as it were, about the future from the past; wherefore memory of the past is necessary in order to take good counsel for the future.

## Second Article.

### Whether Understanding† Is A Part Of Prudence?

*We proceed thus to the Second Article :—*

*Objection* 1. It would seem that understanding is not a part of prudence. When two things are members of a division, one is not part of the other. But intellectual virtue is divided into understanding and prudence, according to *Ethic.* vi. 3. Therefore understanding should not be reckoned a part of prudence.

*Obj.* 2. Further, Understanding is numbered among the gifts of the Holy Ghost, and corresponds to faith, as stated above (Q. VIII., AA. 1, 8). But prudence is a virtue other than faith, as is clear from what has been said above (Q. IV., A. 8: I.-II., Q. LXII., A. 2). Therefore understanding does not pertain to prudence.

*Obj.* 3. Further, Prudence is about singular matters of action (*Ethic.* vi. 7): whereas understanding takes cognizance of universal and immaterial objects (*De Anima* iii. 4). Therefore understanding is not a part of prudence.

*On the contrary,* Tully‡ accounts *intelligence* a part of prudence, and Macrobius§ mentions *understanding,* which comes to the same.

*I answer that,* Understanding denotes here, not the

* *Ad Herenn. de Arte Rhet.* iii.
† Otherwise intuition; Aristotle's word is νοῦς.
‡ *De Inv. Rhet.* ii. 53.          § *In Somn. Scip.* i. 8.

intellectual power, but the right estimate about some final
principle, which is taken as self-evident: thus we are said
to understand the first principles of demonstrations.   Now
every deduction of reason proceeds from certain state-
ments which are taken as primary: wherefore every process
of reasoning must needs proceed from some understanding.
Therefore since prudence is right reason applied to action,
the whole process of prudence must needs have its source
in understanding.    Hence it is that understanding is
reckoned a part of prudence.

*Reply Obj.* 1. The reasoning of prudence terminates, as
in a conclusion, in the particular matter of action, to which,
as stated above (Q. XLVII., AA. 3, 6), it applies the knowledge of some universal principle.   Now a singular conclusion
is argued from a universal and a singular proposition.
Wherefore the reasoning of prudence must proceed from a
twofold understanding.   The one is cognizant of universals,
and this belongs to the understanding which is an intellectual
virtue, whereby we know naturally not only speculative
principles, but also practical universal principles, such as
*One should do evil to no man*, as shown above (Q. XLVII.,
A. 6).   The other understanding, as stated in *Ethic*. vi. 11,
is cognizant of an extreme, *i.e.*, of some primary singular
and contingent practical matter, viz., the minor premiss,
which must needs be singular in the syllogism of prudence,
as stated above (Q. XLVII., AA. 3, 6).   Now this primary
singular is some singular end, as stated in the same place.
Wherefore the understanding which is a part of prudence is
a right estimate of some particular end.

*Reply Obj.* 2. The understanding which is a gift of the
Holy Ghost, is a quick insight into divine things, as shown
above (Q. VIII., AA. 1, 2).   It is in another sense that it is
accounted a part of prudence, as stated above.

*Reply Obj.* 3. The right estimate about a particular end is
called both *understanding,* in so far as its object is a principle,
and *sense,* in so far as its object is a particular.   This is
what the Philosopher means when he says (*Ethic*. v. 11):
*Of such things we need to have the sense, and this is under-*

*standing.* But this is to be understood as referring, not to the particular sense whereby we know proper sensibles, but to the interior sense, whereby we judge of a particular.

### Third Article.
#### WHETHER DOCILITY SHOULD BE ACCOUNTED A PART OF PRUDENCE ?

*We proceed thus to the Third Article :—*

*Objection* 1. It would seem that docility should not be accounted a part of prudence. For that which is a necessary condition of every intellectual virtue, should not be appropriated to one of them. But docility is requisite for every intellectual virtue. Therefore it should not be accounted a part of prudence.

*Obj.* 2. Further, That which pertains to a human virtue is in our power, since it is for things that are in our power that we are praised or blamed. Now it is not in our power to be docile, for this is befitting to some through their natural disposition. Therefore it is not a part of prudence.

*Obj.* 3. Further, Docility is in the disciple: whereas prudence, since it makes precepts, seems rather to belong to teachers, who are also called *preceptors.* Therefore docility is not a part of prudence.

*On the contrary,* Macrobius* following the opinion of Plotinus places docility among the parts of prudence.

*I answer that,* As stated above (A. 2, *ad* 1: Q. XLVII., A. 3) prudence is concerned with particular matters of action, and since such matters are of infinite variety, no one man can consider them all sufficiently; nor can this be done quickly, for it requires length of time. Hence in matters of prudence man stands in very great need of being taught by others, especially by old folk who have acquired a sane understanding of the ends in practical matters. Wherefore the Philosopher says (*Ethic.* vi. 11): *It is right to pay no less attention to the undemonstrated assertions and opinions of such persons as are experienced, older than we are, and prudent,*

* *In Somn. Scip.* i. 8.

*than to their demonstrations, for their experience gives them
an insight into principles.* Thus it is written (Prov. iii. 5):
*Lean not on thy own prudence,* and (Ecclus. vi. 35): *Stand
in the multitude of the ancients (i.e.* the old men), *that are
wise, and join thyself from thy heart to their wisdom.* Now
it is a mark of docility to be ready to be taught: and consequently docility is fittingly reckoned a part of prudence.

*Reply Obj.* 1. Although docility is useful for every intellectual virtue, yet it belongs to prudence chiefly, for the
reason given above.

*Reply Obj.* 2. Man has a natural aptitude for docility even
as for other things connected with prudence. Yet his own
efforts count for much towards the attainment of perfect
docility: and he must carefully, frequently and reverently
apply his mind to the teachings of the learned, neither
neglecting them through laziness, nor despising them
through pride.

*Reply Obj.* 3. By prudence man makes precepts not only
for others, but also for himself, as stated above (Q. XLVII.,
A. 12, *ad* 3). Hence as stated (*ibid.*), even in subjects, there
is place for prudence; to which docility pertains. And yet
even the learned should be docile in some respects, since no
man is altogether self-sufficient in matters of prudence, as
stated above.

### FOURTH ARTICLE.

#### WHETHER SHREWDNESS IS PART OF PRUDENCE?

*We proceed thus to the Fourth Article :—*

*Objection* 1. It would seem that shrewdness is not a part
of prudence. For shrewdness consists in easily finding the
middle term for demonstrations, as stated in *Poster.* i. 34.
Now the reasoning of prudence is not a demonstration since
it deals with contingencies. Therefore shrewdness does not
pertain to prudence.

*Obj.* 2. Further, Good counsel pertains to prudence
according to *Ethic.* vi. 5, 7, 9. Now there is no place in good
counsel for shrewdness* which is *a kind of* εὐστοχία, i.e.,

---

\* *Ibid.* 9; *Poster.* i. 34.

*a happy conjecture :* for the latter is *unreasoning and rapid,
whereas counsel needs to be slow,* as stated in *Ethic.* vi. 9.
Therefore shrewdness should not be accounted a part of
prudence.

*Obj.* 3. Further, Shrewdness as stated above (Q. XLVIII.)
is a *happy conjecture.* Now it belongs to rhetoricians to
make use of conjectures. Therefore shrewdness belongs to
rhetoric rather than to prudence.

*On the contrary,* Isidore says (*Etym.* x.): *A solicitous man
is one who is shrewd and alert (solers citus).* But solicitude
belongs to prudence, as stated above (Q. XLVII., A. 9).
Therefore shrewdness does also.

*I answer that,* Prudence consists in a right estimate about
matters of action. Now a right estimate or opinion is
acquired in two ways, both in practical and in speculative matters, first by discovering it oneself, secondly by
learning it from others. Now just as docility consists in a
man being well disposed to acquire a right opinion from
another man, so shrewdness is an apt disposition to acquire
a right estimate by oneself, yet so that shrewdness be taken
for εὐστοχία, of which it is a part. For εὐστοχία is a happy
conjecture about any matter, while shrewdness is *an easy
and rapid conjecture in finding the middle term* (*Poster.* i. 34).
Nevertheless the philosopher\* who calls shrewdness a part of
prudence, takes it for εὐστοχία in general, hence he says:
*Shrewdness is a habit whereby congruities are discovered rapidly.*

*Reply Obj.* 1. Shrewdness is concerned with the discovery
of the middle term not only in demonstrative, but also in
practical syllogisms, as, for instance, when two men are
seen to be friends they are reckoned to be enemies of a third
one, as the Philosopher says (*ibid.*). In this way shrewdness
belongs to prudence.

*Reply Obj.* 2. The Philosopher adduces the true reason
(*Ethic.* vi. 9) to prove that εὐβουλία, *i.e.,* good counsel, is
not εὐστοχία, which is commended for grasping quickly what
should be done. Now a man may take good counsel, though
he be long and slow in so doing, and yet this does not
discount the utility of a happy conjecture in taking

\* Andronicus; *cf.* Q. XLVIII., *obj.* 1.

good counsel: indeed it is sometimes a necessity, when, for instance, something has to be done without warning. It is for this reason that shrewdness is fittingly reckoned a part of prudence.

*Reply Obj.* 3. Rhetoric also reasons about practical matters, wherefore nothing hinders the same thing belonging both to rhetoric and prudence. Nevertheless, conjecture is taken here not only in the sense in which it is employed by rhetoricians, but also as applicable to all matters whatsoever wherein man is said to conjecture the truth.

## FIFTH ARTICLE.

### WHETHER REASON SHOULD BE RECKONED A PART OF PRUDENCE ?

*We proceed thus to the Fifth Article :—*

*Objection* 1. It would seem that reason should not be reckoned a part of prudence. For the subject of an accident is not a part thereof. But prudence is in the reason as its subject (*Ethic.* vi. 5). Therefore reason should not be reckoned a part of prudence.

*Obj.* 2. Further, That which is common to many, should not be reckoned a part of any one of them; or if it be so reckoned, it should be reckoned a part of that one to which it chiefly belongs. Now reason is necessary in all the intellectual virtues, and chiefly in wisdom and science, which employ a demonstrative reason. Therefore reason should not be reckoned a part of prudence.

*Obj.* 3. Further, Reason as a power does not differ essentially from the intelligence, as stated above (P. I., Q. LXXIX., A. 8). If therefore intelligence be reckoned a part of prudence, it is superfluous to add reason.

*On the contrary,* Macrobius,* following the opinion of Plotinus, numbers reason among the parts of prudence.

*I answer that,* The work of prudence is to take good counsel, as stated in *Ethic.* vi. 7. Now counsel is a research proceeding from certain things to others. But this is the

* *In Somn. Scip.* i.

work of reason.    Wherefore it is requisite for prudence that man should be an apt reasoner.    And since the things required for the perfection of prudence are called requisite or quasi-integral parts of prudence, it follows that reason should be numbered among these parts.

*Reply Obj.* 1. Reason denotes here, not the power of reason, but its good use.

*Reply Obj.* 2. The certitude of reason comes from the intellect.    Yet the need of reason is from a defect in the intellect, since those things in which the intellective power is in full vigour, have no need of reason, for they comprehend the truth by their simple insight, as do God and the angels. On the other hand particular matters of action, wherein prudence guides, are very far from the condition of things intelligible, and so much the farther, as they are less certain and fixed.    Thus matters of art, though they are singular, are nevertheless more fixed and certain, wherefore in many of them there is no room for counsel on account of their certitude, as stated in *Ethic.* iii. 3.    Hence, although in certain other intellectual virtues reason is more certain than in prudence, yet prudence above all requires that man be an apt reasoner, so that he may rightly apply universals to particulars, which latter are various and uncertain.

*Reply Obj.* 3. Although intelligence and reason are not different powers, yet they are named after different acts. For intelligence takes its name from being an intimate penetration of the truth,* while reason is so called from being inquisitive and discursive.    Hence each is accounted a part of reason as explained above (A. 2: Q. XLVII., A. 2, 3).

## SIXTH ARTICLE.

### WHETHER FORESIGHT† SHOULD BE ACCOUNTED A PART OF PRUDENCE ?

*We proceed thus to the Sixth Article :—*

*Objection* 1. It would seem that foresight should not be accounted a part of prudence. For nothing is part of itself. Now

* Cf. II.-II., Q. VIII., A. 1.
† *Providentia,* which may be translated either *providence* or *foresight.*

foresight seems to be the same as prudence, because according to Isidore (*Etym.* x.), *a prudent man is one who sees from afar (porro videns)* : and this is also the derivation of *providentia (foresight)*, according to Boethius (*De Consol.* v.). Therefore foresight is not a part of prudence.

*Obj.* 2. Further, Prudence is only practical, whereas foresight may be also speculative, because *seeing*, whence we have the word *to foresee*, has more to do with speculation than operation.  Therefore foresight is not a part of prudence.

*Obj.* 3. Further, The chief act of prudence is to command, while its secondary act is to judge and to take counsel. But none of these seems to be properly implied by foresight. Therefore foresight is not part of prudence.

*On the contrary* stands the authority of Tully and Macrobius, who number foresight among the parts of prudence, as stated above (Q. XLVIII.).

*I answer that*, As stated above (Q. XLVII., A. 1, *ad* 2, AA. 6, 13), prudence is properly about the means to an end, and its proper work is to set them in due order to the end. And although certain things are necessary for an end, which are subject to divine providence, yet nothing is subject to human providence except the contingent matters of actions which can be done by man for an end.  Now the past has become a kind of necessity, since what has been done cannot be undone.  In like manner, the present as such, has a kind of necessity, since it is necessary that Socrates sit, so long as he sits.

Consequently, future contingents, in so far as they can be directed by man to the end of human life, are the matter of prudence: and each of these things is implied in the word foresight, for it implies the notion of something distant, to which that which occurs in the present has to be directed. Therefore foresight is part of prudence.

*Reply Obj.* 1. Whenever many things are requisite for a unity, one of them must needs be the principal to which all the others are subordinate.  Hence in every whole one part must be formal and predominant, whence the whole has unity.  Accordingly foresight is the principal of all the parts of prudence, since whatever else is required for prudence, is necessary precisely that some particular thing may be rightly directed to its end. Hence it is that the very name of prudence is taken from foresight (*providentia*) as from its principal part.

*Reply Obj.* 2. Speculation is about universal and necessary things, which, in themselves, are not distant, since they are everywhere and always, though they are distant from us, in so far as we fail to know them. Hence foresight does not apply properly to speculative, but only to practical matters.

*Reply Obj.* 3. Right order to an end which is included in the notion of foresight, contains rectitude of counsel, judgment and command, without which no right order to the end is possible.

## SEVENTH ARTICLE.

### WHETHER CIRCUMSPECTION CAN BE A PART OF PRUDENCE ?

*We proceed thus to the Seventh Article :—*

*Objection* 1. It would seem that circumspection cannot be a part of prudence. For circumspection seems to signify looking at one's surroundings. But these are of infinite number, and cannot be considered by the reason wherein is prudence. Therefore circumspection should not be reckoned a part of prudence.

*Obj.* 2. Further, Circumstances seem to be the concern of moral virtues rather than of prudence. But circumspection seems to denote nothing but attention to circumstances. Therefore circumspection apparently belongs to the moral virtues rather than to prudence.

*Obj.* 3. Further, Whoever can see things afar off can much more see things that are near. Now foresight enables a man to look on distant things. Therefore there is no need to account circumspection a part of prudence in addition to foresight.

*On the contrary* stands the authority of Macrobius, quoted above (Q. XLVIII.).

*I answer that,* As stated above (A. 6), it belongs to prudence chiefly to direct something aright to an end; and this is not

Q. 49. Art. 8 THE "SUMMA THEOLOGICA" 44

done aright unless both the end be good, and the means good and suitable.

Since, however, prudence, as stated above (Q. XLVII., A. 3) is about singular matters of action, which contain many combinations of circumstances, it happens that a thing is good in itself and suitable to the end, and nevertheless becomes evil or unsuitable to the end, by reason of some combination of circumstances. Thus to show signs of love to someone seems, considered in itself, to be a fitting way to arouse love in his heart, yet if pride or suspicion of flattery arise in his heart, it will no longer be a means suitable to the end. Hence the need of circumspection in prudence, viz. of comparing the means with the circumstances.

*Reply Obj.* 1. Though the number of possible circumstances be infinite, the number of actual circumstances is not; and the judgment of reason in matters of action is influenced by things which are few in number.

*Reply Obj.* 2. Circumstances are the concern of prudence, because prudence has to fix them; on the other hand they are the concern of moral virtues, in so far as moral virtues are perfected by the fixing of circumstances.

*Reply Obj.* 3. Just as it belongs to foresight to look on that which is by its nature suitable to an end, so it belongs to circumspection to consider whether it be suitable to the end in view of the circumstances. Now each of these presents a difficulty of its own, and therefore each is reckoned a distinct part of prudence.

## EIGHTH ARTICLE.

### WHETHER CAUTION SHOULD BE RECKONED A PART OF PRUDENCE ?

*We proceed thus to the Eighth Article :—*

*Objection* 1. It would seem that caution should not be reckoned a part of prudence. For when no evil is possible, no caution is required. Now no man makes evil use of virtue, as Augustine declares (*De Lib. Arb.* ii. 19). Therefore caution does not belong to prudence which directs the virtues.

*Obj.* 2. Further, To foresee good and to avoid evil belong to the same faculty, just as the same art gives health and cures ill-health. Now it belongs to foresight to foresee good, and consequently, also to avoid evil. Therefore caution should not be accounted a part of prudence, distinct from foresight.

*Obj.* 3. Further, No prudent man strives for the impossible. But no man can take precautions against all possible evils. Therefore caution does not belong to prudence.

*On the contrary*, The Apostle says (Eph. v. 15): *See how you walk cautiously* (Douay, *circumspectly*).

*I answer that*, The things with which prudence is concerned, are contingent matters of action, wherein, even as false is found with true, so is evil mingled with good, on account of the great variety of these matters of action, wherein good is often hindered by evil, and evil has the appearance of good. Wherefore prudence needs caution, so that we may have such a grasp of good as to avoid evil.

*Reply Obj.* 1. Caution is required in moral acts, that we may be on our guard, not against acts of virtue, but against the hindrances to acts of virtue.

*Reply Obj.* 2. It is the same in idea, to ensue good and to avoid the opposite evil, but the avoidance of outward hindrances is different in idea. Hence caution differs from foresight, although they both belong to the one virtue of prudence.

*Reply Obj.* 3. Of the evils which man has to avoid, some are of frequent occurrence; the like can be grasped by reason, and against them caution is directed, either that they may be avoided altogether, or that they may do less harm. Others there are that occur rarely and by chance, and these, since they are infinite in number, cannot be grasped by reason, nor is man able to take precautions against them, although by exercising prudence he is able to prepare against all the surprises of chance, so as to suffer less harm thereby.

# QUESTION L.

## OF THE SUBJECTIVE PARTS OF PRUDENCE.

### (*In Four Articles.*)

WE must, in due sequence, consider the subjective parts of prudence. And since we have already spoken of the prudence with which a man rules himself (Q. XLVII., *seqq.*), it remains for us to discuss the species of prudence whereby a multitude is governed. Under this head there are four points of inquiry: (1) Whether a species of prudence is reignative? (2) Whether political and (3) domestic economy are species of prudence? (4) Whether military prudence is?

### FIRST ARTICLE.

#### WHETHER A SPECIES OF PRUDENCE IS REIGNATIVE?

*We proceed thus to the First Article:—*

*Objection* 1. It would seem that reignative should not be reckoned a species of prudence. For reignative prudence is directed to the preservation of justice, since according to *Ethic.* v. 6 *the prince is the guardian of justice.* Therefore reignative prudence belongs to justice rather than to prudence.

*Obj.* 2. Further, According to the Philosopher (*Polit.* iii. 5) a kingdom (*regnum*) is one of six species of government. But no species of prudence is ascribed to the other five forms of government, which are *aristocracy, polity,* also called *timocracy,** *tyranny, oligarchy and democracy.* Therefore neither should a reignative species be ascribed to a kingdom.

*Obj.* 3. Further, Lawgiving belongs not only to kings, but also to certain others placed in authority, and even to

* Cf. *Ethic.* viii. 10.

the people, according to Isidore (*Etym.* v.). Now the Philosopher (*Ethic.* vi. 8) reckons a part of prudence to be *legislative*. Therefore it is not becoming to substitute reignative prudence in its place.

*On the contrary*, The Philosopher says (*Polit.* iii. 11) that *prudence is a virtue which is proper to the prince*. Therefore a special kind of prudence is reignative.

*I answer that*, As stated above (Q. XLVII., AA. 8, 10), it belongs to prudence to govern and command, so that wherever in human acts we find a special kind of governance and command, there must be a special kind of prudence. Now it is evident that there is a special and perfect kind of governance in one who has to govern not only himself but also the perfect community of a city or kingdom; because a government is the more perfect according as it is more universal, extends to more matters, and attains a higher end. Hence prudence in its special and most perfect sense, belongs to a king who is charged with the government of a city or kingdom: for which reason a species of prudence is reckoned to be reignative.

*Reply Obj.* 1. All matters connected with moral virtue belong to prudence as their guide, wherefore *right reason in accord with prudence* is included in the definition of moral virtue, as stated above (Q. XLVII., A. 5, *ad* 1: I.-II., Q. LVIII., A. 2, *ad* 4). For this reason also the execution of justice, in so far as it is directed to the common good, which is part of the kingly office, needs the guidance of prudence. Hence these two virtues—prudence and justice —belong most properly to a king, according to Jerem. xxiii. 5: *A king shall reign and shall be wise, and shall execute justice and judgment in the earth*. Since, however, direction belongs rather to the king, and execution to his subjects, reignative prudence is reckoned a species of prudence which is directive, rather than to justice which is executive.

*Reply Obj.* 2. A kingdom is the best of all governments, as stated in *Ethic.* viii. 10: wherefore the species of prudence should be denominated rather from a kingdom, yet so as to comprehend under reignative all other rightful forms of government, but not perverse forms which are opposed to virtue, and which, accordingly, do not pertain to prudence.

*Reply Obj.* 3. The Philosopher names reignative prudence after the principal act of a king which is to make laws, and although this applies to the other forms of government, this is only in so far as they have a share of kingly government.

## SECOND ARTICLE.

### WHETHER POLITICAL PRUDENCE IS FITTINGLY ACCOUNTED A PART OF PRUDENCE ?

*We proceed thus to the Second Article :—*

*Objection* 1. It would seem that political prudence is not fittingly accounted a part of prudence. For reignative is a part of political prudence, as stated above (A. 1). But a part should not be reckoned a species with the whole. Therefore political prudence should not be reckoned a part of prudence.

*Obj.* 2. Further, The species of habits are distinguished by their various objects. Now what the ruler has to command is the same as what the subject has to execute. Therefore political prudence as regards the subjects, should not be reckoned a species of prudence distinct from reignative prudence.

*Obj.* 3. Further, Each subject is an individual person. Now each individual person can direct himself sufficiently by prudence commonly so called. Therefore there is no need of a special kind of prudence called political.

*On the contrary,* The Philosopher says (*Ethic.* vi. 8) that *of the prudence which is concerned with the state one kind is a master-prudence and is called legislative ; another kind bears the common name political, and deals with individuals.*

*I answer that,* A slave is moved by his master, and a subject by his ruler, by command, but otherwise than as irrational and inanimate beings are set in motion by their movers. For irrational and inanimate beings are moved only by others and do not put themselves in motion, since they have no free-will whereby to be masters of their own actions, wherefore the rectitude of their government is not in their power but in the power of their movers. On the other hand, men who are slaves or subjects in any sense, are moved by the commands of others in such a way that they move themselves by their free-will; wherefore some kind of rectitude of government is required in them, so that they may direct themselves in obeying their superiors; and to this belongs that species of prudence which is called political.

*Reply Obj.* 1. As stated above, reignative is the most perfect species of prudence, wherefore the prudence of subjects, which falls short of reignative prudence, retains the common name of political prudence, even as in logic a convertible term which does not denote the essence of a thing retains the name of *proper.*

*Reply Obj.* 2. A different aspect of the object diversifies the species of a habit, as stated above (Q. XLVII., A. 5). Now the same actions are considered by the king, but under a more general aspect, as by his subjects who obey: since many obey one king in various departments. Hence reignative prudence is compared to this political prudence of which we are speaking, as mastercraft to handicraft.

*Reply Obj.* 3. Man directs himself by prudence commonly so called, in relation to his own good, but by political prudence, of which we speak, he directs himself in relation to the common good.

### Third Article.

#### WHETHER A PART OF PRUDENCE SHOULD BE RECKONED TO BE DOMESTIC ?

*We proceed thus to the Third Article :—*

*Objection* 1. It would seem that domestic should not be reckoned a part of prudence. For, according to the Philosopher (*Ethic.* vi. 5) *prudence is directed to a good life in general:* whereas domestic prudence is directed to a particular end, viz. wealth, according to *Ethic.* i. 1. Therefore a species of prudence is not domestic.

*Obj.* 2. Further, As stated above (Q. XLVII., A. 13)

prudence is only in good people.   But domestic prudence may be also in wicked people, since many sinners are provident in governing their household.   Therefore domestic prudence should not be reckoned a species of prudence.

*Obj.* 3. Further, Just as in a kingdom there is ruler and subject, so also is there in a household.   If therefore domestic like political is a species of prudence, there should be a paternal corresponding to reignative prudence.   Now there is no such prudence.   Therefore neither should domestic prudence be accounted a species of prudence.

*On the contrary*, The Philosopher states (*Ethic.* vi. 8) that there are various kinds of prudence in the government of a multitude, *one of which is domestic, another legislative, and another political.*

*I answer that*, Different aspects of an object, in respect of universality and particularity, or of totality and partiality, diversify arts and virtues; and in respect of such diversity one act of virtue is principal as compared with another. Now it is evident that a household is a mean between the individual and the city or kingdom, since just as the individual is part of the household, so is the household part of the city or kingdom.   And therefore, just as prudence commonly so called which governs the individual, is distinct from political prudence, so must domestic prudence be distinct from both.

*Reply Obj.* 1. Riches are compared to domestic prudence, not as its last end, but as its instrument, as stated in *Polit.* i. 3.   On the other hand, the end of political prudence is *a good life in general* as regards the conduct of the household. In *Ethic.* i. 1 the Philosopher speaks of riches as the end of political prudence, by way of example and in accordance with the opinion of many.

*Reply Obj.* 2. Some sinners may be provident in certain matters of detail concerning the disposition of their household, but not in regard to *a good life in general* as regards the conduct of the household, for which above all a virtuous life is required.

*Reply Obj.* 3. The father has in his household an authority like that of a king, as stated in *Ethic.* viii. 10, but he has not the full power of a king, wherefore paternal government is not reckoned a distinct species of prudence, like reignative prudence.

## FOURTH ARTICLE.

### WHETHER MILITARY PRUDENCE SHOULD BE RECKONED A PART OF PRUDENCE ?

*We proceed thus to the Fourth Article :—*

*Objection* 1. It would seem that military prudence should not be reckoned a part of prudence. For prudence is distinct from art, according to *Ethic.* vi. 3. Now military prudence seems to be the art of warfare, according to the Philosopher (*Ethic.* iii. 8). Therefore military prudence should not be accounted a species of prudence.

*Obj.* 2. Further, Just as military business is contained under political affairs, so too are many other matters, such as those of tradesmen, craftsmen, and so forth. But there are no species of prudence corresponding to other affairs in the state. Neither therefore should any be assigned to military business.

*Obj.* 3. Further, The soldiers' bravery counts for a great deal in warfare. Therefore military prudence pertains to fortitude rather than to prudence.

*On the contrary,* It is written (Prov. xxiv. 6): *War is managed by due ordering, and there shall be safety where there are many counsels.* Now it belongs to prudence to take counsel. Therefore there is great need in warfare for that species of prudence which is called *military.*

*I answer that,* Whatever things are done according to art or reason, should be made to conform to those which are in accordance with nature, and are established by the Divine Reason. Now nature has a twofold tendency: first, to govern each thing in itself, secondly, to withstand outward assailants and corruptives: and for this reason she has provided animals not only with the concupiscible faculty, whereby they are moved to that which is conducive to their well-being, but also with the irascible power, whereby the animal withstands an assailant.   Therefore in those things also which are in accordance with reason, there should be not only *political* prudence, which disposes in a suitable manner such things as belong to the common good, but also a *military* prudence, whereby hostile attacks are repelled.

*Reply Obj.* 1. Military prudence may be an art, in so far as it has certain rules for the right use of certain external things, such as arms and horses, but in so far as it is directed to the common good, it belongs rather to prudence.

*Reply Obj.* 2. Other matters in the state are directed to the profit of individuals, whereas the business of soldiering is directed to the protection of the entire common good.

*Reply Obj.* 3. The execution of military service belongs to fortitude, but the direction, especially in so far as it concerns the commander in chief, belongs to prudence.

# QUESTION LI.

## OF THE VIRTUES WHICH ARE CONNECTED WITH PRUDENCE.

### (*In Four Articles.*)

In due sequence, we must consider the virtues that are connected with prudence, and which are its quasi-potential parts. Under this head there are four points of inquiry: (1) Whether εὐβουλία is a virtue? (2) Whether it is a special virtue, distinct from prudence? (3) Whether σύνεσις is a special virtue? (4) Whether γνώμη is a special virtue? *

## FIRST ARTICLE.

### WHETHER εὐβουλία IS A VIRTUE?

*We proceed thus to the First Article :—*

*Objection* 1. It would seem that εὐβουλία is not a virtue. For, according to Augustine (*De Lib. Arb.* ii. 18, 19) *no man makes evil use of virtue.* Now some make evil use of εὐβουλία or good counsel, either through devising crafty counsels in order to achieve evil ends, or through committing sin in order that they may achieve good ends, as those who rob that they may give alms. Therefore εὐβουλία is not a virtue.

*Obj.* 2. Further, Virtue is a perfection, according to *Phys.* vii. But εὐβουλία is concerned with counsel, which implies doubt and research, and these are marks of imperfection. Therefore εὐβουλία is not a virtue.

* These three may be rendered as the faculties of deliberating well (εὐβουλία), of judging well according to common law (σύνεσις), and of judging well according to general law (γνώμη).

*Obj.* 3. Further, Virtues are connected with one another, as stated above (I.-II., Q. LXV.). Now εὐβουλία is not connected with the other virtues, since many sinners take good-counsel, and many godly men are slow in taking counsel. Therefore εὐβουλία is not a virtue.

*On the contrary*, According to the Philosopher (*Ethic.* vi. 9) *εὐβουλία is a right counselling*. Now the perfection of virtue consists in right reason. Therefore εὐβουλία is a virtue.

*I answer that*, As stated above (Q. XLVII., A. 4) the nature of a human virtue consists in making a human act good. Now among the acts of man, it is proper to him to take counsel, since this denotes a research of the reason about the actions he has to perform and whereof human life consists, for the speculative life is above man, as stated in *Ethic.* x. But εὐβουλία signifies goodness of counsel, for it is derived from εὐ, good, and βουλή, counsel, being *a good counsel* or rather *a disposition to take good-counsel*. Hence it is evident that εὐβουλία is a human virtue.

*Reply Obj.* 1. There is no good-counsel either in deliberating for an evil end, or in discovering evil means for attaining a good end, even as in speculative matters, there is no good reasoning either in coming to a false conclusion, or in coming to a true conclusion from false premisses through employing an unsuitable middle term. Hence both the aforesaid processes are contrary to εὐβουλία, as the Philosopher declares (*Ethic.* vi. 9).

*Reply Obj.* 2. Although virtue is essentially a perfection, it does not follow that whatever is the matter of a virtue implies perfection. For man needs to be perfected by virtues in all his parts, and this not only as regards the acts of reason, of which counsel is one, but also as regards the passions of the sensitive appetite, which are still more imperfect.

It may also be replied that human virtue is a perfection according to the mode of man, who is unable by simple insight to comprehend with certainty the truth of things, especially in matters of action which are contingent.

*Reply Obj.* 3. In no sinner as such is εὐβουλία to be found: since all sin is contrary to taking good-counsel. For good-counsel requires not only the discovery or devising of fit means for the end, but also other circumstances. Such are suitable time, so that one be neither too slow nor too quick in taking counsel, and the mode of taking counsel, so that one be firm in the counsel taken, and other like due circumstances, which sinners fail to observe when they sin. On the other hand, every virtuous man takes good-counsel in those things which are directed to the end of virtue, although perhaps he does not take good-counsel in other particular matters, for instance in matters of trade, or warfare, or the like.

## SECOND ARTICLE.

### WHETHER εὐβουλία IS A SPECIAL VIRTUE, DISTINCT FROM PRUDENCE?

*We proceed thus to the Second Article :—*

*Objection* 1. It would seem that εὐβουλία is not a distinct virtue from prudence. For, according to the Philosopher (*Ethic.* vi. 5), the *prudent man is, seemingly, one who takes good-counsel.* Now this belongs to εὐβουλία, as stated above. Therefore εὐβουλία is not distinct from prudence.

*Obj.* 2. Further, Human acts to which human virtues are directed, are specified chiefly by their end, as stated above (I.-II., Q. I., A. 3; Q. XVIII., AA. 4, 6). Now εὐβουλία and prudence are directed to the same end, as stated in *Ethic.* vi. 9, not indeed to some particular end, but to the common end of all life. Therefore εὐβουλία is not a distinct virtue from prudence.

*Obj.* 3. Further, In speculative sciences, research and decision belong to the same science. Therefore in like manner these belong to the same virtue in practical matters. Now research belongs to εὐβουλία, while decision belongs to prudence. Therefore εὐβουλία is not a distinct virtue from prudence.

*On the contrary,* Prudence is preceptive, according to

*Ethic.* vi. 10. But this does not apply to εὐβουλία. Therefore εὐβουλία is a distinct virtue from prudence.

*I answer that*, As stated above (A. 1), virtue is properly directed to an act which it renders good; and consequently virtues must differ according to different acts, especially when there is a different kind of goodness in the acts. For, if various acts contained the same kind of goodness, they would belong to the same virtue: thus the goodness of love, desire and joy depends on the same, wherefore all these belong to the same virtue of charity.

Now acts of the reason that are ordained to action are diverse, nor have they the same kind of goodness: since it is owing to different causes, that a man acquires good-counsel, good judgment, or good command, inasmuch as these are sometimes separated from one another. Consequently εὐβουλία which makes man take good-counsel must needs be a distinct virtue from prudence, which makes man command well. And since, counsel is directed to command as to that which is principal, so εὐβουλία is directed to prudence as to a principal virtue, without which it would be no virtue at all, even as neither are the moral virtues, without prudence, nor the other virtues, without charity.

*Reply Obj.* 1. It belongs to prudence to take good-counsel by commanding it, to εὐβουλία by eliciting it.

*Reply Obj.* 2. Different acts are directed in different degrees to the one end which is *a good life in general :** for counsel comes first, judgment follows, and command comes last. The last named has an immediate relation to the last end: whereas the other two acts are related thereto remotely. Nevertheless these have certain proximate ends of their own, the end of counsel being the discovery of what has to be done, and the end of judgment, certainty. Hence this proves not that εὐβουλία is not a distinct virtue from prudence, but that it is subordinate thereto, as a secondary to a principal virtue.

*Reply Obj.* 3. Even in speculative matters the rational science of dialectics, which is directed to research and discovery, is distinct from demonstrative science, which decides the truth.

* *Ethic.* vi. 5.

### Third Article.

#### WHETHER σύνεσις IS A VIRTUE ?

*We proceed thus to the Third Article :—*

*Objection* 1. It would seem that σύνεσις is not a virtue. Virtues are not in us by nature, according to *Ethic.* ii. 1. But σύνεσις is natural to some, as the Philosopher states (*Ethic.* vi. 11). Therefore σύνεσις is not a virtue.

*Obj.* 2. Further, As stated in the same book (10), σύνεσις is nothing but *a faculty of judging*. But judgment without command can be even in the wicked. Since then virtue is only in the good, it seems that σύνεσις is not a virtue.

*Obj.* 3. Further, There is never a defective command, unless there be a defective judgment, at least in a particular matter of action; for it is in this that every wicked man errs. If therefore σύνεσις be reckoned a virtue directed to good judgment, it seems that there is no need for any other virtue directed to good command: and consequently prudence would be superfluous, which is not reasonable. Therefore σύνεσις is not a virtue.

*On the contrary,* Judgment is more perfect than counsel. But εὐβουλία, or good-counsel, is a virtue. Much more, therefore, is σύνεσις a virtue, as being good judgment.

*I answer that,* σύνεσις signifies a right judgment, not indeed about speculative matters, but about particular practical matters, about which also is prudence. Hence in Greek some, in respect of σύνεσις are said to be σύνετοι, i.e. *persons of sense,* or εὐσύνετοι, i.e. *men of good sense,* just as on the other hand, those who lack this virtue are called ἀσύνετοι i.e. *senseless.*

Now different acts which cannot be ascribed to the same cause, must correspond to different virtues. And it is evident that goodness of counsel and goodness of judgment are not reducible to the same cause, for many can take good-counsel, without having good sense so as to judge well. Even so, in speculative matters some are good at research, through their reason being quick at arguing from one thing to another (which seems to be due to a disposition of their power of imagination, which has a facility in forming phantasms), and yet such persons sometimes lack good judgment (and this is due to a defect in the intellect arising chiefly from a defective disposition of the common sense which fails to judge aright). Hence there is need, besides εὐβουλία, for another virtue, which judges well, and this is called σύνεσις.

*Reply Obj.* 1. Right judgment consists in the cognitive power apprehending a thing just as it is in reality, and this is due to the right disposition of the apprehensive power. Thus if a mirror be well disposed the forms of bodies are reflected in it just as they are, whereas if it be ill disposed, the images therein appear distorted and misshapen. Now that the cognitive power be well disposed to receive things just as they are in reality, is radically due to nature, but, as to its consummation, is due to practice or to a gift of grace, and this in two ways. First directly, on the part of the cognitive power itself, for instance, because it is imbued, not with distorted, but with true and correct ideas: this belongs to σύνεσις, which in this respect is a special virtue. Secondly indirectly, through the good disposition of the appetitive power, the result being that one judges well of the objects of appetite: and thus a good judgment of virtue results from the habits of moral virtue; but this judgment is about the ends, whereas σύνεσις is rather about the means.

*Reply Obj.* 2. In wicked men there may be right judgment of a universal principle, but their judgment is always corrupt in the particular matter of action, as stated above (Q. XLVII., A. 13).

*Reply Obj.* 3. Sometimes after judging aright we delay to execute or execute negligently or inordinately. Hence after the virtue which judges aright there is a further need of a final and principal virtue, which commands aright, and this is prudence.

### Fourth Article.

#### WHETHER γνώμη IS A SPECIAL VIRTUE ?

*We proceed thus to the Fourth Article :—*

*Objection* 1. It would seem that γνώμη is not a special virtue distinct from σύνεσις. For a man is said, in respect of σύνεσις, to have good judgment. Now no man can be said to have good judgment, unless he judge aright in all things. Therefore σύνεσις extends to all matters of judgment, and consequently there is no other virtue of good judgment called γνώμη.

*Obj.* 2. Further, Judgment is midway between counsel and precept. Now there is only one virtue of good counsel, viz. εὐβουλία, and only one virtue of good command, viz. prudence. Therefore there is only one virtue of good judgment, viz. σύνεσις.

*Obj.* 3. Further, Rare occurrences wherein there is need to depart from the common law, seem for the most part to happen by chance, and with such things reason is not concerned, as stated in *Physic.* ii. 5. Now all the intellectual virtues depend on right reason. Therefore there is no intellectual virtue about such matters.

*On the contrary*, The Philosopher concludes (*Ethic.* vi. 11) that γνώμη is a special virtue.

*I answer that* cognitive habits differ according to higher and lower principles: thus in speculative matters wisdom considers higher principles than science does, and consequently is distinguished from it; and so must it be also in practical matters. Now it is evident that what is beside the order of a lower principle or cause, is sometimes reducible to the order of a higher principle; thus monstrous births of animals are beside the order of the active seminal force, and yet they come under the order of a higher principle, namely, of a heavenly body, or higher still, of divine providence. Hence by considering the active seminal force one could not pronounce a sure judgment on such monstrosities, and yet this is possible if we consider divine providence.

Now it happens sometimes that something has to be done which is not covered by the common rules of actions, for instance in the case of the enemy of one's country, when it would be wrong to give him back his deposit, or in other similar cases. Hence it is necessary to judge of such matters according to higher principles than the common laws, according to which σύνεσις judges: and corresponding to such higher principles it is necessary to have a higher virtue of judgment, which is called γνώμη, and which denotes a certain discrimination in judgment.

*Reply Obj.* 1. Σύνεσις judges rightly about all actions that are covered by the common rules: but certain things have to be judged beside these common rules, as stated above.

*Reply Obj.* 2. Judgment about a thing should be formed from the proper principles thereof, whereas research is made by employing also common principles. Wherefore also in speculative matters, dialectics which aims at research proceeds from common principles; while demonstration which tends to judgment, proceeds from proper principles. Hence εὐβουλία to which the research of counsel belongs is one for all, but not so σύνεσις, whose act is judicial. Command considers in all matters the one aspect of good, wherefore prudence also is only one.

*Reply Obj.* 3. It belongs to divine providence alone to consider all things that may happen beside the common course. On the other hand, among men, he who is most discerning can judge a greater number of such things by his reason: this belongs to γνώμη, which denotes a certain discrimination in judgment.

# QUESTION LII.

## OF THE GIFT OF COUNSEL.

### (*In Four Articles.*)

WE must now consider the gift of counsel which corresponds to prudence. Under this head there are four points of inquiry: (1) Whether counsel should be reckoned among the seven gifts of the Holy Ghost ? (2) Whether the gift of counsel corresponds to prudence ? (3) Whether the gift of counsel remains in heaven ? (4) Whether the fifth beatitude, *Blessed are the merciful*, etc. corresponds to the gift of counsel ?

### FIRST ARTICLE.

#### WHETHER COUNSEL SHOULD BE RECKONED AMONG THE GIFTS OF THE HOLY GHOST ?

*We proceed thus to the First Article :—*

*Objection* 1. It would seem that counsel should not be reckoned among the gifts of the Holy Ghost. The gifts of the Holy Ghost are given as a help to the virtues, according to Gregory (*Moral.* ii. 49). Now for the purpose of taking counsel, man is sufficiently perfected by the virtue of prudence, or even of εὐβουλία, as is evident from what has been said (Q. XLVII., AA. 1, *ad* 2; Q. LI., AA. 1, 2). Therefore counsel should not be reckoned among the gifts of the Holy Ghost.

*Obj.* 2. Further, The difference between the seven gifts of the Holy Ghost and the gratuitous graces seems to be that the latter are not given to all, but are divided among various people, whereas the gifts of the Holy Ghost are given to all who have the Holy Ghost. But counsel seems to be one of those things which are given by the Holy Ghost specially to certain persons, according to 1 Machab. ii. 65: *Behold, . . . your brother Simon is a man of counsel*. Therefore counsel should be numbered among the gratuitous graces rather than among the seven gifts of the Holy Ghost.

*Obj.* 3. Further, It is written (Rom. viii. 14): *Whosoever are led by the Spirit of God, they are the sons of God*. But counselling is not consistent with being led by another. Since then the gifts of the Holy Ghost are most befitting the children of God, who *have received the spirit of adoption of sons*, it would seem that counsel should not be numbered among the gifts of the Holy Ghost.

*On the contrary*, It is written (Isa. xi. 2): *(The Spirit of the Lord) shall rest upon him . . . the spirit of counsel, and of fortitude*.

*I answer that*, As stated above (I.-II., Q. LXVIII., A. 1), the gifts of the Holy Ghost are dispositions whereby the soul is rendered amenable to the motion of the Holy Ghost. Now God moves everything according to the mode of the thing moved: thus He moves the corporeal creature through time and place, and the spiritual creature through time, but not through place, as Augustine declares (*Gen. ad lit.* viii. 20, 22). Again, it is proper to the rational creature to be moved through the research of reason to perform any particular action, and this research is called counsel. Hence the Holy Ghost is said to move the rational creature by way of counsel, wherefore counsel is reckoned among the gifts of the Holy Ghost.

*Reply Obj.* 1. Prudence or εὐβουλία, whether acquired or infused, directs man in the research of counsel, according to principles that the reason can grasp; hence prudence or εὐβουλία makes man take good counsel either for himself or for another. Since, however, human reason is unable to grasp the singular and contingent things which may occur, the result is that *the thoughts of mortal men are fearful, and our counsels uncertain* (Wis. ix. 14). Hence in the research of counsel, man requires to be directed by God who comprehends all things: and this is done through the gift of counsel, whereby man is directed as though counselled by God, just as, in human affairs, those who are unable to take counsel for themselves, seek counsel from those who are wiser.

*Reply Obj.* 2. That a man be of such good counsel as to counsel others, may be due to a gratuitous grace; but that a man be counselled by God as to what he ought to do in matters necessary for salvation is common to all holy persons.

*Reply Obj.* 3. The children of God are moved by the Holy Ghost according to their mode, without prejudice to their free-will which is the *faculty of will and reason.*\* Accordingly the gift of counsel is befitting the children of God in so far as the reason is instructed by the Holy Ghost about what we have to do.

## SECOND ARTICLE.

### WHETHER THE GIFT OF COUNSEL CORRESPONDS TO THE VIRTUE OF PRUDENCE ?

*We proceed thus to the Second Article :—*

*Objection* 1. It would seem that the gift of counsel does not fittingly correspond to the virtue of prudence. For *the highest point of that which is underneath touches that which is above*, as Dionysius observes (*Div. Nom.* vii.), even as a man comes into contact with the angel in respect of his intellect. Now cardinal virtues are inferior to the gifts, as stated above (I.-II., Q. LXVIII., A. 8). Since, then, counsel is the first and lowest act of prudence, while command is its highest act, and judgment comes between, it seems that the gift corresponding to prudence is not counsel, but rather a gift of judgment or command.

*Obj.* 2. Further, One gift suffices to help one virtue, since the higher a thing is the more one it is, as proved in *De Causis*. Now prudence is helped by the gift of knowledge, which is not only speculative but also practical, as shown above (Q. IX., A. 3). Therefore the gift of counsel does not correspond to the virtue of prudence.

*Obj.* 3. Further, It belongs properly to prudence to direct, as stated above (Q. XLVII., A. 8). But it belongs to the

\* *Sentent.* iii. D. 24.

gift of counsel that man should be directed by God, as stated above (A. 1).   Therefore the gift of counsel does not correspond to the virtue of prudence.

*On the contrary*, The gift of counsel is about what has to be done for the sake of the end.   Now prudence is about the same matter.   Therefore they correspond to one another.

*I answer that*, A lower principle of movement is helped chiefly, and is perfected through being moved by a higher principle of movement, as a body through being moved by a spirit.   Now it is evident that the rectitude of human reason is compared to the Divine Reason, as a lower motive principle to a higher: for the Eternal Reason is the supreme rule of all human rectitude.   Consequently prudence, which denotes rectitude of reason, is chiefly perfected and helped through being ruled and moved by the Holy Ghost, and this belongs to the gift of counsel, as stated above (A. 1). Therefore the gift of counsel corresponds to prudence, as helping and perfecting it.

*Reply Obj.* 1. To judge and command belongs not to the thing moved, but to the mover.   Wherefore, since in the gifts of the Holy Ghost, the position of the human mind is of one moved rather than of a mover, as stated above (A. 1: I-II., Q. LXVIII., A. 1), it follows that it would be unfitting to call the gift corresponding to prudence by the name of command or judgment rather than of counsel, whereby it is possible to signify that the counselled mind is moved by another counselling it.

*Reply Obj.* 2. The gift of knowledge does not directly correspond to prudence, since it deals with speculative matters: yet by a kind of extension it helps it.   On the other hand the gift of counsel corresponds to prudence directly, because it is concerned about the same things.

*Reply Obj.* 3. The mover that is moved, moves through being moved.   Hence the human mind, from the very fact that it is directed by the Holy Ghost, is enabled to direct itself and others.

## Third Article.

### Whether the Gift of Counsel Remains in Heaven?

*We proceed thus to the Third Article :—*

*Objection* 1. It would seem that the gift of counsel does not remain in heaven. For counsel is about what has to be done for the sake of an end. But in heaven nothing will have to be done for the sake of an end, since there man possesses the last end. Therefore the gift of counsel is not in heaven.

*Obj.* 2. Further, Counsel implies doubt, for it is absurd to take counsel in matters that are evident, as the Philosopher observes (*Ethic* iii. 3). Now all doubt will cease in heaven. Therefore there is no counsel in heaven.

*Obj.* 3. Further, The saints in heaven are most conformed to God, according to 1 Jo. iii. 2, *When He shall appear, we shall be like to Him*. But counsel is not becoming to God, according to Rom. xi. 34, *Who hath been His counsellor ?* Therefore neither to the saints in heaven is the gift of counsel becoming.

*On the contrary*, Gregory says (*Moral.* xvii. 12): *When either the guilt or the righteousness of each nation is brought into the debate of the heavenly Court, the guardian of that nation is said to have won in the conflict, or not to have won.*

*I answer that*, As stated above (A. 2: I-II., Q. LXVIII., A. 1), the gifts of the Holy Ghost are connected with the motion of the rational creature by God. Now we must observe two points concerning the motion of the human mind by God. First, that the disposition of that which is moved, differs while it is being moved from its disposition when it is in the term of movement. Indeed if the mover is the principle of the movement alone, when the movement ceases, the action of the mover ceases as regards the thing moved, since it has already reached the term of movement, even as a house, after it is built, ceases being built by the builder. On the other hand, when the mover is cause not only of the movement, but also of the form to which the

movement tends, then the action of the mover does not
cease even after the form has been attained: thus the sun
lightens the air even after it is lightened.   In this way, then,
God causes in us virtue and knowledge, not only when we
first acquire them, but also as long as we persevere in them:
and it is thus that God causes in the blessed a knowledge of
what is to be done, not as though they were ignorant, but
by continuing that knowledge in them.

Nevertheless there are things which the blessed, whether
angels or men, do not know: such things are not essential
to blessedness, but concern the government of things according to Divine providence.   As regards these, we must make
a further observation, namely, that God moves the mind
of the blessed in one way, and the mind of the wayfarer,
in another.   For God moves the mind of the wayfarer in
matters of action, by soothing the pre-existing anxiety of
doubt; whereas there is simple nescience in the mind of the
blessed as regards the things they do not know.   From
this nescience the angel's mind is cleansed, according to
Dionysius (*Cœl. Hier.* vii.), nor does there precede in them
any research of doubt, for they simply turn to God; and this
is to take counsel of God, for as Augustine says (*Gen. ad lit.*
v. 19) *the angels take counsel of God about things beneath
them :* wherefore the instruction which they receive from
God in such matters is called *counsel.*

Accordingly the gift of counsel is in the blessed, in so far
as God preserves in them the knowledge that they have,
and enlightens them in their nescience of what is to be done.

*Reply Obj.* 1. Even in the blessed there are acts directed
to an end, or resulting, as it were, from their attainment
of the end, such as the acts of praising God, or of helping
on others to the end which they themselves have attained,
for example the ministrations of the angels, and the prayers
of the saints.   In this respect the gift of counsel finds a
place in them.

*Reply Obj.* 2. Doubt belongs to counsel according to the
present state of life, but not to that counsel which takes
place in heaven.   Even so neither have the theological

virtues quite the same acts in heaven as on the way thither.

*Reply Obj.* 3. Counsel is in God, not as receiving but as giving it: and the saints in heaven are conformed to God, as receivers to the source whence they receive.

### FOURTH ARTICLE.

#### WHETHER THE FIFTH BEATITUDE, WHICH IS THAT OF MERCY, CORRESPONDS TO THE GIFT OF COUNSEL?

*We proceed thus to the Fourth Article :*

*Objection* 1. It would seem that the fifth beatitude, which is that of mercy, does not correspond to the gift of counsel. For all the beatitudes are acts of virtue, as stated above (I.-II., Q. LXIX., A. 1). Now we are directed by counsel in all acts of virtue. Therefore the fifth beatitude does not correspond more than any other to counsel.

*Obj.* 2. Further, Precepts are given about matters necessary for salvation, while counsel is given about matters which are not necessary for salvation. Now mercy is necessary for salvation, according to James ii. 13, *Judgment without mercy to him that hath not done mercy.* On the other hand poverty is not necessary for salvation, but belongs to the life of perfection, according to Matth. xix. 21. Therefore the beatitude of poverty corresponds to the gift of counsel, rather than the beatitude of mercy.

*Obj.* 3. Further, The fruits result from the beatitudes, for they denote a certain spiritual delight resulting from perfect acts of virtue. Now none of the fruits correspond to the gift of counsel, as appears from Gal v. 22, 23. Therefore neither does the beatitude of mercy correspond to the gift of counsel.

*On the contrary,* Augustine says (*De Serm. Dom.* iv.): *Counsel is befitting the merciful, because the one remedy is to be delivered from evils so great, to pardon, and to give.*

*I answer that,* Counsel is properly about things useful for an end. Hence such things as are of most use for an end, should above all correspond to the gift of counsel. Now such is mercy, according to 1 Tim. iv. 8, *Godliness\* is profitable to all things*. Therefore the beatitude of mercy specially corresponds to the gift of counsel, not as eliciting but as directing mercy.

*Reply Obj*. 1. Although counsel directs in all the acts of virtue, it does so in a special way in works of mercy, for the reason given above.

*Reply Obj*. 2. Counsel considered as a gift of the Holy Ghost guides us in all matters that are directed to the end of eternal life, whether they be necessary for salvation or not, and yet not every work of mercy is necessary for salvation.

*Reply Obj*. 3. Fruit denotes something ultimate. Now the ultimate in practical matters consists not in knowledge but in an action which is the end. Hence nothing pertaining to practical knowledge is numbered among the fruits, but only such things as pertain to action, in which practical knowledge is the guide. Among these we find *goodness* and *benignity* which correspond to mercy.

* *Pietas* whence our English word *pity* which is the same as mercy. Cf. footnote on II.-II., Q. XXX., A. 1.

# QUESTION LIII.

## OF IMPRUDENCE.

### (*In Six Articles.*)

WE must now consider the vices opposed to prudence. For Augustine says (*Contra Julian.* iv. 3): *There are vices opposed to every virtue, not only vices that are in manifest opposition to virtue, as temerity is opposed to prudence, but also vices which have a kind of kinship and not a true but a spurious likeness to virtue; thus in opposition to prudence we have craftiness.*

Accordingly we must consider first of all those vices which are in evident opposition to prudence, those namely which are due to a defect either of prudence or of those things which are requisite for prudence, and secondly those vices which have a false resemblance to prudence, those namely which are due to abuse of the things required for prudence. And since solicitude pertains to prudence, the first of these considerations will be twofold: (1) Of imprudence: (2) Of negligence which is opposed to solicitude.

Under the first head there are six points of inquiry: (1) Concerning imprudence, whether it is a sin? (2) Whether it is a special sin? (3) Of precipitation or temerity: (4) Of thoughtlessness: (5) Of inconstancy: (6) Concerning the origin of these vices.

### FIRST ARTICLE.

#### WHETHER IMPRUDENCE IS A SIN?

*We proceed thus to the First Article :—*

*Objection* 1. It would seem that imprudence is not a sin. For every sin is voluntary, according to Augustine;*

* *De Vera Relig.* xiv.

whereas imprudence is not voluntary, since no man wishes
to be imprudent.   Therefore imprudence is not a sin.

*Obj*. 2.  Further, None but original sin comes to man with
his birth.   But imprudence comes to man with his birth,
wherefore the young are imprudent; and yet it is not original
sin which is opposed to original justice.   Therefore imprudence is not a sin.

*Obj*. 3.  Further, Every sin is taken away by repentance.
But imprudence is not taken away by repentance.   Therefore imprudence is not a sin.

*On the contrary*, The spiritual treasure of grace is not taken
away save by sin.   But it is taken away by imprudence,
according to Prov. xxi. 20, *There is a treasure to be desired,
and oil in the dwelling of the just, and the imprudent* (Douay,
*foolish*) *man shall spend it*.   Therefore imprudence is a sin.

*I answer that*, Imprudence may be taken in two ways,
first, as a privation, secondly, as a contrary.   Properly
speaking it is not taken as a negation, so as merely to signify
the absence of prudence, for this can be without any sin.
Taken as a privation, imprudence denotes lack of that
prudence which a man can and ought to have, and in this
sense imprudence is a sin by reason of a man's negligence
in striving to have prudence.

Imprudence is taken as a contrary, in so far as the movement or act of reason is in opposition to prudence: for instance,
whereas the right reason of prudence acts by taking counsel,
the imprudent man despises counsel, and the same applies
to the other conditions which require consideration in the
act of prudence.   In this way imprudence is a sin in respect
of prudence considered under its proper aspect, since it is
not possible for a man to act against prudence, except by
infringing the rules on which the right reason of prudence
depends.   Wherefore, if this should happen through aversion
from the Divine Law, it will be a mortal sin, as when a man
acts precipitately through contempt and rejection of the
Divine teaching: whereas if he act beside the Law and without contempt, and without detriment to things necessary
for salvation, it will be a venial sin.

*Reply Obj.* 1. No man desires the deformity of imprudence, but the rash man wills the act of imprudence, because he wishes to act precipitately. Hence the Philosopher says (*Ethic.* vi. 5) that *he who sins willingly against prudence is less to be commended.*

*Reply Obj.* 2. This argument takes imprudence in the negative sense. It must be observed however that lack of prudence or of any other virtue is included in the lack of original justice which perfected the entire soul. Accordingly all such lack of virtue may be ascribed to original sin.

*Reply Obj.* 3. Repentance restores infused prudence, and thus the lack of this prudence ceases; but acquired prudence is not restored as to the habit, although the contrary act is taken away, wherein properly speaking the sin of imprudence consists.

## SECOND ARTICLE.

### WHETHER IMPRUDENCE IS A SPECIAL SIN ?

*We proceed thus to the Second Article :—*

*Objection* 1. It would seem that imprudence is not a special sin. For whoever sins, acts against right reason, i.e. against prudence. But imprudence consists in acting against prudence, as stated above (A. 1). Therefore imprudence is not a special sin.

*Obj.* 2. Further, Prudence is more akin to moral action than knowledge is. But ignorance which is opposed to knowledge, is reckoned one of the general causes of sin. Much more therefore should imprudence be reckoned among those causes.

*Obj.* 3. Further, Sin consists in the corruption of the circumstances of virtue, wherefore Dionysius says (*Div. Nom.* iv.) that *evil results from each single defect.* Now many things are requisite for prudence; for instance, reason, intelligence, docility, and so on, as stated above (QQ. XLVIII., XLIX.). Therefore there are many species of imprudence, so that it is not a special sin.

*On the contrary*, Imprudence is opposed to prudence, as

stated above (A. 1).   Now prudence is a special virtue.
Therefore imprudence too is one special vice.

*I answer that*, A vice or sin may be styled general in two
ways; first, absolutely, because, to wit, it is general in
respect of all sins; secondly, because it is general in respect
of certain vices, which are its species.   In the first way, a
vice may be said to be general on two counts: first, essentially,
because it is predicated of all sins: and in this way imprudence is not a general sin, as neither is prudence a general
virtue: since it is concerned with special acts, namely the
very acts of reason: secondly, by participation; and in this
way imprudence is a general sin: for, just as all the virtues
have a share of prudence, in so far as it directs them, so have
all vices and sins a share of imprudence, because no sin can
occur, without some defect in an act of the directing reason,
which defect belongs to imprudence.

If, on the other hand, a sin be called general, not simply
but in some particular genus, that is, as containing several
species of sin, then imprudence is a general sin.   For it
contains various species in three ways.   First, by opposition
to the various subjective parts of prudence, for just as we
distinguish the prudence that guides the individual, from
other kinds that govern communities, as stated above
(Q. XLVIII.: Q. L., A. 1), so also we distinguish various
kinds of imprudence.—Secondly, in respect of the quasi-
potential parts of prudence, which are virtues connected
with it, and correspond to the several acts of reason.   Thus,
by defect of *counsel* to which εὐβουλία corresponds,
*precipitation* or *temerity* is a species of imprudence; by
defect of *judgment*, to which σύνεσις and γνώμη refer,
there is *thoughtlessness;* while *inconstancy* and *negligence*
correspond to the *command* which is the proper act of
prudence.—Thirdly, this may be taken by way of opposition
to those things which are requisite for prudence, which
are the quasi-integral parts of prudence.   Since however
all these things are intended for the direction of the aforesaid three acts of reason, it follows that all the opposite
defects are reducible to the four parts mentioned above.

Thus incautiousness and incircumspection are included in *thoughtlessness*, lack of docility, memory, or reason is referable to *precipitation;* improvidence, lack of intelligence and of shrewdness, belong to *negligence* and *inconstancy*.

*Reply Obj.* 1. This argument considers generality by participation.

*Reply Obj.* 2. Since knowledge is further removed from morality than prudence is, according to their respective proper natures, it follows that ignorance has the nature of mortal sin, not of itself, but on account either of a preceding negligence, or of the consequent result, and for this reason it is reckoned one of the general causes of sin. On the other hand imprudence, by its very nature, denotes a moral vice; and for this reason it can be called a special sin.

*Reply Obj.* 3. When various circumstances are corrupted for the same motive, the species of sin is not multiplied: thus it is the same species of sin to take what is not one's own, where one ought not, and when one ought not. If, however, there be various motives, there are various species: for instance, if one man were to take another's property from where he ought not, so as to wrong a sacred place, this would constitute the species called sacrilege, while if another were to take another's property when he ought not, merely through the lust of possession, this would be a case of simple avarice. Hence the lack of those things which are requisite for prudence, does not constitute a diversity of species, except in so far as they are directed to different acts of reason, as stated above.

## THIRD ARTICLE.

### WHETHER PRECIPITATION IS A SIN INCLUDED IN IMPRUDENCE ?

*We proceed thus to the Third Article :—*

*Objection* 1. It would seem that precipitation is not a sin included in imprudence. Imprudence is opposed to the virtue of prudence; whereas precipitation is opposed to the gift of counsel, according to Gregory, who says (*Moral.* ii. 49) that the gift of *counsel is given as a remedy to precipitation*.

Therefore precipitation is not a sin contained under imprudence.

*Obj.* 2. Further, Precipitation seemingly pertains to rashness.   Now rashness implies presumption, which pertains to pride.   Therefore precipitation is not a vice contained under imprudence.

*Obj.* 3. Further, Precipitation seems to denote inordinate haste.   Now sin happens in counselling not only through being over hasty but also through being over slow, so that the opportunity for action passes by, and through corruption of other circumstances, as stated in *Ethic.* vi. 9.   Therefore there is no reason for reckoning precipitation as a sin contained under imprudence, rather than slowness, or something else of the kind pertaining to inordinate counsel.

*On the contrary*, It is written (Prov. iv. 19): *The way of the wicked is darksome, they know not where they fall.*   Now the darksome ways of ungodliness belong to imprudence. Therefore imprudence leads a man to fall or to be precipitate.

*I answer that*, Precipitation is ascribed metaphorically to acts of the soul, by way of similitude to bodily movement. Now a thing is said to be precipitated as regards bodily movement, when it is brought down from above by the impulse either of its own movement or of another's, and not in orderly fashion by degrees.   Now the summit of the soul is the reason, and the base is reached in the action performed by the body; while the steps that intervene by which one ought to descend in orderly fashion are *memory* of the past, *intelligence* of the present, *shrewdness* in considering the future outcome, *reasoning* which compares one thing with another, *docility* in accepting the opinions of others.   He that takes counsel descends by these steps in due order, whereas if a man is rushed into action by the impulse of his will or of a passion, without taking these steps, it will be a case of precipitation.   Since then inordinate counsel pertains to imprudence, it is evident that the vice of precipitation is contained under imprudence.

*Reply Obj.* 1. Rectitude of counsel belongs to the gift of counsel and to the virtue of prudence; albeit in different ways, as stated above (Q. LII., A. 2), and consequently precipitation is opposed to both.

*Reply Obj.* 2. Things are said to be done rashly when they are not directed by reason: and this may happen in two ways; first through the impulse of the will or of a passion, secondly through contempt of the directing rule; and this is what is meant by rashness properly speaking, wherefore it appears to proceed from that root of pride, which refuses to submit to another's ruling. But precipitation refers to both, so that rashness is contained under precipitation, although precipitation refers rather to the first.

*Reply Obj.* 3. Many things have to be considered in the research of reason; hence the Philosopher declares (*Ethic.* vi. 9) that *one should be slow in taking counsel.* Hence precipitation is more directly opposed to rectitude of counsel than over slowness is, for the latter bears a certain likeness to right counsel.

### Fourth Article.

#### WHETHER THOUGHTLESSNESS IS A SPECIAL SIN INCLUDED IN IMPRUDENCE ?

*We proceed thus to the Fourth Article :—*

*Objection* 1. It would seem that thoughtlessness is not a special sin included in imprudence. For the Divine law does not incite us to any sin, according to Ps. xviii. 8, *The law of the Lord is unspotted :* and yet it incites us to be thoughtless, according to Matth. x. 19, *Take no thought how or what to speak.* Therefore thoughtlessness is not a sin.

*Obj.* 2. Further, Whoever takes counsel must needs give thought to many things. Now precipitation is due to a defect of counsel and therefore to a defect of thought. Therefore precipitation is contained under thoughtlessness: and consequently thoughtlessness is not a special sin.

*Obj.* 3. Further, Prudence consists in acts of the practical reason, viz. *counsel, judgment* about what has been counselled, and *command.** Now thought precedes all these acts, since it belongs also to the speculative intellect.

* Cf. Q. XLVII., A. 8.

Therefore thoughtlessness is not a special sin contained under imprudence.

*On the contrary*, It is written (Prov. iv. 25): *Let thy eyes look straight on, and let thine eye-lids go before thy steps*. Now this pertains to prudence, while the contrary pertains to thoughtlessness. Therefore thoughtlessness is a special sin contained under imprudence.

*I answer that*, Thought signifies the act of the intellect in considering the truth about something. Now just as research belongs to the reason, so judgment belongs to the intellect. Wherefore in speculative matters a demonstrative science is said to exercise judgment, in so far as it judges the truth of the results of research by tracing those results back to the first indemonstrable principles. Hence thought pertains chiefly to judgment; and consequently the lack of right judgment belongs to the vice of thoughtlessness, in so far, to wit, as one fails to judge rightly through contempt or neglect of those things on which a right judgment depends. It is therefore evident that thoughtlessness is a sin.

*Reply Obj*. 1. Our Lord did not forbid us to take thought, when we have the opportunity, about what we ought to do or say, but, in the words quoted, He encourages His disciples, so that when they had no opportunity of taking thought, either through lack of knowledge or through a sudden call, they should trust in the guidance of God alone, because *as we know not what to do, we can only turn our eyes to* God, according to 2 Paral. xx. 12: else if man, instead of doing what he can, were to be content with awaiting God's assistance, he would seem to tempt God.

*Reply Obj*. 2. All thought about those things of which counsel takes cognizance, is directed to the formation of a right judgment, wherefore this thought is perfected in judgment. Consequently thoughtlessness is above all opposed to the rectitude of judgment.

*Reply Obj*. 3. Thoughtlessness is to be taken here in relation to a determinate matter, namely, that of human action, wherein more things have to be thought about for the purpose of right judgment, than in speculative matters, because actions are about singulars.

## FIFTH ARTICLE.

### WHETHER INCONSTANCY IS A VICE CONTAINED UNDER IMPRUDENCE ?

*We proceed thus to the Fifth Article :—*

*Objection* 1. It would seem that inconstancy is not a vice contained under imprudence.  For inconstancy consists seemingly in a lack of perseverance in matters of difficulty. But perseverance in difficult matters belongs to fortitude. Therefore inconstancy is opposed to fortitude rather than to prudence.

*Obj.* 2. Further, It is written (James iii. 16): *Where jealousy* (Douay, *envy*) *and contention are, there are inconstancy and every evil work*.  But jealousy pertains to envy. Therefore inconstancy pertains not to imprudence but to envy.

*Obj.* 3. Further, A man would seem to be inconstant who fails to persevere in what he has proposed to do.  Now this is a mark of *incontinency* in pleasurable matters, and of *effeminacy* or *squeamishness* in unpleasant matters, according to *Ethic*. vii. 7.  Therefore inconstancy does not pertain to imprudence.

*On the contrary*, It belongs to prudence to prefer the greater good to the lesser.  Therefore to forsake the greater good belongs to imprudence.  Now this is inconstancy. Therefore inconstancy belongs to imprudence.

*I answer that*, Inconstancy denotes withdrawal from a definite good purpose.  Now the origin of this withdrawal is in the appetite, for a man does not withdraw from a previous good purpose, except on account of something being inordinately pleasing to him: nor is this withdrawal completed except through a defect of reason, which is deceived in rejecting what before it had rightly accepted. And since it can resist the impulse of the passions, if it fail to do this, it is due to its own weakness in not standing to the good purpose it has conceived ; hence inconstancy, as to its completion, is due to a defect in the reason.

Now just as all rectitude of the practical reason belongs in some degree to prudence, so all lack of that rectitude belongs to imprudence. Consequently inconstancy, as to its completion, belongs to imprudence. And just as precipitation is due to a defect in the act of counsel, and thoughtlessness to a defect in the act of judgment, so inconstancy arises from a defect in the act of command. For a man is stated to be inconstant because his reason fails in commanding what has been counselled and judged.

*Reply Obj.* 1. The good of prudence is shared by all the moral virtues, and accordingly perseverance in good belongs to all moral virtues, chiefly, however, to fortitude which suffers a greater impulse to the contrary.

*Reply Obj.* 2. Envy and anger which are the source of contention, cause inconstancy on the part of the appetite, to which power the origin of inconstancy is due, as stated above.

*Reply Obj.* 3. Continency and perseverance seem to be not in the appetitive power, but in the reason. For the continent man suffers evil concupiscences, and the persevering man suffers grievous sorrows (which points to a defect in the appetitive power); but reason stands firm, in the continent man, against concupiscence, and in the persevering man, against sorrow. Hence continency and perseverance seem to be species of constancy which pertains to reason; and to this power inconstancy pertains also.

## Sixth Article.

### WHETHER THE AFORESAID VICES ARISE FROM LUST ?

*We proceed thus to the Sixth Article :—*

*Objection* 1. It would seem that the aforesaid vices do not arise from lust. For inconstancy arises from envy, as stated above (A. 5, *ad* 2). But envy is a distinct vice from lust. Therefore the aforesaid vices do not arise from lust.

*Obj.* 2. Further, It is written (James i. 8): *A double-minded man is inconstant in all his ways.* Now duplicity does not seem to pertain to lust, but rather to deceitfulness, which is a daughter of covetousness, according to Gregory (*Moral.* xxxi. 45). Therefore the aforesaid vices do not arise from lust.

*Obj.* 3. Further, The aforesaid vices are connected with some defect of reason. Now spiritual vices are more akin to the reason than carnal vices. Therefore the aforesaid vices arise from spiritual vices rather than from carnal vices.

*On the contrary,* Gregory declares (*Moral.* xxxi. 45) that the aforesaid vices arise from lust.

*I answer that,* As the Philosopher states (*Ethic.* vi. 5) *pleasure above all corrupts the estimate of prudence,* and chiefly sexual pleasure which absorbs the mind, and draws it to sensible delight. Now the perfection of prudence and of every intellectual virtue consists in abstraction from sensible objects. Wherefore, since the aforesaid vices involve a defect of prudence and of the practical reason, as stated above (AA. 2, 5), it follows that they arise chiefly from lust.

*Reply Obj.* 1. Envy and anger cause inconstancy by drawing away the reason to something else; whereas lust causes inconstancy by destroying the judgment of reason entirely. Hence the Philosopher says (*Ethic.* vii. 6) that *the man who is incontinent through anger listens to reason, yet not perfectly, whereas he who is incontinent through lust does not listen to it at all.*

*Reply Obj.* 2. Duplicity also is something resulting from lust, just as inconstancy is, if by duplicity we understand fluctuation of the mind from one thing to another. Hence Terence says (*Eunuch.*, act 1, sc. 1) that *love leads to war, and likewise to peace and truce.*

*Reply Obj.* 3. Carnal vices destroy the judgment of reason so much the more as they lead us away from reason.

# QUESTION LIV.

## OF NEGLIGENCE.

### (*In Three Articles*.)

WE must now consider negligence, under which head there are three points of inquiry: (1) Whether negligence is a special sin? (2) To which virtue is it opposed? (3) Whether negligence is a mortal sin?

## FIRST ARTICLE.

### WHETHER NEGLIGENCE IS A SPECIAL SIN?

*We proceed thus to the First Article :—*

*Objection* 1. It would seem that negligence is not a special sin. For negligence is opposed to diligence. But diligence is required in every virtue. Therefore negligence is not a special sin.

*Obj.* 2. Further, That which is common to every sin is not a special sin. Now negligence is common to every sin, because he who sins neglects that which withdraws him from sin, and he who perseveres in sin neglects to be contrite for his sin. Therefore negligence is not a special sin.

*Obj.* 3. Further, Every special sin has a determinate matter. But negligence seems to have no determinate matter: since it is neither about evil or indifferent things, (for no man is accused of negligence if he omit them), nor about good things, for if these be done negligently, they are no longer good. Therefore it seems that negligence is not a special vice.

*On the contrary*, Sins committed through negligence, are

distinguished from those which are committed through contempt.

*I answer that*, Negligence denotes lack of due solicitude. Now every lack of a due act is sinful: wherefore it is evident that negligence is a sin, and that it must needs have the character of a special sin according as solicitude is the act of a special virtue. For certain sins are special through being about a special matter, as lust is about sexual matters, while some vices are special on account of their having a special kind of act which extends to all kinds of matter, and such are all vices affecting an act of reason, since every act of reason extends to any kind of moral matter. Since then solicitude is a special act of reason, as stated above (Q. XLVII., A. 9), it follows that negligence, which denotes lack of solicitude, is a special sin.

*Reply Obj.* 1. Diligence seems to be the same as solicitude, because the more we love (*diligimus*) a thing the more solicitous are we about it. Hence diligence, no less than solicitude, is required for every virtue, in so far as due acts of reason are requisite for every virtue.

*Reply Obj.* 2. In every sin there must needs be a defect affecting an act of reason, for instance a defect in counsel or the like. Hence just as precipitation is a special sin on account of a special act of reason which is omitted, namely counsel, although it may be found in any kind of sin; so negligence is a special sin on account of the lack of a special act of reason, namely solicitude, although it is found more or less in all sins.

*Reply Obj.* 3. Properly speaking the matter of negligence is a good that one ought to do, not that it is a good when it is done negligently, but because on account of negligence it incurs a lack of goodness, whether a due act be entirely omitted through lack of solicitude, or some due circumstance be omitted.

## Second Article.

### WHETHER NEGLIGENCE IS OPPOSED TO PRUDENCE?

*We proceed thus to the Second Article :—*

*Objection* 1. It would seem that negligence is not opposed to prudence. For negligence seems to be the same as idleness or laziness, which belongs to sloth, according to Gregory (*Moral.* xxxi. 45). Now sloth is not opposed to prudence, but to charity, as stated above (Q. XXXV., A. 3). Therefore negligence is not opposed to prudence.

*Obj.* 2. Further, Every sin of omission seems to be due to negligence. But sins of omission are not opposed to prudence, but to the executive moral virtues. Therefore negligence is not opposed to prudence.

*Obj.* 3. Further, Imprudence relates to some act of reason. But negligence does not imply a defect of counsel, for that is *precipitation,* nor a defect of judgment, since that is *thoughtlessness,* nor a defect of command, because that is *inconstancy.* Therefore negligence does not pertain to imprudence.

*Obj.* 4. Further, It is written (Eccles. vii. 19): *He that feareth God, neglecteth nothing.* But every sin is excluded by the opposite virtue. Therefore negligence is opposed to fear rather than to prudence.

*On the contrary,* It is written (Ecclus. xx. 7): *A babbler and a fool* (*imprudens*) *will regard no time.* Now this is due to negligence. Therefore negligence is opposed to prudence.

*I answer that,* Negligence is directly opposed to solicitude. Now solicitude pertains to the reason, and rectitude of solicitude to prudence. Hence, on the other hand, negligence pertains to imprudence. This appears from its very name, because, as Isidore observes (*Etym.* x.) *a negligent man is one who fails to choose* (*nec eligens*): and the right choice of the means belongs to prudence. Therefore negligence pertains to imprudence.

*Reply Obj.* 1. Negligence is a defect in the internal

act, to which choice also belongs: whereas idleness and laziness denote slowness of execution, yet so that idleness denotes slowness in setting about the execution, while laziness denotes remissness in the execution itself. Hence it is becoming that laziness should arise from sloth, which is *an oppressive sorrow*, i.e. hindering, the mind from action.*

*Reply Obj.* 2. Omission regards the external act, for it consists in failing to perform an act which is due. Hence it is opposed to justice, and is an effect of negligence, even as the execution of a just deed is the effect of right reason.

*Reply Obj.* 3. Negligence regards the act of command, which solicitude also regards. Yet the negligent man fails in regard to this act otherwise than the inconstant man: for the inconstant man fails in commanding, being hindered as it were, by something, whereas the negligent man fails through lack of a prompt will.

*Reply Obj.* 4. The fear of God helps us to avoid all sins, because according to Prov. xv. 27, *by the fear of the Lord everyone declineth from evil*. Hence fear makes us avoid negligence, yet not as though negligence were directly opposed to fear, but because fear incites man to acts of reason. Wherefore also it has been stated above (I.-II., Q. XLIV., A. 2) when we were treating of the passions, that *fear makes us take counsel*.

## THIRD ARTICLE.

### WHETHER NEGLIGENCE CAN BE A MORTAL SIN?

*We proceed thus to the Third Article :—*

*Objection* 1. It would seem that negligence cannot be a mortal sin. For a gloss of Gregory† on Job ix. 28, *I feared all my works*, etc. says that *too little love of God aggravates the former*, viz. negligence. But wherever there is mortal sin, the love of God is done away with altogether. Therefore negligence is not a mortal sin.

*Obj.* 2. Further, A gloss on Ecclus. vii. 34, *For thy negligences purify thyself with a few*, says: *Though the offering*

* Cf. Q. XXXV. 1; I.-II., Q. XXXV. 8.          † *Moral.* ix. 34.

*be small it cleanses the negligences of many sins.* Now this would not be, if negligence were a mortal sin. Therefore negligence is not a mortal sin.

*Obj.* 3. Further, Under the law certain sacrifices were prescribed for mortal sins, as appears from the book of Leviticus. Yet no sacrifice was prescribed for negligence. Therefore negligence is not a mortal sin.

*On the contrary,* It is written (Prov. xix. 16): *He that neglecteth his own life* (Vulg., *way*) *shall die.*

*I answer that,* As stated above (A. 2, *ad* 3), negligence arises out of a certain remissness of the will, the result being a lack of solicitude on the part of the reason in commanding what it should command, or as it should command. Accordingly negligence may happen to be a mortal sin in two ways. First on the part of that which is omitted through negligence. If this be either an act or a circumstance necessary for salvation, it will be a mortal sin. Secondly on the part of the cause: for if the will be so remiss about Divine things, as to fall away altogether from the charity of God, such negligence is a mortal sin, and this is the case chiefly when negligence is due to contempt.

But if negligence consists in the omission of an act or circumstance that is not necessary for salvation, it is not a mortal but a venial sin, provided the negligence arise, not from contempt, but from some lack of fervour, to which venial sin is an occasional obstacle.

*Reply Obj.* 1. Man may be said to love God less in two ways. First through lack of the fervour of charity, and this causes the negligence that is a venial sin: secondly through lack of charity itself, in which sense we say that a man loves God less when he loves Him with a merely natural love; and this causes the negligence that is a mortal sin.

*Reply Obj.* 2. According to the same authority (*ibid.*) a small offering made with a humble mind and out of pure love, cleanses man not only from venial but also from mortal sin

*Reply Obj.* 3. When negligence consists in the omission

of that which is necessary for salvation, it is drawn to the other more manifest genus of sin. Because those sins that consist of inward actions, are more hidden, wherefore no special sacrifices were prescribed for them in the Law, since the offering of sacrifices was a kind of public confession of sin, whereas hidden sins should not be confessed in public.

# QUESTION LV.

## OF VICES OPPOSED TO PRUDENCE BY WAY OF RESEMBLANCE.

### (*In Eight Articles.*)

WE must now consider those vices opposed to prudence, which have a resemblance thereto. Under this head there are eight points of inquiry: (1) Whether prudence of the flesh is a sin? (2) Whether it is a mortal sin? (3) Whether craftiness is a special sin? (4) Of guile: (5) Of fraud: (6) Of solicitude about temporal things: (7) Of solicitude about the future: (8) Of the origin of these vices.

## FIRST ARTICLE.

### WHETHER PRUDENCE OF THE FLESH IS A SIN?

*We proceed thus to the First Article :—*

*Objection* 1. It would seem that prudence of the flesh is not a sin. For prudence is more excellent than the other moral virtues, since it governs them all. But no justice or temperance is sinful. Neither therefore is any prudence a sin.

*Obj.* 2. Further, It is not a sin to act prudently for an end which it is lawful to love. But it is lawful to love the flesh, *for no man ever hated his own flesh* (Eph. v. 29). Therefore prudence of the flesh is not a sin.

*Obj.* 3. Further, Just as man is tempted by the flesh, so too is he tempted by the world and the devil. But no prudence of the world, or of the devil is accounted a sin. Therefore neither should any prudence of the flesh be accounted among sins.

*On the contrary*, No man is an enemy to God save for wickedness, according to Wis. xiv. 9, *To God the wicked and his wickedness are hateful alike.* Now it is written (Rom. viii. 7): *The prudence* (Vulg.,—*wisdom*) *of the flesh is an enemy to God.* Therefore prudence of the flesh is a sin.

*I answer that,* As stated above (Q. XLVII., A. 13), prudence regards things which are directed to the end of life as a whole. Hence prudence of the flesh signifies properly the prudence of a man who looks upon carnal goods as the last end of his life. Now it is evident that this is a sin, because it involves a disorder in man with respect to his last end, which does not consist in the goods of the body, as stated above (I.-II., Q. II., A. 5). Therefore prudence of the flesh is a sin.

*Reply Obj.* 1. Justice and temperance include in their very nature that which ranks them among the virtues, viz. equality and the curbing of concupiscence; hence they are never taken in a bad sense. On the other hand prudence is so called from foreseeing (*providendo*), as stated above (Q. XLVII., A. 1: Q. XLIX., A. 6), which can extend to evil things also. Therefore, although prudence is taken simply in a good sense, yet, if something be added, it may be taken in a bad sense: and it is thus that prudence of the flesh is said to be a sin.

*Reply Obj.* 2. The flesh is on account of the soul, as matter is on account of the form, and the instrument on account of the principal agent. Hence the flesh is loved lawfully, if it be directed to the good of the soul as its end. If, however, a man place his last end in a good of the flesh, his love will be inordinate and unlawful, and it is thus that the prudence of the flesh is directed to the love of the flesh.

*Reply Obj.* 3. The devil tempts us, not through the good of the appetible object, but by way of suggestion. Wherefore, since prudence implies direction to some appetible end, we do not speak of *prudence of the devil*, as of a prudence directed to some evil end, which is the aspect under which the world and the flesh tempt us, in so far as worldly or carnal goods are proposed to our appetite. Hence we speak of *carnal* and again of *worldly* prudence, according to Luke xvi. 8, *The children of this world are more prudent* (Douay,—*wiser*) *in their generation*, etc.   The Apostle includes all in the *prudence of the flesh*, because we covet the external things of the world on account of the flesh.

We may also reply that since prudence is in a certain sense called *wisdom*, as stated above (Q. XLVII., A. 2, *ad* 1), we may distinguish a threefold prudence corresponding to the three kinds of temptation.   Hence it is written (James iii. 15) that there is a wisdom which is *earthly, sensual and devilish*, as explained above (Q. XLV., A. 1, *ad* 1), when we were treating of wisdom.

### SECOND ARTICLE.

#### WHETHER PRUDENCE OF THE FLESH IS A MORTAL SIN?

*We proceed thus to the Second Article :—*

*Objection* 1. It would seem that prudence of the flesh is a mortal sin.   For it is a mortal sin to rebel against the Divine law, since this implies contempt of God.   Now *the prudence* (Douay,—*wisdom*) *of the flesh . . . is not subject to the law of God* (Rom. viii. 7).   Therefore prudence of the flesh is a mortal sin.

*Obj.* 2. Further, Every sin against the Holy Ghost is a mortal sin.   Now prudence of the flesh seems to be a sin against the Holy Ghost, for *it cannot be subject to the law of God* (Rom. viii. 7), and so it seems to be an unpardonable sin, which is proper to the sin against the Holy Ghost. Therefore prudence of the flesh is a mortal sin.

*Obj.* 3. Further, The greatest evil is opposed to the greatest good, as stated in *Ethic.* viii. 10.   Now prudence of the flesh is opposed to that prudence which is the chief of the moral virtues.   Therefore prudence of the flesh is chief among mortal sins, so that it is itself a mortal sin.

*On the contrary*, That which diminishes a sin has not of itself the nature of a mortal sin.   Now the thoughtful quest of things pertaining to the care of the flesh, which seems to pertain to carnal prudence, diminishes sin.*   Therefore

* Cf. Prov. vi. 30.

prudence of the flesh has not of itself the nature of a mortal sin.

*I answer that*, As stated above (Q. XLVII., A. 2, *ad* 1: A. 13), a man is said to be prudent in two ways. First, simply, i.e. in relation to the end of life as a whole. Secondly, relatively, i.e. in relation to some particular end; thus a man is said to be prudent in business or something else of the kind. Accordingly if prudence of the flesh be taken as corresponding to prudence in its absolute signification, so that a man place the last end of his whole life in the care of the flesh, it is a mortal sin, because he turns away from God by so doing, since he cannot have several last ends, as stated above (I.-II., Q. I., A. 5).

If, on the other hand, prudence of the flesh be taken as corresponding to particular prudence, it is a venial sin. For it happens sometimes that a man has an inordinate affection for some pleasure of the flesh, without turning away from God by a mortal sin; in which case he does not place the end of his whole life in carnal pleasure. To apply oneself to obtain this pleasure is a venial sin and pertains to prudence of the flesh. But if a man actually refers the care of the flesh to a good end, as when one is careful about one's food in order to sustain one's body, this is no longer prudence of the flesh, because then one uses the care of the flesh as a means to an end.

*Reply Obj.* 1. The Apostle is speaking of that carnal prudence whereby a man places the end of his whole life in the goods of the flesh, and this is a mortal sin.

*Reply Obj.* 2. Prudence of the flesh does not imply a sin against the Holy Ghost. For when it is stated that *it cannot be subject to the law of God*, this does not mean that he who has prudence of the flesh, cannot be converted and submit to the law of God, but that carnal prudence itself cannot be subject to God's law, even as neither can injustice be just, nor heat cold, although that which is hot may become cold.

*Reply Obj.* 3. Every sin is opposed to prudence, just as prudence is shared by every virtue. But it does not follow

# # # tion

that every sin opposed to prudence is most grave, but only when it is opposed to prudence in some very grave matter.

## Third Article.
### Whether Craftiness is a Special Sin?

*We proceed thus to the Third Article:—*

*Objection* 1. It would seem that craftiness is not a special sin. For the words of Holy Writ do not induce anyone to sin; and yet they induce us to be crafty, according to Prov. i. 4, *To give craftiness* (Douay,—*subtlety*) *to little ones.* Therefore craftiness is not a sin.

*Obj.* 2. Further, It is written (Prov. xiii. 16): *The crafty* (Douay,—*prudent*) *man doth all things with counsel.* Therefore, he does so either for a good or for an evil end. If for a good end, there is no sin seemingly, and if for an evil end, it would seem to pertain to carnal or worldly prudence. Therefore craftiness is not a special sin distinct from prudence of the flesh.

*Obj.* 3. Further, Gregory expounding the words of Job xii., *The simplicity of the just man is laughed to scorn,* says (*Moral.* x. 29): *The wisdom of this world is to hide one's thoughts by artifice, to conceal one's meaning by words, to represent error as truth, to make out the truth to be false,* and further on he adds: *This prudence is acquired by the young, it is learnt at a price by children.* Now the above things seem to belong to craftiness. Therefore craftiness is not distinct from carnal or worldly prudence, and consequently it seems not to be a special sin.

*On the contrary,* The Apostle says (2 Cor. iv. 2): *We renounce the hidden things of dishonesty, not walking in craftiness, nor adulterating the word of God.* Therefore craftiness is a sin.

*I answer that,* Prudence is *right reason applied to action,* Just as science is *right reason applied to knowledge.* In speculative matters one may sin against rectitude of knowledge in two ways; in one way when the reason is led to a false conclusion that appears to be true; in another way when the reason proceeds from false premisses, that appear to be true, either to a true or to a false conclusion. Even so a sin may be against prudence, through having some resemblance thereto, in two ways. First, when the purpose of the reason is directed to an end which is good not in truth but in appearance, and this pertains to prudence of the flesh; secondly, when, in order to obtain a certain end, whether good or evil, a man uses means that are not true but fictitious and counterfeit, and this belongs to the sin of craftiness. This is consequently a sin opposed to prudence, and distinct from prudence of the flesh.

*Reply Obj.* 1. As Augustine observes (*Contra Julian.* iv. 3) just as prudence is sometimes improperly taken in a bad sense, so is craftiness sometimes taken in a good sense, and this on account of their mutual resemblance. Properly speaking, however, craftiness is taken in a bad sense, as the Philosopher states in *Ethic.* vi. 12.

*Reply Obj.* 2. Craftiness can take counsel both for a good end and for an evil end: nor should a good end be pursued by means that are false and counterfeit but by such as are true. Hence craftiness is a sin if it be directed to a good end.

*Reply Obj.* 3. Under *worldly prudence* Gregory included everything that can pertain to false prudence, so that it comprises craftiness also.


FOURTH ARTICLE.

WHETHER GUILE IS A SIN PERTAINING TO CRAFTINESS?

*We proceed thus to the Fourth Article :—*

*Objection* 1. It would seem that guile is not a sin pertaining to craftiness. For sin, especially mortal, has no place in perfect men. Yet a certain guile is to be found in them, according to 2 Cor. xii. 16, *Being crafty I caught you by guile.* Therefore guile is not always a sin.

*Obj.* 2. Further, Guile seems to pertain chiefly to the tongue, according to Ps. v. 11, *They dealt deceitfully with their tongues.* Now craftiness like prudence is in the

very act of reason. Therefore guile does not pertain to
craftiness.

*Obj*. 3. Further, It is written (Prov. xii. 20): *Guile* (Douay,
*—Deceit*) *is in the heart of them that think evil things*.
But the thought of evil things does not always pertain to
craftiness. Therefore guile does not seem to belong to
craftiness.

*On the contrary*, Craftiness aims at lying in wait, according
to Eph. iv. 14, *By cunning craftiness by which they lie in wait
to deceive:* and guile aims at this also. Therefore guile
pertains to craftiness.

*I answer that*, As stated above (A. 3), it belongs to craftiness
to adopt ways that are not true but counterfeit and apparently true, in order to attain some end either good or evil.
Now the adopting of such ways may be subjected to a
twofold consideration; first, as regards the process of thinking them out, and this belongs properly to craftiness, even
as thinking out right ways to a due end belongs to prudence.
Secondly the adopting of suchlike ways may be considered
with regard to their actual execution, and in this way it
belongs to guile. Hence guile denotes a certain execution
of craftiness, and accordingly belongs thereto.

*Reply Obj*. 1. Just as craftiness is taken properly in a bad
sense, and improperly in a good sense, so too is guile which
is the execution of craftiness.

*Reply Obj*. 2. The execution of craftiness with the purpose
of deceiving, is effected first and foremost by words, which
hold the chief place among those signs whereby a man
signifies something to another man, as Augustine states (*De
Doctr. Christ*. ii. 3), hence guile is ascribed chiefly to speech.
Yet guile may happen also in deeds, according to Ps. civ. 25,
*And to deal deceitfully with his servants*. Guile is also in the
heart, according to Ecclus. xix. 23, *His interior is full of
deceit*, but this is to devise deceits, according to Ps. xxxvii.
13: *They studied deceits all the day long*.

*Reply Obj*. 3. Whoever purposes to do some evil deed,
must needs devise certain ways of attaining his purpose,
and for the most part he devises deceitful ways, whereby the

more easily to obtain his end. Nevertheless it happens sometimes that evil is done openly and by violence without craftiness and guile; but as this is more difficult, it is of less frequent occurrence.

### FIFTH ARTICLE.

#### WHETHER FRAUD PERTAINS TO CRAFTINESS

*We proceed thus to the Fifth Article :—*

*Objection* 1. It would seem that fraud does not pertain to craftiness. For a man does not deserve praise if he allows himself to be deceived, which is the object of craftiness; and yet a man deserves praise for allowing himself to be defrauded, according to 1 Cor. vi. 7, *Why do you not rather suffer yourselves to be defrauded ?* Therefore fraud does not belong to craftiness.

*Obj.* 2. Further, Fraud seems to consist in unlawfully taking or receiving external things, for it is written (Acts v. 1) that *a certain man named Ananias with Saphira his wife, sold a piece of land, and by fraud kept back part of the price of the land.* Now it pertains to injustice or illiberality to take possession of or retain external things unjustly. Therefore fraud does not belong to craftiness which is opposed to prudence.

*Obj.* 3. Further, No man employs craftiness against himself. But the frauds of some are against themselves, for it is written (Prov. i. 18) concerning some *that they practise frauds* (Douay,—*deceits*) *against their own souls.* Therefore fraud does not belong to craftiness.

*On the contrary,* The object of fraud is to deceive, according to Job xiii. 9, *Shall he be deceived as a man, with your fraudulent* (Douay,—*deceitful*) *dealings ?* Now craftiness is directed to the same object. Therefore fraud pertains to craftiness.

*I answer that,* Just as *guile* consists in the execution of craftiness, so also does *fraud.* But they seem to differ in the fact that *guile* belongs in general to the execution of craftiness, whether this be effected by words, or by deeds, whereas *fraud* belongs more properly to the execution of craftiness by deeds.

*Reply Obj.* 1. The Apostle does not counsel the faithful to be deceived in their knowledge, but to bear patiently the effect of being deceived, and to endure wrongs inflicted on them by fraud.

*Reply Obj.* 2. The execution of craftiness may be carried out by another vice, just as the execution of prudence by the virtues: and accordingly nothing hinders fraud from pertaining to covetousness or illiberality.

*Reply Obj.* 3. Those who commit frauds, do not design anything against themselves or their own souls; it is through God's just judgment that what they plot against others, recoils on themselves, according to Ps. vii. 16, *He is fallen into the hole he made.*


## Sixth Article.

### WHETHER IT IS LAWFUL TO BE SOLICITOUS ABOUT TEMPORAL MATTERS ?

*We proceed thus to the Sixth Article :—*

*Objection* 1. It would seem lawful to be solicitous about temporal matters.   Because a superior should be solicitous for his subjects, according to Rom. xii. 8, *He that ruleth, with solicitude.*   Now according to the Divine ordering, man is placed over temporal things, according to Ps. viii. 8, *Thou hast subjected all things under his feet,* etc.   Therefore man should be solicitous about temporal things.

*Obj.* 2. Further, Everyone is solicitous about the end for which he works.   Now it is lawful for a man to work for the temporal things whereby he sustains life, wherefore the Apostle says (2 Thess. iii. 10): *If any man will not work, neither let him eat.*   Therefore it is lawful to be solicitous about temporal things.

*Obj.* 3. Further, Solicitude about works of mercy is praiseworthy, according to 2 Tim. i. 17, *When he was come to Rome, he carefully sought me.*   Now solicitude about temporal things is sometimes connected with works of mercy; for instance, when a man is solicitous to watch over the interests of orphans and poor persons. Therefore solicitude about temporal things is not unlawful.

*On the contrary,* Our Lord said (Matth. vi. 31): *Be not solicitous, . . . saying, What shall we eat, or what shall we drink, or wherewith shall we be clothed ?* And yet such things are very necessary.

*I answer that,* Solicitude denotes an earnest endeavour to obtain something. Now it is evident that the endeavour is more earnest when there is fear of failure, so that there is less solicitude when success is assured. Accordingly solicitude about temporal things may be unlawful in three ways. First on the part of the object of solicitude; that is, if we seek temporal things as an end. Hence Augustine says (*De Operibus Monach.* xxvi.): *When Our Lord said: ' Be not solicitous,' etc., He intended to forbid them either to make such things their end, or for the sake of these things to do whatever they were commanded to do in preaching the Gospel.* Secondly, solicitude about temporal things may be unlawful, through too much earnestness in endeavouring to obtain temporal things, the result being that a man is drawn away from spiritual things which ought to be the chief object of his search, wherefore it is written (Matth. xiii. 22) that *the care of this world . . . chokes up the word.* Thirdly, through over much fear, when, to wit, a man fears to lack necessary things if he do what he ought to do. Now our Lord gives three motives for laying aside this fear. First, on account of the yet greater favours bestowed by God on man, independently of his solicitude, viz. his body and soul (Matth. vi. 26); secondly, on account of the care with which God watches over animals and plants without the assistance of man, according to the requirements of their nature; thirdly, because of Divine providence, through ignorance of which the gentiles are solicitous in seeking temporal goods before all others. Consequently He concludes that we should be solicitous most of all about spiritual goods, hoping that temporal goods also may be granted us according to our needs, if we do what we ought to do.

*Reply Obj.* 1. Temporal goods are subjected to man that he may use them according to his needs, not that he may place his end in them and be over solicitous about them.

*Reply Obj.* 2. The solicitude of a man who gains his bread by bodily labour is not superfluous but proportionate; hence Jerome says on Matth. vi. 31, *Be not solicitous*, that *labour is necessary, but solicitude must be banished*, namely superfluous solicitude which unsettles the mind.

*Reply Obj.* 3. In the works of mercy solicitude about temporal things is directed to charity as its end, wherefore it is not unlawful, unless it be superfluous.


SEVENTH ARTICLE.

WHETHER WE SHOULD BE SOLICITOUS ABOUT THE FUTURE ?

*We proceed thus to the Seventh Article :—*

*Objection* 1. It would seem that we should be solicitous about the future.   For it is written (Prov. vi. 6-8): *Go to the ant, O sluggard, and consider her ways and learn wisdom ; which, although she hath no guide, nor master . . . provideth her meat for herself in the summer, and gathereth her food in the harvest.*   Now this is to be solicitous about the future. Therefore solicitude about the future is praiseworthy.

*Obj.* 2. Further, Solicitude pertains to prudence.   But prudence is chiefly about the future, since its principal part is *foresight of future things*, as stated above (Q. XLIX., A. 6, *ad* 1).   Therefore it is virtuous to be solicitous about the future.

*Obj.* 3. Further, Whoever puts something by that he may keep it for the morrow, is solicitous about the future.   Now we read (Jo. xii. 6) that Christ had a bag for keeping things in, which Judas carried, and (Acts iv. 34-37) that the Apostles kept the price of the land, which had been laid at their feet.   Therefore it is lawful to be solicitous about the future.

*On the contrary*, Our Lord said (Matth. vi. 34): *Be not . . . solicitous for tomorrow;* where *tomorrow* stands for the future, as Jerome says in his commentary on this passage.

*I answer that*, No work can be virtuous, unless it be vested with its due circumstances, and among these is the due time, according to Eccles. viii. 6, *There is a time and opportunity for every business;* which applies not only to external deeds but also to internal solicitude. For every time has its own fitting proper solicitude; thus solicitude about the crops belongs to the summer time, and solicitude about the vintage to the time of autumn. Accordingly if a man were solicitous about the vintage during the summer, he would be needlessly forestalling the solicitude belonging to a future time. Hence Our Lord forbids suchlike excessive solicitude, saying: *Be . . . not solicitous for tomorrow,* wherefore He adds, *for the morrow will be solicitous for itself,* that is to say, the morrow will have its own solicitude, which will be burden enough for the soul. This is what He means by adding: *Sufficient for the day is the evil thereof,* namely, the burden of solicitude.

*Reply Obj.* 1. The ant is solicitous at a befitting time, and it is this that is proposed for our example.

*Reply Obj.* 2. Due foresight of the future belongs to prudence. But it would be an inordinate foresight or solicitude about the future, if a man were to seek temporal things, to which the terms *past* and *future* apply, as ends, or if he were to seek them in excess of the needs of the present life, or if he were to forestall the time for solicitude.

*Reply Obj.* 3. As Augustine says (*De Serm. Dom. in monte,* ii. 17), *when we see a servant of God taking thought lest he lack these needful things, we must not judge him to be solicitous for the morrow, since even Our Lord deigned for our example to have a purse, and we read in the Acts of the Apostles that they procured the necessary means of livelihood in view of the future on account of a threatened famine. Hence Our Lord does not condemn those who, according to human custom, provide themselves with such things, but those who oppose themselves to God for the sake of these things.*

## EIGHTH ARTICLE.

### WHETHER THESE VICES ARISE FROM COVETOUSNESS ?

*We proceed thus to the Eighth Article :—*

*Objection* 1. It would seem that these vices do not arise from covetousness. As stated above (Q. XLIII., A. 6) lust is the chief cause of lack of rectitude in the reason. Now these vices are opposed to right reason, i.e. to prudence. Therefore they arise chiefly from lust; especially since the Philosopher says (*Ethic.* vii. 6) that *Venus is full of guile and her girdle is many coloured* and that *he who is incontinent in desire acts with cunning.*

*Obj.* 2. Further, These vices bear a certain resemblance to prudence, as stated above (Q. XLVII., A. 13). Now, since prudence is in the reason, the more spiritual vices seem to be more akin thereto, such as pride and vainglory. Therefore the aforesaid vices seem to arise from pride rather than from covetousness.

*Obj.* 3. Further, Men make use of stratagems not only in laying hold of other people's goods, but also in plotting murders, the former of which pertains to covetousness, and the latter to anger. Now the use of stratagems pertains to craftiness, guile, and fraud. Therefore the aforesaid vices arise not only from covetousness, but also from anger.

*On the contrary,* Gregory (*Moral.* xxxi. 45) states that fraud is a daughter of covetousness.

*I answer that,* As stated above (A. 3: Q. XLVII., A. 13), carnal prudence and craftiness, as well as guile and fraud, bear a certain resemblance to prudence in some kind of use of the reason. Now among all the moral virtues it is justice wherein the use of right reason appears chiefly, for justice is in the rational appetite. Hence the undue use of reason appears chiefly in the vices opposed to justice, the chief of which is covetousness. Therefore the aforesaid vices arise chiefly from covetousness.

*Reply Obj.* 1. On account of the vehemence of pleasure and of concupiscence, lust entirely suppresses the reason from exercising its act: whereas in the aforesaid vices there is some use of reason, albeit inordinate. Hence these vices do not arise directly from lust.—When the Philosopher says that *Venus is full of guile,* he is referring to a certain resemblance, in so far as she carries man away suddenly, just as he is moved in deceitful actions, yet not by means of craftiness but rather by the vehemence of concupiscence and pleasure; wherefore he adds that *Venus doth cozen the wits of the wisest man.**

*Reply Obj.* 2. To do anything by stratagem seems to be due to pusillanimity: because a magnanimous man wishes to act openly, as the Philosopher says (*Ethic.* iv. 3). Wherefore, as pride resembles or apes magnanimity, it follows that the aforesaid vices which make use of fraud and guile, do not arise directly from pride, but rather from covetousness, which seeks its own profit and sets little by excellence.

*Reply Obj.* 3. Anger's movement is sudden, hence it acts with precipitation, and without counsel, contrary to the use of the aforesaid vices, though these use counsel inordinately. That men use stratagems in plotting murders, arises not from anger but rather from hatred, because the angry man desires to harm manifestly, as the Philosopher states (*Rhet.* ii. 2, 3).†

* Cf. *Iliad* xiv. 214-217.          † Cf. *Ethic.* vii. 6.

## QUESTION LVI.

### OF THE PRECEPTS RELATING TO PRUDENCE.

*(In Two Articles.)*

WE must now consider the precepts relating to prudence, under which head there are two points of inquiry: (1) The precepts of prudence: (2) The precepts relating to the opposite vices.

### FIRST ARTICLE.

#### WHETHER THE PRECEPTS OF THE DECALOGUE SHOULD HAVE INCLUDED A PRECEPT OF PRUDENCE?

*We proceed thus to the First Article :—*

*Objection* 1. It would seem that the precepts of the decalogue should have included a precept of prudence. For the chief precepts should include a precept of the chief virtue. Now the chief precepts are those of the decalogue. Since then prudence is the chief of the moral virtues, it seems that the precepts of the decalogue should have included a precept of prudence.

*Obj.* 2. Further, The teaching of the Gospel contains the Law especially with regard to the precepts of the decalogue. Now the teaching of the Gospel contains a precept of prudence (Matth. x. 16): *Be ye . . . prudent* (Douay,—*wise*) *as serpents.* Therefore the precepts of the decalogue should have included a precept of prudence.

*Obj.* 3. Further, The other lessons of the Old Testament are directed to the precepts of the decalogue: wherefore it is written (Malach. iv. 4): *Remember the law of Moses My servant, which I commanded him in Horeb.* Now the other lessons of the Old Testament include precepts of prudence;

for instance (Prov. iii. 5): *Lean not upon thy own prudence* and further on (iv. 25): *Let thine eyelids go before thy steps.* Therefore the Law also should have contained a precept of prudence, especially among the precepts of the decalogue.

*The contrary* however appears to anyone who goes through the precepts of the decalogue.

*I answer that,* As stated above (I.-II., Q. C., A. 3; A. 5, *ad* 1) when we were treating of precepts, the commandments of the decalogue being given to the whole people, are a matter of common knowledge to all, as coming under the purview of natural reason. Now foremost among the things dictated by natural reason are the ends of human life, which are to the practical order what naturally known principles are to the speculative order, as shown above (Q. XLVII., A. 6). Now prudence is not about the end, but about the means, as stated above (*ibid.*). Hence it was not fitting that the precepts of the decalogue should include a precept relating directly to prudence. And yet all the precepts of the decalogue are related to prudence, in so far as it directs all virtuous acts.

*Reply Obj.* 1. Although prudence is simply foremost among all the moral virtues, yet justice, more than any other virtue, regards its object under the aspect of something due, which is a necessary condition for a precept, as stated above (Q. XLIV., A. 1: I.-II., Q. XCIX., AA. 1, 5). Hence it behoved the chief precepts of the Law, which are those of the decalogue, to refer to justice rather than to prudence.

*Reply Obj.* 2. The teaching of the Gospel is the doctrine of perfection. Therefore it needed to instruct man perfectly in all matters relating to right conduct, whether ends or means: wherefore it behoved the Gospel teaching to contain precepts also of prudence.

*Reply Obj.* 3. Just as the rest of the teaching of the Old Testament is directed to the precepts of the decalogue as its end, so it behoved man to be instructed by the subsequent lessons of the Old Testament about the act of prudence which is directed to the means.

## SECOND ARTICLE.

### WHETHER THE PROHIBITIVE PRECEPTS RELATING TO THE VICES OPPOSED TO PRUDENCE ARE FITTINGLY PROPOUNDED IN THE OLD LAW ?

*We proceed thus to the Second Article :—*

*Objection* 1. It would seem that the prohibitive precepts relating to the vices opposed to prudence are unfittingly propounded in the Old Law.   For such vices as imprudence and its parts which are directly opposed to prudence are not less opposed thereto, than those which bear a certain resemblance to prudence, such as craftiness and vices connected with it.   Now the latter vices are forbidden in the Law: for it is written (Levit. xix. 13): *Thou shalt not calumniate thy neighbour,* and (Deut. xxv. 13): *Thou shalt not have divers weights in thy bag, a greater and a less.*   Therefore there should have also been prohibitive precepts about the vices directly opposed to prudence.

*Obj.* 2. Further, There is room for fraud in other things than in buying and selling.   Therefore the Law unfittingly forbade fraud solely in buying and selling.

*Obj.* 3. Further, There is the same reason for prescribing an act of virtue as for prohibiting the act of a contrary vice. But acts of prudence are not prescribed in the Law.   Therefore neither should any contrary vices have been forbidden in the Law.

*The contrary,* however, appears from the precepts of the Law which are quoted in the first objection.

*I answer that,* As stated above (A. 1), justice, above all, regards the aspect of something due, which is a necessary condition for a precept, because justice tends to render that which is due to another, as we shall state further on (Q. LVIII., A. 2).   Now craftiness, as to its execution, is committed chiefly in matters of justice, as stated above (Q. LV., A. 8): and so it was fitting that the Law should contain precepts forbidding the execution of craftiness, in so far as this pertains to injustice, as when a man uses guile and fraud in calumniating another or in stealing his goods.

*Reply Obj.* 1. Those vices that are manifestly opposed to prudence, do not pertain to injustice in the same way as the execution of craftiness, and so they are not forbidden in the Law, as fraud and guile are, which latter pertain to injustice.

*Reply Obj.* 2. All guile and fraud committed in matters of injustice, can be understood to be forbidden in the prohibition of calumny (Levit. xix. 13). Yet fraud and guile are wont to be practised chiefly in buying and selling, according to Ecclus. xxvi. 28, *A huckster shall not be justified from the sins of the lips:* and it is for this reason that the Law contained a special precept forbidding fraudulent buying and selling.

*Reply Obj.* 3. All the precepts of the Law that relate to acts of justice pertain to the execution of prudence, even as the precepts prohibitive of stealing, calumny and fraudulent selling pertain to the execution of craftiness.

# QUESTION LVII.

## OF RIGHT.

### (*In Four Articles.*)

AFTER considering prudence we must in due sequence consider justice, the consideration of which will be fourfold: (1) Of justice: (2) Of its parts: (3) Of the corresponding gift: (4) Of the precepts relating to justice.

Four points will have to be considered about justice: (1) Right: (2) Justice itself: (3) Injustice: (4) Judgment.

Under the first head there are four points of inquiry: (1) Whether right is the object of justice? (2) Whether right is fittingly divided into natural and positive right? (3) Whether the right of nations is the same as natural right? (4) Whether right of dominion and paternal right are distinct species?

## FIRST ARTICLE.

### WHETHER RIGHT IS THE OBJECT OF JUSTICE?

*We proceed thus to the First Article :—*

*Objection* 1. It would seem that right is not the object of justice. For the jurist Celsus says* that *right is the art of goodness and equality*. Now art is not the object of justice, but is by itself an intellectual virtue. Therefore right is not the object of justice.

*Obj.* 2. Further, *Law*, according to Isidore (*Etym.* v. 3), *is a kind of right*. Now law is the object not of justice but of prudence, wherefore the Philosopher reckons *legislative* as one of the parts of prudence.† Therefore right is not the object of justice.

* Digest. i. 1; *De Just. et Jure* i.
† *Ethic.* vi. 8.

*Obj.* 3. Further, Justice, before all, subjects man to God: for Augustine says (*De Moribus Eccl.* xv.) that *justice is love serving God alone, and consequently governing aright all things subject to man.*   Now right (*jus*) does not pertain to Divine things, but only to human affairs, for Isidore says (*Etym.* v. 2) that '*fas*' *is the Divine law, and* ' *jus,*' *the human law.*   Therefore right is not the object of justice.

*On the contrary,* Isidore says (*ibid.*) that *jus* (*right*) *is so called because it is just.*   Now the *just* is the object of justice, for the Philosopher declares (*Ethic.* v. 1) that *all are agreed in giving the name of justice to the habit which makes men capable of doing just actions.*

*I answer that,* It is proper to justice, as compared with the other virtues, to direct man in his relations with others: because it denotes a kind of equality, as its very name implies; indeed we are wont to say that things are adjusted when they are made equal, for equality is in reference of one thing to some other.  On the other hand the other virtues perfect man in those matters only which befit him in relation to himself.  Accordingly that which is right in the works of the other virtues, and to which the intention of the virtue tends as to its proper object, depends on its relation to the agent only, whereas the right in a work of justice, besides its relation to the agent, is set up by its relation to others.  Because a man's work is said to be just when it is related to some other by way of some kind of equality, for instance the payment of the wage due for a service rendered.   And so a thing is said to be just, as having the rectitude of justice, when it is the term of an act of justice, without taking into account the way in which it is done by the agent: whereas in the other virtues nothing is declared to be right unless it is done in a certain way by the agent.  For this reason justice has its own special proper object over and above the other virtues, and this object is called the just, which is the same as *right.*  Hence it is evident that right is the object of justice.

*Reply Obj.* 1. It is usual for words to be distorted from their original signification so as to mean something else:

thus the word *medicine* was first employed to signify a remedy used for curing a sick person, and then it was drawn to signify the art by which this is done. In like manner the word *jus* (right) was first of all used to denote the just thing itself, but afterwards it was transferred to designate the art whereby it is known what is just, and further to denote the place where justice is administered, thus a man is said to appear *in jure*,* and yet further, we say even that a man, who has the office of exercising justice, administers the *jus* even if his sentence be unjust.

*Reply Obj.* 2. Just as there pre-exists in the mind of the craftsman an expression of the things to be made externally by his craft, which expression is called the rule of his craft, so too there pre-exists in the mind an expression of the particular just work which the reason determines, and which is a kind of rule of prudence. If this rule be expressed in writing, it is called a *law*, which according to Isidore (*Etym.* v. I) is *a written decree :* and so law is not the same as right, but an expression of right.

*Reply Obj.* 3. Since justice implies equality, and since we cannot offer God an equal return, it follows that we cannot make Him a perfectly just repayment. For this reason the Divine law is not properly called *jus* but *fas*, because, to wit, God is satisfied if we accomplish what we can. Nevertheless justice tends to make man repay God as much as he can, by subjecting his mind to Him entirely.

## SECOND ARTICLE.

### WHETHER RIGHT IS FITTINGLY DIVIDED INTO NATURAL RIGHT AND POSITIVE RIGHT ?

*We proceed thus to the Second Article:—*

*Objection* I. It would seem that right is not fittingly divided into natural right and positive right. For that which is natural is unchangeable, and is the same for all. Now nothing of the kind is to be found in human affairs, since all the rules of human right fail in certain cases, nor do they

* In English we speak of a court of law, a barrister at law, etc.

obtain force everywhere. Therefore there is no such thing as natural right.

*Obj.* 2. Further, A thing is called *positive* when it proceeds from the human will. But a thing is not just, simply because it proceeds from the human will, else a man's will could not be unjust. Since then the *just* and the *right* are the same, it seems that there is no positive right.

*Obj.* 3. Further, Divine right is not natural right, since it transcends human nature. In like manner, neither is it positive right, since it is based not on human, but on Divine authority. Therefore right is unfittingly divided into natural and positive.

*On the contrary,* The Philosopher says (*Ethic.* v. 7) that *political justice is partly natural and partly legal,* i.e. established by law.

*I answer that,* As stated above (A. 1) the *right* or the *just* is a work that is adjusted to another person according to some kind of equality. Now a thing can be adjusted to a man in two ways: first by its very nature, as when a man gives so much that he may receive equal value in return, and this is called *natural right.* In another way a thing is adjusted or commensurated to another person, by agreement, or by common consent, when, to wit, a man deems himself satisfied, if he receive so much. This can be done in two ways: first by private agreement, as that which is confirmed by an agreement between private individuals; secondly, by public agreement, as when the whole community agrees that something should be deemed as though it were adjusted and commensurated to another person, or when this is decreed by the prince who is placed over the people, and acts in its stead, and this is called *positive right.*

*Reply Obj.* 1. That which is natural to one whose nature is unchangeable, must needs be such always and everywhere. But man's nature is changeable, wherefore that which is natural to man may sometimes fail. Thus the restitution of a deposit to the depositor is in accordance with natural equality, and if human nature were always right, this would always have to be observed; but since it happens sometimes that man's will is unrighteous, there are cases in which a deposit should not be restored, lest a man of unrighteous will make evil use of the thing deposited: as when a madman or an enemy of the common weal demands the return of his weapons.

*Reply Obj.* 2. The human will can, by common agreement, make a thing to be just provided it be not, of itself, contrary to natural justice, and it is in such matters that positive right has its place. Hence the Philosopher says (*Ethic.* v. 7) that *in the case of the legal just, it does not matter in the first instance whether it takes one form or another, it only matters when once it is laid down.* If, however, a thing is, of itself, contrary to natural right, the human will cannot make it just, for instance by decreeing that it is lawful to steal or to commit adultery. Hence it is written (Isa. x. 1): *Woe to them that make wicked laws.*

*Reply Obj.* 3. The Divine right is that which is promulgated by God. Such things are partly those that are naturally just, yet their justice is hidden to man, and partly are made just by God's decree. Hence also Divine right may be divided in respect of these two things, even as human right is. For the Divine law commands certain things because they are good, and forbids others, because they are evil, while others are good because they are prescribed, and others evil because they are forbidden.

### THIRD ARTICLE.

#### WHETHER THE RIGHT OF NATIONS IS THE SAME AS THE NATURAL RIGHT?

*We proceed thus to the Third Article :—*

*Objection* 1. It would seem that the right of nations is the same as the natural right. For all men do not agree save in that which is natural to them. Now all men agree in the right of nations; since the jurist* says that *the right of nations is that which is in use among all nations.* Therefore the right of nations is the natural right.

* Ulpian: Digest. i. 1; *De Just. et Jure* i.

*Obj.* 2. Further, Slavery among men is natural, for some are naturally slaves according to the Philosopher (*Polit.* i. 2). Now *slavery belongs to the right of nations*, as Isidore states (*Etym.* v. 4). Therefore the right of nations is a natural right.

*Obj.* 3. Further, Right as stated above (A. 2) is divided into natural and positive. Now the right of nations is not a positive right, since all nations never agreed to decree anything by common agreement. Therefore the right of nations is a natural right.

*On the contrary,* Isidore says (*Etym.* v. 4) that *right is either natural, or civil, or right of nations,* and consequently the right of nations is distinct from natural right.

*I answer that,* As stated above (A. 2), the natural right or just is that which by its very nature is adjusted to or commensurate with another person. Now this may happen in two ways; first, according as it is considered absolutely: thus a male by its very nature is commensurate with the female to beget offspring by her, and a parent is commensurate with the offspring to nourish it. Secondly a thing is naturally commensurate with another person, not according as it is considered absolutely, but according to something resultant from it, for instance the possession of property. For if a particular piece of land be considered absolutely, it contains no reason why it should belong to one man more than to another, but if it be considered in respect of its adaptability to cultivation, and the unmolested use of the land, it has a certain commensuration to be the property of one and not of another man, as the Philosopher shows (*Polit.* ii. 2).

Now it belongs not only to man but also to other animals to apprehend a thing absolutely: wherefore the right which we call natural, is common to us and other animals according to the first kind of commensuration. But the right of nations falls short of natural right in this sense, as the jurist* says because *the latter is common to all animals, while the former is common to men only.* On the other hand to consider a thing by comparing it with what results from it,

* Digest., *loc. cit.*

is proper to reason, wherefore this same is natural to man in respect of natural reason which dictates it. Hence the jurist Gaius says (*ibid.* 9): *Whatever natural reason decrees among all men, is observed by all equally, and is called the right of nations.* This suffices for the *Reply* to the *First Objection*.

*Reply Obj.* 2. Considered absolutely, the fact that this particular man should be a slave rather than another man, is based, not on natural reason, but on some resultant utility, in that it is useful to this man to be ruled by a wiser man, and to the latter to be helped by the former, as the Philosopher states (*Polit.* i. 2). Wherefore slavery which belongs to the right of nations is natural in the second way, but not in the first.

*Reply Obj.* 3. Since natural reason dictates matters which are according to the right of nations, as implying a proximate equality, it follows that they need no special institution, for they are instituted by natural reason itself, as stated by the authority quoted above.

## FOURTH ARTICLE.

### WHETHER PATERNAL RIGHT AND RIGHT OF DOMINION SHOULD BE DISTINGUISHED AS SPECIAL SPECIES?

*We proceed thus to the Fourth Article :—*

*Objection* 1. It would seem that *paternal right* and *right of dominion* should not be distinguished as special species. For it belongs to justice to render to each one what is his, as Ambrose states (*De Offic.* i. 24). Now right is the object of justice, as stated above (A. 1). Therefore right belongs to each one equally; and we ought not to distinguish the rights of fathers and masters as distinct species.

*Obj.* 2. Further, The law is an expression of what is just, as stated above (A. 1, *ad* 2). Now a law looks to the common good of a city or kingdom, as stated above (I.-II., Q. XC., A. 2), but not to the private good of an individual or even of one household. Therefore there is no need for a special right of dominion or paternal right, since the master and the father pertain to a household, as stated in *Polit.* i. 2.

*Obj.* 3. Further, There are many other differences of degrees among men, for instance some are soldiers, some are priests, some are princes. Therefore some special kind of right should be allotted to them.

*On the contrary,* The Philosopher (*Ethic.* v. 6) distinguishes right of dominion, paternal right and so on as species distinct from civil right.

*I answer that,* Right or just depends on commensuration with another person. Now *another* has a twofold signification. First, it may denote something that is other simply, as that which is altogether distinct; as, for example, two men neither of whom is subject to the other, and both of whom are subjects of the ruler of the state; and between these according to the Philosopher (*Ethic.* v. 6) there is the *just* simply. Secondly a thing is said to be other from something else, not simply, but as belonging in some way to that something else: and in this way, as regards human affairs, a son belongs to his father, since he is part of him somewhat, as stated in *Ethic.* viii. 12, and a slave belongs to his master, because he is his instrument, as stated in *Polit.* i. 2.* Hence a father is not compared to his son as to another simply, and so between them there is not the just simply, but a kind of just, called *paternal.* In like manner neither is there the just simply, between master and servant, but that which is called *dominative.* A wife, though she is something belonging to the husband, since she stands related to him as to her own body, as the Apostle declares (Eph. v. 28), is nevertheless more distinct from her husband, than a son from his father, or a slave from his master: for she is received into a kind of social life, that of matrimony, wherefore according to the Philosopher (*Ethic.* v. 6) there is more scope for justice between husband and wife than between father and son, or master and slave, because, as husband and wife have an immediate relation to the community of the household, as stated in *Polit.* i. 2, 5, it follows that between them there is *domestic justice* rather than *civic.*

*Reply Obj.* 1. It belongs to justice to render to each one

* Cf. *Ethic* viii. 11.

his right, the distinction between individuals being pre-supposed: for if a man gives himself his due, this is not strictly called *just*. And since what belongs to the son is his father's, and what belongs to the slave is his master's, it follows that properly speaking there is not justice of father to son, or of master to slave.

*Reply Obj.* 2. A son, as such, belongs to his father, and a slave, as such, belongs to his master; yet each, considered as a man, is something having separate existence and distinct from others. Hence in so far as each of them is a man, there is justice towards them in a way: and for this reason too there are certain laws regulating the relations of a father to his son, and of a master to his slave; but in so far as each is something belonging to another, the perfect idea of *right* or *just* is wanting to them.

*Reply Obj.* 3. All other differences between one person and another in a state, have an immediate relation to the community of the state and to its ruler, wherefore there is just towards them in the perfect sense of justice. This *just* however is distinguished according to various offices, hence when we speak of *military*, or *magisterial*, or *priestly* right, it is not as though such rights fell short of the simply right, as when we speak of *paternal* right, or right of *dominion*, but for the reason that something proper is due to each class of person in respect of his particular office.

# QUESTION LVIII.

## OF JUSTICE.

### (*In Twelve Articles.*)

WE must now consider justice. Under this head there are twelve points of inquiry: (1) What is justice? (2) Whether justice is always towards another? (3) Whether it is a virtue? (4) Whether it is in the will as its subject? (5) Whether it is a general virtue? (6) Whether, as a general virtue, it is essentially the same as every virtue? (7) Whether there is a particular justice? (8) Whether particular justice has a matter of its own? (9) Whether it is about passions, or about operations only? (10) Whether the mean of justice is the real mean? (11) Whether the act of justice is to render to everyone his own? (12) Whether justice is the chief of the moral virtues?

## FIRST ARTICLE.

### WHETHER JUSTICE IS FITTINGLY DEFINED AS BEING THE PERPETUAL AND CONSTANT WILL TO RENDER TO EACH ONE HIS RIGHT?

*We proceed thus to the First Article :—*

*Objection* 1. It would seem that lawyers have unfittingly defined justice as being *the perpetual and constant will to render to each one his right.** For, according to the Philosopher (*Ethic.* v. 1), justice is a habit which makes a man *capable of doing what is just, and of being just in action and in intention.* Now *will* denotes a power, or also an act. Therefore justice is unfittingly defined as being a will.

*Obj.* 2. Further, Rectitude of the will is not the will;

* Digest. i. 1; *De Just. et Jure* 10.

else if the will were its own rectitude, it would follow that
no will is unrighteous. Yet, according to Anselm (*De
Veritate* xii.), justice is rectitude. Therefore justice is not
the will.

*Obj.* 3. Further, No will is perpetual save God's. If
therefore justice is a perpetual will, in God alone will there
be justice.

*Obj.* 4. Further, Whatever is perpetual is constant, since
it is unchangeable. Therefore it is needless in defining
justice, to say that it is both *perpetual* and *constant.*

*Obj.* 5. Further, It belongs to the sovereign to give each
one his right. Therefore, if justice gives each one his
right, it follows that it is in none but the sovereign: which
is absurd.

*Obj.* 6. Further, Augustine says (*De Moribus Eccl.* xv.)
that *justice is love serving God alone.* Therefore it does
not render to each one his right.

*I answer that,* The aforesaid definition of justice is fitting
if understood aright. For since every virtue is a habit
that is the principle of a good act, a virtue must needs be
defined by means of the good act bearing on the matter
proper to that virtue. Now the proper matter of justice
consists of those things that belong to our intercourse with
other men, as shall be shown further on (A. 2). Hence the
act of justice in relation to its proper matter and object is
indicated in the words, *Rendering to each one his right,*
since, as Isidore says (*Etym.* x.), *a man is said to be just
because he respects the rights* (jus) *of others.*

Now in order that an act bearing upon any matter whatever be virtuous, it requires to be voluntary, stable, and firm,
because the Philosopher says (*Ethic.* ii. 4) that in order for
an act to be virtuous it needs first of all to be done *knowingly,* secondly to be done *by choice,* and *for a due end,*
thirdly to be done *immovably.* Now the first of these is
included in the second, since *what is done through ignorance
is involuntary* (*Ethic.* iii. 1). Hence the definition of justice
mentions first the *will,* in order to show that the act of
justice must be voluntary; and mention is made afterwards

of its *constancy* and *perpetuity* in order to indicate the firmness of the act.

Accordingly, this is a complete definition of justice; save that the act is mentioned instead of the habit, which takes its species from that act, because habit implies relation to act. And if anyone would reduce it to the proper form of a definition, he might say that *justice is a habit whereby a man renders to each one his due by a constant and perpetual will :* and this is about the same definition as that given by the Philosopher (*Ethic.* v. 5) who says that *justice is a habit whereby a man is said to be capable of doing just actions in accordance with his choice.*

*Reply Obj.* 1. Will here denotes the act, not the power: and it is customary among writers to define habits by their acts: thus Augustine says (*Tract. in Joan.* xl.) that *faith is to believe what one sees not.*

*Reply Obj.* 2. Justice is the same as rectitude, not essentially but causally; for it is a habit which rectifies the deed and the will.

*Reply Obj.* 3. The will may be called perpetual in two ways. First on the part of the will's act which endures for ever, and thus God's will alone is perpetual. Secondly on the part of the subject, because, to wit, a man wills to do a certain thing always, and this is a necessary condition of justice. For it does not satisfy the conditions of justice that one wish to observe justice in some particular matter for the time being, because one could scarcely find a man willing to act unjustly in every case; and it is requisite that one should have the will to observe justice at all times and in all cases.

*Reply Obj.* 4. Since *perpetual* does not imply perpetuity of the act of the will, it is not superfluous to add *constant :* for while the *perpetual will* denotes the purpose of observing justice always, *constant* signifies a firm perseverance in this purpose.

*Reply Obj.* 5. A judge renders to each one what belongs to him, by way of command and direction, because a judge is the *personification of justice,* and *the sovereign is its guardian* (*Ethic.* v. 4). On the other hand, the subjects render to each one what belongs to him, by way of execution.

*Reply Obj.* 6. Just as love of God includes love of our neighbour, as stated above (Q. XXV., A. 1), so too the service of God includes rendering to each one his due.

## SECOND ARTICLE.

### WHETHER JUSTICE IS ALWAYS TOWARDS ANOTHER?

*We proceed thus to the Second Article :—*

*Objection* 1. It would seem that justice is not always towards another. For the Apostle says (Rom. iii. 22) that *the justice of God is by faith of Jesus Christ.* Now faith does not concern the dealings of one man with another. Neither therefore does justice.

*Obj.* 2. Further, According to Augustine (*De Moribus Eccl.* xv.), *it belongs to justice that man should direct to the service of God his authority over the things that are subject to him.* Now the sensitive appetite is subject to man, according to Gen. iv. 7, where it is written: *The lust thereof,* viz. of sin, *shall be under thee, and thou shalt have dominion over it.* Therefore it belongs to justice to have dominion over one's own appetite: so that justice is towards oneself.

*Obj.* 3. Further, The justice of God is eternal. But nothing else is co-eternal with God. Therefore justice is not essentially towards another.

*Obj.* 4. Further, Man's dealings with himself need to be rectified no less than his dealings with another. Now man's dealings are rectified by justice, according to Prov. xi. 5, *The justice of the upright shall make his way prosperous.* Therefore justice is about our dealings not only with others, but also with ourselves.

*On the contrary,* Tully says (*De Officiis* i. 7) that *the object of justice is to keep men together in society and mutual intercourse.* Now this implies relationshp of one man to another. Therefore justice is concerned only about our dealings with others.

*I answer that,* As stated above (Q. LVII., A, 1) since

justice by its name implies equality, it denotes essentially relation to another, for a thing is equal, not to itself, but to another. And forasmuch as it belongs to justice to rectify human acts, as stated above (Q. LVII., A. 1: I.-II., Q. CXIII., A. 1) this otherness which justice demands must needs be between beings capable of action. Now actions belong to supposits* and wholes and, properly speaking, not to parts and forms or powers, for we do not say properly that the hand strikes, but a man with his hand, nor that heat makes a thing hot, but fire by heat, although such expressions may be employed metaphorically. Hence, justice properly speaking demands a distinction of supposits, and consequently is only in one man towards another. Nevertheless in one and the same man we may speak metaphorically of his various principles of action such as the reason, the irascible, and the concupiscible, as though they were so many agents: so that metaphorically in one and the same man there is said to be justice in so far as the reason commands the irascible and concupiscible, and these obey reason; and in general in so far as to each part of man is ascribed what is becoming to it. Hence the Philosopher (*Ethic.* v. 11) calls this *metaphorical justice*.

*Reply Obj.* 1. The justice which faith works in us, is that whereby the ungodly is justified: it consists in the due co-ordination of the parts of the soul, as stated above (I.-II., Q. CXIII., A. 1) where we were treating of the justification of the ungodly. Now this belongs to metaphorical justice, which may be found even in a man who lives all by himself.

This suffices for the *Reply* to the *Second Objection*.

*Reply Obj.* 3. God's justice is from eternity in respect of the eternal will and purpose (and it is chiefly in this that justice consists); although it is not eternal as regards its effect, since nothing is co-eternal with God.

*Reply Obj.* 4. Man's dealings with himself are sufficiently rectified by the rectification of the passions by the other moral virtues. But his dealings with others need a special

* *Cf.* P. I., Q. XXIX., A. 2.

rectification, not only in relation to the agent, but also in relation to the person to whom they are directed.   Hence about such dealings there is a special virtue, and this is justice.

### THIRD ARTICLE.

#### WHETHER JUSTICE IS A VIRTUE ?

*We proceed thus to the Third Article :—*

*Objection* 1. It would seem that justice is not a virtue.  For it is written (Luke xvii. 10): *When you shall have done all these things that are commanded you, say : We are unprofitable servants ; we have done that which we ought to do.*  Now it is not unprofitable to do a virtuous deed: for Ambrose says (*De Offic.* ii. 6): *We look to a profit that is estimated not by pecuniary gain but by the acquisition of godliness.*  Therefore to do what one ought to do, is not a virtuous deed.  And yet it is an act of justice.  Therefore justice is not a virtue.

*Obj.* 2. Further, That which is done of necessity, is not meritorious.  But to render to a man what belongs to him, as justice requires, is of necessity.  Therefore it is not meritorious.  Yet it is by virtuous actions that we gain merit.  Therefore justice is not a virtue.

*Obj.* 3. Further, Every moral virtue is about matters of action.  Now those things which are wrought externally are not things concerning behaviour but concerning handicraft, according to the Philosopher (*Metaph.* ix.).*  Therefore since it belongs to justice to produce externally a deed that is just in itself, it seems that justice is not a moral virtue.

*On the contrary,* Gregory says (*Moral.* ii. 49) that *the entire structure of good works is built on four virtues,* viz. temperance, prudence, fortitude and justice.

*I answer that,* A human virtue is one *which renders a human act and man himself good*:† and this can be applied to justice.  For a man's act is made good through attaining the rule of reason, which is the rule whereby human acts are regulated.  Hence, since justice regulates human operations, it is evident that it renders man's operations good, and, as

* Didot ed., viii. 8.          † *Ethic.* ii. 6.

Tully declares (*De Officiis* i. 7), good men are so called chiefly from their justice, wherefore, as he says again (*ibid.*) *the lustre of virtue appears above all in justice.*

*Reply Obj.* 1. When a man does what he ought, he brings no gain to the person to whom he does what he ought, but only abstains from doing him a harm. He does however profit himself, in so far as he does what he ought, spontaneously and readily, and this is to act virtuously. Hence it is written (Wis. viii. 7) that Divine wisdom *teacheth temperance, and prudence, and justice, and fortitude, which are such things as men* (i.e. virtuous men) *can have nothing more profitable in life.*

*Reply Obj.* 2. Necessity is twofold. One arises from *constraint*, and this removes merit, since it runs counter to the will. The other arises from the obligation of a *command*, or from the necessity of obtaining an end, when, to wit, a man is unable to achieve the end of virtue without doing some particular thing. The latter necessity does not remove merit, when a man does voluntarily that which is necessary in this way. It does however exclude the credit of supererogation, according to 1 Cor. ix. 16, *If I preach the Gospel, it is no glory to me, for a necessity lieth upon me.*

*Reply Obj.* 3. Justice is concerned about external things, not by making them, which pertains to art, but by using them in our dealings with other men.

## FOURTH ARTICLE.

### WHETHER JUSTICE IS IN THE WILL AS ITS SUBJECT?

*We proceed thus to the Fourth Article :—*

*Objection* 1. It would seem that justice is not in the will as its subject. For justice is sometimes called truth. But truth is not in the will, but in the intellect. Therefore justice is not in the will as its subject.

*Obj.* 2. Further, Justice is about our dealings with others. Now it belongs to the reason to direct one thing in relation

to another.    Therefore justice is not in the will as its subject
but in the reason.

*Obj.* 3. Further, Justice is not an intellectual virtue, since
it is not directed to knowledge; wherefore it follows that it is
a moral virtue.    Now the subject of moral virtue is the
faculty which is *rational by participation,* viz. the irascible
and the concupiscible, as the Philosopher declares (*Ethic.*
i. 13).    Therefore justice is not in the will as its subject, but
in the irascible and concupiscible.

*On the contrary,* Anselm says (*De Verit.* xii.) that *justice
is rectitude of the will observed for its own sake.*

*I answer that,* The subject of a virtue is the power whose
act that virtue aims at rectifying.    Now justice does not
aim at directing an act of the cognitive power, for we are
not said to be just through knowing something aright.
Hence the subject of justice is not the intellect or reason
which is a cognitive power.    But since we are said to be
just through doing something aright, and because the
proximate principle of action is the appetitive power,
justice must needs be in some appetitive power as its
subject.

Now the appetite is twofold; namely, the will which is in
the reason, and the sensitive appetite which follows on
sensitive apprehension, and is divided into the irascible and
the concupiscible, as stated in the First Part (Q. LXXXI.,
A. 2).    Again the act of rendering his due to each man
cannot proceed from the sensitive appetite, because sensitive
apprehension does not go so far as to be able to consider the
relation of one thing to another; but this is proper to the
reason.    Therefore justice cannot be in the irascible or
concupiscible as its subject, but only in the will: hence the
Philosopher (*Ethic.* v. 1) defines justice by an act of the will,
as may be seen above (A. 1).

*Reply Obj.* 1. Since the will is the rational appetite, when
the rectitude of the reason which is called truth is imprinted
on the will on account of its nighness to the reason, this im-
print retains the name of truth; and hence it is that justice
sometimes goes by the name of truth.

*Reply Obj.* 2. The will is borne towards its object consequently on the apprehension of reason: wherefore, since the reason directs one thing in relation to another, the will can will one thing in relation to another, and this belongs to justice.

*Reply Obj.* 3. Not only the irascible and concupiscible parts are *rational by participation*, but the entire *appetitive* faculty, as stated in *Ethic.* i. 13, because all appetite is subject to reason. Now the will is contained in the appetitive faculty, wherefore it can be the subject of moral virtue.

## FIFTH ARTICLE.

### WHETHER JUSTICE IS A GENERAL VIRTUE ?

*We proceed thus to the Fifth Article :—*

*Objection* 1. It would seem that justice is not a general virtue. For justice is specified with the other virtues, according to Wis. viii. 7, *She teacheth temperance and prudence, and justice, and fortitude.* Now the *general* is not specified or reckoned together with the species contained under the same *general.* Therefore justice is not a general virtue.

*Obj.* 2. Further, As justice is accounted a cardinal virtue, so are temperance and fortitude. Now neither temperance nor fortitude is reckoned to be a general virtue. Therefore neither should justice in any way be reckoned a general virtue.

*Obj.* 3. Further, Justice is always towards others, as stated above (A. 2). But a sin committed against one's neighbour cannot be a general sin, because it is condivided with sin committed against oneself. Therefore neither is justice a general virtue.

*On the contrary*, The Philosopher says (*Ethic.* v. 1) that *justice is every virtue.*

*I answer that*, Justice, as stated above (A. 2) directs man in his relations with other men. Now this may happen in two ways: first as regards his relations with individuals, secondly as regards his relations with others in general, in so far as a man who serves a community, serves all those who are included in that community.  Accordingly justice in its proper acceptation can be directed to another in both these senses.  Now it is evident that all who are included in a community, stand in relation to that community as parts to a whole; while a part, as such, belongs to a whole, so that whatever is the good of a part can be directed to the good of the whole.  It follows therefore that the good of any virtue, whether such virtue direct man in relation to himself, or in relation to certain other individual persons, is referable to the common good, to which justice directs: so that all acts of virtue can pertain to justice, in so far as it directs man to the common good.  It is in this sense that justice is called a general virtue.  And since it belongs to the law to direct to the common good, as stated above (I.-II., Q. XC., A. 2), it follows that the justice which is in this way styled general, is called *legal justice*, because thereby man is in harmony with the law which directs the acts of all the virtues to the common good.

*Reply Obj.* 1. Justice is specified or enumerated with the other virtues, not as a general but as a special virtue, as we shall state further on (AA. 7, 12).

*Reply Obj.* 2. Temperance and fortitude are in the sensitive appetite, viz. in the concupiscible and irascible.  Now these powers are appetitive of certain particular goods, even as the senses are cognitive of particulars.  On the other hand justice is in the intellective appetite as its subject, which can have the universal good as its object, knowledge whereof belongs to the intellect.  Hence justice can be a general virtue rather than temperance or fortitude.

*Reply Obj.* 3. Things referable to oneself are referable to another, especially in regard to the common good.  Wherefore legal justice, in so far as it directs to the common good, may be called a general virtue: and in like manner injustice may be called a general sin; hence it is written (1 Jo. iii. 4) that all *sin is iniquity*.

SIXTH ARTICLE.

## WHETHER JUSTICE, AS A GENERAL VIRTUE, IS ESSENTIALLY THE SAME AS ALL VIRTUE ?

*We proceed thus to the Sixth Article :—*

*Objection* 1. It would seem that justice, as a general virtue, is essentially the same as all virtue. For the Philosopher says (*Ethic.* v. 1) that *virtue and legal justice are the same as all virtue, but differ in their mode of being.* Now things that differ merely in their mode of being or logically do not differ essentially. Therefore justice is essentially the same as every virtue.

*Obj.* 2. Further, Every virtue that is not essentially the same as all virtue is a part of virtue. Now the aforesaid justice, according to the Philosopher (*ibid.*) *is not a part but the whole of virtue.* Therefore the aforesaid justice is essentially the same as all virtue.

*Obj.* 3. Further, The essence of a virtue does not change through that virtue directing its act to some higher end even as the habit of temperance remains essentially the same even though its act be directed to a Divine good. Now it belongs to legal justice that the acts of all the virtues are directed to a higher end, namely the common good of the multitude, which transcends the good of one single individual. Therefore it seems that legal justice is essentially all virtue.

*Obj.* 4. Further, Every good of a part can be directed to the good of the whole, so that if it be not thus directed it would seem without use or purpose. But that which is in accordance with virtue cannot be so. Therefore it seems that there can be no act of any virtue, that does not belong to general justice, which directs to the common good; and so it seems that general justice is essentially the same as all virtue.

*On the contrary,* The Philosopher says (*Ethic.* v. 1) that *many are able to be virtuous in matters affecting themselves, but are unable to be virtuous in matters relating to others,* and

(*Pol.* iii. 2) that *the virtue of the good man is not strictly the same as the virtue of the good citizen*. Now the virtue of a good citizen is general justice, whereby a man is directed to the common good. Therefore general justice is not the same as virtue in general, and it is possible to have one without the other.

*I answer that*, A thing is said to be *general* in two ways. First, by *predication :* thus *animal* is general in relation to man and horse and the like: and in this sense that which is general must needs be essentially the same as the things in relation to which it is general, for the reason that the genus belongs to the essence of the species, and forms part of its definition. Secondly a thing is said to be general *virtually ;* thus a universal cause is general in relation to all its effects, the sun, for instance, in relation to all bodies that are illumined, or transmuted by its power; and in this sense there is no need for that which is *general* to be essentially the same as those things in relation to which it is general, since cause and effect are not essentially the same. Now it is in the latter sense that, according to what has been said (A. 5), legal justice is said to be a general virtue, in as much, to wit, as it directs the acts of the other virtues to its own end, and this is to move all the other virtues by its command; for just as charity may be called a general virtue in so far as it directs the acts of all the virtues to the Divine good, so too is legal justice, in so far as it directs the acts of all the virtues to the common good. Accordingly, just as charity which regards the Divine good as its proper object, is a special virtue in respect of its essence, so too legal justice is a special virtue in respect of its essence, in so far as it regards the common good as its proper object. And thus it is in the sovereign principally and by way of a master-craft, while it is secondarily and administratively in his subjects.

However the name of legal justice can be given to every virtue, in so far as every virtue is directed to the common good by the aforesaid legal justice, which though special essentially is nevertheless virtually general. Speaking in this way, legal justice is essentially the same as all virtue, but differs therefrom logically: and it is in this sense that the Philosopher speaks.

Wherefore the *Replies* to the *First* and *Second Objections* are manifest.

*Reply Obj.* 3. This argument again takes legal justice for the virtue commanded by legal justice.

*Reply Obj.* 4. Every virtue strictly speaking directs its act to that virtue's proper end: that it should happen to be directed to a further end either always or sometimes, does not belong to that virtue considered strictly, for it needs some higher virtue to direct it to that end. Consequently there must be one supreme virtue essentially distinct from every other virtue, which directs all the virtues to the common good; and this virtue is legal justice.

## SEVENTH ARTICLE.

### WHETHER THERE IS A PARTICULAR BESIDES A GENERAL JUSTICE ?

*We proceed thus to the Seventh Article :—*

*Objection* 1. It would seem that there is not a particular besides a general justice. For there is nothing superfluous in the virtues, as neither is there in nature. Now general justice directs man sufficiently in all his relations with other men. Therefore there is no need for a particular justice.

*Obj.* 2. Further, The species of a virtue does not vary according to *one* and *many*. But legal justice directs one man to another in matters relating to the multitude, as shown above (AA. 5, 6). Therefore there is not another species of justice directing one man to another in matters relating to the individual.

*Obj.* 3. Further, Between the individual and the general public stands the household community. Consequently, if in addition to general justice there is a particular justice corresponding to the individual, for the same reason there should be a domestic justice directing man to the common good of a household: and yet this is not the case. Therefore neither should there be a particular besides a legal justice.

*On the contrary*, Chrysostom in his commentary on Matth. v. 6, *Blessed are they that hunger and thirst after justice*, says (*Hom.* xv. *in Matth.*): *By justice He signifies either the general virtue, or the particular virtue which is opposed to covetousness.*

*I answer that*, As stated above (A. 6), legal justice is not essentially the same as every virtue, and besides legal justice which directs man immediately to the common good, there is a need for other virtues to direct him immediately in matters relating to particular goods: and these virtues may be relative to himself or to another individual person. Accordingly, just as in addition to legal justice there is a need for particular virtues to direct man in relation to himself, such as temperance and fortitude, so too besides legal justice there is need for particular justice to direct man in his relations to other individuals.

*Reply Obj.* 1. Legal justice does indeed direct man sufficiently in his relations towards others. As regards the common good it does so immediately, but as to the good of the individual, it does so mediately. Wherefore there is need for particular justice to direct a man immediately to the good of another individual.

*Reply Obj.* 2. The common good of the realm and the particular good of the individual differ not only in respect of the *many* and the *few*, but also under a formal aspect. For the aspect of the *common* good differs from the aspect of the *individual* good, even as the aspect of *whole* differs from that of *part*. Wherefore the Philosopher says (*Polit.* i. 1) that *they are wrong who maintain that the State and the home and the like differ only as many and few and not specifically*.

*Reply Obj.* 3. The household community, according to the Philosopher (*Polit.* i. 2), differs in respect of a threefold fellowship; namely *of husband and wife, father and son, master and slave*, in each of which one person is, as it were, part of the other. Wherefore between such persons there is not justice simply, but a species of justice, viz. *domestic* justice, as stated in *Ethic.* v. 6.

### Eighth Article.

#### WHETHER PARTICULAR JUSTICE HAS A SPECIAL MATTER?

*We proceed thus to the Eighth Article :—*

*Objection* 1. It would seem that particular justice has no special matter. Because a gloss on Gen. ii. 14, *The fourth river is Euphrates*, says : *Euphrates signifies ' fruitful';* *nor is it stated through what country it flows, because justice pertains to all the parts of the soul.* Now this would not be the case, if justice had a special matter, since every special matter belongs to a special power. Therefore particular justice has no special matter.

*Obj.* 2. Further, Augustine says (*QQ.* lxxxiii., qu. 61) that *the soul has four virtues whereby, in this life, it lives spiritually, viz. temperance, prudence, fortitude and justice;* and he says that *the fourth is justice, which pervades all the virtues.* Therefore particular justice, which is one of the four cardinal virtues, has no special matter.

*Obj.* 3. Further, Justice directs man sufficiently in matters relating to others. Now a man can be directed to others in all matters relating to this life. Therefore the matter of justice is general and not special.

*On the contrary*, The Philosopher reckons (*Ethic.* v. 2) particular justice to be specially about those things which belong to social life.

*I answer that*, Whatever can be rectified by reason is the matter of moral virtue, for this is defined in reference to right reason, according to the Philosopher (*Ethic.* ii. 6). Now the reason can rectify not only the internal passions of the soul, but also external actions, and also those external things of which man can make use. And yet it is in respect of external actions and external things by means of which men can communicate with one another, that the relation of one man to another is to be considered; whereas it is in respect of internal passions that we consider man's rectitude in himself. Consequently, since justice is directed to others, it is not about the entire matter of moral virtue, but only about external actions and things, under a certain special aspect of the object, in so far as one man is related to another through them.

*Reply Obj.* 1. It is true that justice belongs essentially to one part of the soul, where it resides as in its subject; and this is the will which moves by its command all the other parts of the soul; and accordingly justice belongs to all the parts of the soul, not directly but by a kind of diffusion.

*Reply Obj.* 2. As stated above (I.-II., Q. LXI., AA. 3, 4), the cardinal virtues may be taken in two ways: first as special virtues, each having a determinate matter; secondly, as certain general modes of virtue. In this latter sense Augustine speaks in the passage quoted: for he says that *prudence is knowledge of what we should seek and avoid, temperance is the curb on the lust for fleeting pleasures, fortitude is strength of mind in bearing with passing trials, justice is the love of God and our neighbour which pervades the other virtues, that is to say, is the common principle of the entire order between one man and another.*

*Reply Obj.* 3. A man's internal passions which are a part of moral matter, are not in themselves directed to another man, which belongs to the specific nature of justice; yet their effects, i.e. external actions, are capable of being directed to another man. Consequently it does not follow that the matter of justice is general.

### NINTH ARTICLE.

#### WHETHER JUSTICE IS ABOUT THE PASSIONS?

*We proceed thus to the Ninth Article :—*

*Objection* 1. It would seem that justice is about the passions. For the Philosopher says (*Ethic.* ii. 3) that *moral virtue is about pleasure and pain.* Now pleasure or delight, and pain are passions, as stated above* when we were treating of the passions. Therefore justice, being a moral virtue, is about the passions.

*Obj.* 2. Further, Justice is the means of rectifying a man's operations in relation to another man. Now suchlike

* I.-II., Q. XXIII., A. 4; Q. XXXI., A. 1; Q. XXXV., A. 1.

operations cannot be rectified unless the passions be rectified, because it is owing to disorder of the passions that there is disorder in the aforesaid operations: thus sexual lust leads to adultery, and overmuch love of money leads to theft. Therefore justice must needs be about the passions.

*Obj.* 3. Further, Even as particular justice is towards another person so is legal justice. Now legal justice is about the passions, else it would not extend to all the virtues, some of which are evidently about the passions. Therefore justice is about the passions.

*On the contrary,* The Philosopher says (*Ethic.* v. 1) that justice is about operations.

*I answer that,* The true answer to this question may be gathered from a twofold source. First from the subject of justice i.e. from the will, whose movements or acts are not passions, as stated above (I.-II., Q. XXII., A. 3: Q. LIX., A. 4), for it is only the sensitive appetite whose movements are called passions. Hence justice is not about the passions, as are temperance and fortitude, which are in the irascible and concupiscible parts. Secondly, on the part of the matter, because justice is about a man's relations with another, and we are not directed immediately to another by the internal passions. Therefore justice is not about the passions.

*Reply Obj.* 1. Not every moral virtue is about pleasure and pain as its proper matter, since fortitude is about fear and daring: but every moral virtue is directed to pleasure and pain, as to ends to be acquired, for, as the Philosopher says (*Ethic.* vii. 11), *pleasure and pain are the principal end in respect of which we say that this is an evil, and that a good :* and in this way too they belong to justice, since *a man is not just unless he rejoice in just actions* (*Ethic.* i. 8).

*Reply Obj.* 2. External operations are as it were between external things, which are their matter, and internal passions, which are their origin. Now it happens sometimes that there is a defect in one of these, without there being a defect in the other. Thus a man may steal another's property, not through the desire to have the thing, but through the will to hurt the man; or vice versa, a man may covet another's property without wishing to steal it.  Accordingly the directing of operations in so far as they tend towards external things, belongs to justice, but in so far as they arise from the passions, it belongs to the other moral virtues which are about the passions. Hence justice hinders theft of another's property, in so far as stealing is contrary to the equality that should be maintained in external things, while liberality hinders it as resulting from an immoderate desire for wealth.  Since, however, external operations take their species, not from the internal passions but from external things as being their objects, it follows that, external operations are essentially the matter of justice rather than of the other moral virtues.

*Reply Obj.* 3. The common good is the end of each individual member of a community, just as the good of the whole is the end of each part.  On the other hand the good of one individual is not the end of another individual: wherefore legal justice which is directed to the common good, is more capable of extending to the internal passions whereby man is disposed in some way or other in himself, than particular justice which is directed to the good of another individual: although legal justice extends chiefly to other virtues in the point of their external operations, in so far, to wit, as *the law commands us to perform the actions of a courageous person . . . the actions of a temperate person . . . and the actions of a gentle person* (*Ethic.* v. 5).

## TENTH ARTICLE.

### WHETHER THE MEAN OF JUSTICE IS THE REAL MEAN ?

*We proceed thus to the Tenth Article :—*

*Objection* 1. It would seem that the mean of justice is not the real mean.  For the generic nature remains entire in each species.  Now moral virtue is defined (*Ethic.* ii. 6) to be *an elective habit which observes the mean fixed, in our regard, by reason*.  Therefore justice observes the rational and not the real mean.

*Obj.* 2. Further, In things that are good simply, there is neither excess nor defect, and consequently neither is there a mean; as is clearly the case with the virtues, according to *Ethic.* ii. 6. Now justice is about things that are good simply, as stated in *Ethic.* v. Therefore justice does not observe the real mean.

*Obj.* 3. Further, The reason why the other virtues are said to observe the rational and not the real mean, is because in their case the mean varies according to different persons, since what is too much for one is too little for another (*Ethic.* ii. 6). Now this is also the case in justice: for one who strikes a prince does not receive the same punishment as one who strikes a private individual. Therefore justice also observes, not the real, but the rational mean.

*On the contrary*, The Philosopher says (*Ethic.* ii. 6, v. 4) that the mean of justice is to be taken according to *arithmetical* proportion, so that it is the real mean.

*I answer that*, As stated above (A. 9: I.-II., Q. LIX., A. 4), the other moral virtues are chiefly concerned with the passions, the regulation of which is gauged entirely by a comparison with the very man who is the subject of those passions, in so far as his anger and desire are vested with their various due circumstances. Hence the mean in suchlike virtues is measured not by the proportion of one thing to another, but merely by comparison with the virtuous man himself, so that with them the mean is only that which is fixed by reason in our regard.

On the other hand the matter of justice is external operation, in so far as an operation or the thing used in that operation is duly proportionate to another person, wherefore the mean of justice consists in a certain proportion of equality between the external thing and the external person. Now equality is the real mean between greater and less, as stated in *Metaph.* x.:* wherefore justice observes the real mean.

*Reply Obj.* 1. This real mean is also the rational mean, wherefore justice satisfies the conditions of a moral virtue.

*Reply Obj.* 2. We may speak of a thing being good simply

* Didot ed., ix. 5. Cf. *Ethic.* v. 4.

in two ways. First a thing may be good in every way:
thus the virtues are good; and there is neither mean nor
extremes in things that are good simply in this sense.
Secondly a thing is said to be good simply through being
good absolutely i.e. in its nature, although it may become
evil through being abused. Such are riches and honours;
and in the like it is possible to find excess, deficiency and
mean, as regards men who can use them well or ill: and it is
in this sense that justice is about things that are good simply.

*Reply Obj*. 3. The injury inflicted bears a different
proportion to a prince from that which it bears to a private
person: wherefore each injury requires to be equalized
by vengeance in a different way: and this implies a real
and not merely a rational diversity

### Eleventh Article.

#### WHETHER THE ACT OF JUSTICE IS TO RENDER TO EACH ONE HIS OWN ?

*We proceed thus to the Eleventh Article :—*

*Objection* 1. It would seem that the act of justice is not to
render to each one his own. For Augustine (*De Trin*. xiv. 9)
ascribes to justice the act of succouring the needy. Now
in succouring the needy we give them what is not theirs
but ours. Therefore the act of justice does not consist in
rendering to each one his own.

*Obj*. 2. Further, Tully says (*De Offic*. i. 7) that *beneficence
which we may call kindness or liberality, belongs to justice.*
Now it pertains to liberality to give to another of one's
own, not of what is his. Therefore the act of justice does
not consist in rendering to each one his own.

*Obj*. 3. Further, It belongs to justice not only to distribute
things duly, but also to repress injurious actions, such as
murder, adultery and so forth. But the rendering to each
one of what is his seems to belong solely to the distribution
of things. Therefore the act of justice is not sufficiently
described by saying that it consists in rendering to each
one his own.

*On the contrary,* Ambrose says (*De Offic.* i. 24): *It is justice that renders to each one what is his, and claims not another's property ; it disregards its own profit in order to preserve the common equity.*

*I answer that,* As stated above (AA. 8, 10), the matter of justice is an external operation, in so far as either it or the thing we use by it is made proportionate to some other person to whom we are related by justice.   Now each man's own is that which is due to him according to equality of proportion.   Therefore the proper act of justice is nothing else than to render to each one his own.

*Reply Obj.* 1. Since justice is a cardinal virtue, other secondary virtues, such as mercy, liberality and the like are connected with it, as we shall state further on (Q. LXXX., A. 1).   Wherefore to succour the needy, which belongs to mercy or pity, and to be liberally beneficent, which pertains to liberality, are by a kind of reduction ascribed to justice as to their principal virtue.

This suffices for the *Reply* to the *Second Objection.*

*Reply Obj.* 3. As the Philosopher states (*Ethic.* v. 4), in matters of justice, the name of *profit* is extended to whatever is excessive, and whatever is deficient is called *loss.*   The reason for this is that justice is first of all and more commonly exercised in voluntary interchanges of things, such as buying and selling, wherein those expressions are properly employed; and yet they are transferred to all other matters of justice.   The same applies to the rendering to each one of what is his own.

## TWELFTH ARTICLE.

### WHETHER JUSTICE STANDS FOREMOST AMONG ALL MORAL VIRTUES ?

*We proceed thus to the Twelfth Article :—*

*Objection* 1. It would seem that justice does not stand foremost among all the moral virtues.   Because it belongs to justice to render to each one what is his, whereas it belongs to liberality to give of one's own, and this is more virtuous.   Therefore liberality is a greater virtue than justice.

*Obj.* 2. Further, Nothing is adorned by a less excellent thing than itself. Now magnanimity is the ornament both of justice and of all the virtues, according to *Ethic.* iv. 3. Therefore magnanimity is more excellent than justice.

*Obj.* 3. Further, Virtue is about that which is *difficult* and *good*, as stated in *Ethic.* ii. 3. But fortitude is about more difficult things than justice is, since it is about dangers of death, according to *Ethic.* iii. 6. Therefore fortitude is more excellent than justice.

*On the contrary,* Tully says (*De Offic.* i. 7): *Justice is the most resplendent of the virtues, and gives its name to a good man.*

*I answer that,* If we speak of legal justice, it is evident that it stands foremost among all the moral virtues, for as much as the common good transcends the individual good of one person. In this sense the Philosopher declares (*Ethic.* v. 1) that *the most excellent of the virtues would seem to be justice, and more glorious than either the evening or the morning star.* But, even if we speak of particular justice, it excels the other moral virtues for two reasons. The first reason may be taken from the subject, because justice is in the more excellent part of the soul, viz. the rational appetite or will, whereas the other moral virtues are in the sensitive appetite, whereunto appertain the passions which are the matter of the other moral virtues. The second reason is taken from the object, because the other virtues are commendable in respect of the sole good of the virtuous person himself, whereas justice is praiseworthy in respect of the virtuous person being well disposed towards another, so that justice is somewhat the good of another person, as stated in *Ethic.* v. 1. Hence the Philosopher says (*Rhet.* i. 9): *The greatest virtues must needs be those which are most profitable to other persons, because virtue is a faculty of doing good to others. For this reason the greatest honours are accorded the brave and the just, since bravery is useful to others in warfare, and justice is useful to others both in warfare and in time of peace.*

*Reply Obj.* 1. Although the liberal man gives of his own, yet he does so in so far as he takes into consideration the good of his own virtue, while the just man gives to another what is his, through consideration of the common good. Moreover justice is observed towards all, whereas liberality cannot extend to all.    Again liberality which gives of a man's own is based on justice, whereby one renders to each man what is his.

*Reply Obj.* 2. When magnanimity is added to justice it increases the latter's goodness; and yet without justice it would not even be a virtue.

*Reply Obj.* 3. Although fortitude is about the most difficult things, it is not about the best, for it is only useful in warfare, whereas justice is useful both in war and in peace, as stated above.

# QUESTION LIX.

## OF INJUSTICE.

### (*In Four Articles.*)

WE must now consider injustice, under which head there are four points of inquiry: (1) Whether injustice is a special vice? (2) Whether it is proper to the unjust man to do unjust deeds? (3) Whether one can suffer injustice willingly? (4) Whether injustice is a mortal sin according to its genus?

### FIRST ARTICLE.

#### WHETHER INJUSTICE IS A SPECIAL VICE?

*We proceed thus to the First Article :—*

*Objection* 1. It would seem that injustice is not a special vice. For it is written (1 Jo. iii. 4): *All sin is iniquity.** Now iniquity would seem to be the same as injustice, because justice is a kind of equality, so that injustice is apparently the same as inequality or iniquity. Therefore injustice is not a special sin.

*Obj.* 2. Further, No special sin is contrary to all the virtues. But injustice is contrary to all the virtues: for as regards adultery it is opposed to chastity, as regards murder it is opposed to meekness, and in like manner as regards the other sins. Therefore injustice is not a special sin.

*Obj.* 3. Further, Injustice is opposed to justice which is in the will. But every sin is in the will, as Augustine declares (*De Duabus Anim*. x.). Therefore injustice is not a special sin.

* Vulg.,—*Whosoever committeth sin, committeth also iniquity ; and sin is iniquity.*

*On the contrary*, Injustice is contrary to justice. But justice is a special virtue. Therefore injustice is a special vice.

*I answer that*, Injustice is twofold. First there is illegal injustice which is opposed to legal justice: and this is essentially a special vice, in so far as it regards a special object, namely the common good which it contemns; and yet it is a general vice, as regards the intention, since contempt of the common good may lead to all kinds of sin. Thus too all vices, as being repugnant to the common good, have the character of injustice, as though they arose from injustice, in accord with what has been said above about justice (Q. LVIII., AA. 5, 6). Secondly we speak of injustice in reference to an inequality between one person and another, when one man wishes to have more goods, riches for example, or honours, and less evils, such as toil and losses, and thus injustice has a special matter and is a particular vice opposed to particular justice.

*Reply Obj.* 1. Even as legal justice is referred to human common good, so Divine justice is referred to the Divine good, to which all sin is repugnant, and in this sense all sin is said to be iniquity.

*Reply Obj.* 2. Even particular justice is indirectly opposed to all the virtues; in so far, to wit, as even external acts pertain both to justice and to the other moral virtues, although in different ways as stated above (Q. LVIII., A. 9, *ad* 2).

*Reply Obj.* 3. The will, like the reason, extends to all moral matters, i.e. passions and those external operations that relate to another person. On the other hand justice perfects the will solely in the point of its extending to operations that relate to another: and the same applies to injustice.

## Second Article.

### Whether a Man is Called Unjust Through Doing an Unjust Thing?

*We proceed thus to the Second Article :—*

*Objection* 1. It would seem that a man is called unjust through doing an unjust thing. For habits are specified by

their objects, as stated above (I.-II., Q. LIV., A. 2). Now
the proper object of justice is the just, and the proper object
of injustice is the unjust. Therefore a man should be
called just through doing a just thing, and unjust through
doing an unjust thing.

*Obj.* 2. Further, The Philosopher declares (*Ethic.* v. 9)
that they hold a false opinion who maintain that it is in
a man's power to do suddenly an unjust thing, and that
a just man is no less capable of doing what is unjust than
an unjust man. But this opinion would not be false unless
it were proper to the unjust man to do what is unjust.
Therefore a man is to be deemed unjust from the fact that
he does an unjust thing.

*Obj.* 3. Further, Every virtue bears the same relation
to its proper act, and the same applies to the contrary
vices. But whoever does what is intemperate, is said to
be intemperate. Therefore whoever does an unjust thing,
is said to be unjust.

*On the contrary*, The Philosopher says (*Ethic.* v. 6) that
*a man may do an unjust thing without being unjust.*

*I answer that*, Even as the object of justice is something
equal in external things, so too the object of injustice is
something unequal, through more or less being assigned
to some person than is due to him. To this object the habit
of injustice is compared by means of its proper act which
is called an injustice. Accordingly it may happen in
two ways that a man who does an unjust thing, is not
unjust: first, on account of a lack of correspondence
between the operation and its proper object. For the
operation takes its species and name from its direct and
not from its indirect object: and in things directed to an
end the direct is that which is intended, and the indirect
is what is beside the intention. Hence if a man do that
which is unjust, without intending to do an unjust thing,
for instance if he do it through ignorance, being unaware
that it is unjust, properly speaking he does an unjust
thing, not directly, but only indirectly, and, as it were,
doing materially that which is unjust: hence such an opera-

tion is not called an injustice. Secondly, this may happen on account of a lack of proportion between the operation and the habit. For an injustice may sometimes arise from a passion, for instance, anger or desire, and sometimes from choice, for instance when the injustice itself is the direct object of one's complacency. In the latter case properly speaking it arises from a habit, because whenever a man has a habit, whatever befits that habit is, of itself, pleasant to him. Accordingly, to do what is unjust intentionally and by choice is proper to the unjust man, in which sense the unjust man is one who has the habit of injustice: but a man may do what is unjust, unintentionally or through passion, without having the habit of injustice.

*Reply Obj.* 1. A habit is specified by its object in its direct and formal acceptation, not in its material and indirect acceptation.

*Reply Obj.* 2. It is not easy for any man to do an unjust thing from choice, as though it were pleasing for its own sake and not for the sake of something else: this is proper to one who has the habit, as the Philosopher declares (*ibid.*).

*Reply Obj.* 3. The object of temperance is not something established externally, as is the object of justice: the object of temperance, i.e. the temperate thing, depends entirely on proportion to the man himself. Consequently what is accidental and unintentional cannot be said to be temperate either materially or formally. In like manner neither can it be called intemperate: and in this respect there is dissimilarity between justice and the other moral vitues; but as regards the proportion between operation and habit, there is similarity in all respects.

## THIRD ARTICLE.

### WHETHER WE CAN SUFFER INJUSTICE WILLINGLY?

*We proceed thus to the Third Article :—*

*Objection* 1. It would seem that one can suffer injustice willingly. For injustice is inequality, as stated above (A. 2). Now a man by injuring himself, departs from equality, even as by injuring another. Therefore a man can do an injustice to himself, even as to another. But whoever does himself an injustice, does so involuntarily. Therefore a man can voluntarily suffer injustice especially if it be inflicted by himself.

*Obj.* 2. Further, No man is punished by the civil law, except for having committed some injustice. Now suicides were formerly punished according to the law of the state by being deprived of an honourable burial, as the Philosopher declares (*Ethic.* v. 11). Therefore a man can do himself an injustice, and consequently it may happen that a man suffers injustice voluntarily.

*Obj.* 3. Further, No man does an injustice save to one who suffers that injustice. But it may happen that a man does an injustice to one who wishes it, for instance if he sell him a thing for more than it is worth. Therefore a man may happen to suffer an injustice voluntarily.

*On the contrary,* To suffer an injustice and to do an injustice are contraries. Now no man does an injustice against his will. Therefore on the other hand no man suffers an injustice except against his will.

*I answer that,* Action by its very nature proceeds from an agent, whereas passion as such is from another: wherefore the same thing in the same respect cannot be both agent and patient, as stated in *Phys.* iii. 1, viii. 5. Now the proper principle of action in man is the will, wherefore man does properly and essentially what he does voluntarily, and on the other hand a man suffers properly what he suffers against his will, since in so far as he is willing, he is a principle in himself, and so, considered thus, he is active rather than passive   Accordingly we must conclude that properly and strictly speaking no man can do an injustice except voluntarily, nor suffer an injustice save involuntarily; but that accidentally and materially so to speak, it is possible for that which is unjust in itself either to be done involuntarily (as when a man does anything unintentionally), or to be suffered voluntarily (as when a man voluntarily gives to another more than he owes him).

*Reply Obj.* 1. When one man gives voluntarily to another that which he does not owe him, he causes neither injustice nor inequality. For a man's ownership depends on his will, so there is no disproportion if he forfeit something of his own free-will, either by his own or by another's action.

*Reply Obj.* 2. An individual person may be considered in two ways. First, with regard to himself; and thus, if he inflict an injury on himself, it may come under the head of some other kind of sin, intemperance for instance or imprudence, but not injustice; because injustice no less than justice, is always referred to another person. Secondly, this or that man may be considered as belonging to the State as part thereof, or as belonging to God, as His creature and image; and thus a man who kills himself, does an injury, not indeed to himself, but to the State and to God. Wherefore he is punished in accordance with both Divine and human law, even as the Apostle declares in respect of the fornicator (1 Cor. iii. 17): *If any man violate the temple of God, him shall God destroy.*

*Reply Obj.* 3. Suffering is the effect of external action. Now in the point of doing and suffering injustice, the material element is that which is done externally, considered in itself, as stated above (A. 2), and the formal and essential element is on the part of the will of agent and patient, as stated above (A. 2). Accordingly we must reply that injustice suffered by one man and injustice done by another man always accompany one another, in the material sense. But if we speak in the formal sense a man can do an injustice with the intention of doing an injustice, and yet the other man does not suffer an injustice, because he suffers voluntarily; and on the other hand a man can suffer an injustice if he suffer an injustice against his will, while the man who does the injury unknowingly, does an injustice, not formally but only materially.

## Fourth Article.

### WHETHER WHOEVER DOES AN INJUSTICE SINS MORTALLY ?

*We proceed thus to the Fourth Article :—*

*Objection* 1. It would seem that not everyone who does an injustice sins mortally.   For venial sin is opposed to mortal sin.   Now it is sometimes a venial sin to do an injury: for the Philosopher says (*Ethic.* v. 8) in reference to those who act unjustly: *Whatever they do not merely in ignorance but through ignorance is a venial matter.*   Therefore not everyone that does an injustice sins mortally.

*Obj.* 2. Further, He who does an injustice in a small matter, departs but slightly from the mean.   Now this seems to be insignificant and should be accounted among the least of evils, as the Philosopher declares (*Ethic.* ii. 9).   Therefore not everyone that does an injustice sins mortally.

*Obj.* 3. Further, Charity is the *mother of all the virtues,** and it is through being contrary thereto that a sin is called mortal.   But not all the sins contrary to the other virtues are mortal.   Therefore neither is it always a mortal sin to do an injustice.

*On the contrary,* Whatever is contrary to the law of God is a mortal sin.   Now whoever does an injustice does that which is contrary to the law of God, since it amounts either to theft, or to adultery, or to murder, or to something of the kind, as will be shown further on (Q. LXIV. *seqq.*). Therefore whoever does an injustice sins mortally.

*I answer that,* As stated above (I.-II., Q. LXXII., A. 5), when we were treating of the distinction of sins, a mortal sin is one that is contrary to charity which gives life to the soul.   Now every injury inflicted on another person is of itself contrary to charity, which moves us to will the good of another.   And so since injustice always consists in an injury inflicted on another person, it is evident that to do an injustice is a mortal sin according to its genus.

*Reply Obj.* 1. This saying of the Philosopher is to be

* Peter Lombard, *Sentent.* iii. D. 23.

understood as referring to ignorance of fact, which he calls *ignorance of particular circumstances,*\* and which deserves pardon, and not to ignorance of the law which does not excuse: and he who does an injustice through ignorance, does no injustice except accidentally, as stated above (A. 2).

*Reply Obj.* 2. He who does an injustice in small matters falls short of the perfection of an unjust deed, in so far as what he does may be deemed not altogether contrary to the will of the person who suffers therefrom: for instance, if a man take an apple or some such thing from another man, in which case it is probable that the latter is not hurt or displeased.

*Reply Obj.* 3. The sins which are contrary to the other virtues are not always hurtful to another person, but imply a disorder affecting human passions: hence there is no comparison.

\* *Ethic.* iii. 1.

# QUESTION LX.

## OF JUDGMENT.

### (*In Six Articles.*)

In due sequence we must consider judgment, under which head there are six points of inquiry: (1) Whether judgment is an act of justice ? (2) Whether it is lawful to judge ? (3) Whether judgment should be based on suspicions ? (4) Whether doubts should be interpreted favourably ? (5) Whether judgment should always be given according to the written law ? (6) Whether judgment is perverted by being usurped ?

### First Article.

#### WHETHER JUDGMENT IS AN ACT OF JUSTICE ?

*We proceed thus to the First Article :—*

*Objection* 1. It would seem that judgment is not an act of justice. The Philosopher says (*Ethic.* i. 3) that *everyone judges well of what he knows,* so that judgment would seem to belong to the cognitive faculty. Now the cognitive faculty is perfected by prudence. Therefore judgment belongs to prudence rather than to justice, which is in the will, as stated above (Q. LVIII., A. 4).

*Obj.* 2. Further, The Apostle says (1 Cor. ii. 15): *The spiritual man judgeth all things.* Now man is made spiritual chiefly by the virtue of charity, which *is poured forth in our hearts by the Holy Ghost Who is given to us* (Rom. v. 5). Therefore judgment belongs to charity rather than to justice.

*Obj.* 3. Further, It belongs to every virtue to judge aright of its proper matter, because *the virtuous man is the rule and measure in everything*, according to the Philosopher (*Ethic.* iii. 4). Therefore judgment does not belong to justice any more than to the other moral virtues.

*Obj.* 4. Further, Judgment would seem to belong only to judges. But the act of justice is to be found in every just man. Since then judges are not the only just men, it seems that judgment is not the proper act of justice.

*On the contrary,* It is written (Ps. xciii. 15): *Until justice be turned into judgment.*

*I answer that,* Judgment properly denotes the act of a judge as such. Now a judge (*judex*) is so called because he asserts the right (*jus dicens*) and right is the object of justice, as stated above (Q. LVII., A. 1). Consequently the original meaning of the word *judgment* is a statement or decision of the just or right. Now to decide rightly about virtuous deeds proceeds, properly speaking, from the virtuous habit; thus a chaste person decides rightly about matters relating to chastity. Therefore judgment, which denotes a right decision about what is just, belongs properly to justice. For this reason the Philosopher says (*Ethic.* v. 4) that *men have recourse to a judge as to one who is the personification of justice.*

*Reply Obj.* 1. The word *judgment*, from its original meaning of a right decision about what is just, has been extended to signify a right decision in any matter whether speculative or practical. Now a right judgment in any matter requires two things. The first is the virtue itself that pronounces judgment: and in this way, judgment is an act of reason, because it belongs to the reason to pronounce or define. The other is the disposition of the one who judges, on which depends his aptness for judging aright. In this way, in matters of justice, judgment proceeds from justice, even as in matters of fortitude, it proceeds from fortitude. Accordingly judgment is an act of justice in so far as justice inclines one to judge aright, and of prudence in so far as prudence pronounces judgment: wherefore σύνεσις which belongs to prudence is said to *judge rightly*, as stated above (Q. LI., A. 3).

*Reply Obj.* 2. The spiritual man, by reason of the habit of charity, has an inclination to judge aright of all things according to the Divine rules; and it is in conformity with these that he pronounces judgment through the gift of wisdom: even as the just man pronounces judgment through the virtue of prudence conformably with the ruling of the law.

*Reply Obj.* 3. The other virtues regulate man in himself, whereas justice regulates man in his dealings with others, as shown above (Q. LVIII., A. 2). Now man is master in things concerning himself, but not in matters relating to others. Consequently where the other virtues are in question, there is no need for judgment other than that of a virtuous man, taking judgment in its broader sense, as explained above (*ad* i.). But in matters of justice, there is further need for the judgment of a superior, who is *able to reprove both, and to put his hand between both.** Hence judgment belongs more specially to justice than to any other virtue.

*Reply Obj.* 4. Justice is in the sovereign as a master-virtue,† commanding and prescribing what is just; while it is in the subjects, as an executive and administrative virtue. Hence judgment, which denotes a decision of what is just, belongs to justice, considered as existing chiefly in one who has authority.

## Second Article.

### WHETHER IT IS LAWFUL TO JUDGE ?

*We proceed thus to the Second Article :—*

*Objection* 1. It would seem unlawful to judge. For nothing is punished except what is unlawful. Now those who judge are threatened with punishment, which those who judge not will escape, according to Matth. vii. 1, *Judge not, and ye shall not be judged*. Therefore it is unlawful to judge.

*Obj.* 2. Further, It is written (Rom. xiv. 4): *Who art thou that judgest another man's servant. To his own lord he standeth or falleth*. Now God is the Lord of all. Therefore to no man is it lawful to judge.

*Obj.* 3. Further, No man is sinless, according to 1 Jo. i. 8,

* Job ix. 33.                    † Cf. Q. LVIII., A. 6.

*If we say that we have no sin, we deceive ourselves.* Now it
is unlawful for a sinner to judge, according to Rom. ii. 1,
*Thou art inexcusable, O man, whosoever thou art, that judgest ;
for wherein thou judgest another, thou condemnest thyself,
for thou dost the same things which thou judgest.* Therefore
to no man is it lawful to judge.

*On the contrary,* It is written (Deut. xvi. 18): *Thou shalt
appoint judges and magistrates in all thy gates . . . that
they may judge the people with just judgment.*

*I answer that,* Judgment is lawful in so far as it is an act
of justice. Now it follows from what has been stated above
(A. 1, *ad* 1, 3) that three conditions are requisite for a judgment to be an act of justice: first, that it proceed from the
inclination of justice; secondly, that it come from one who
is in authority; thirdly, that it be pronounced according
to the right ruling of prudence. If any one of these be lacking, the judgment will be faulty and unlawful. First, when
it is contrary to the rectitude of justice, and then it is called
*perverted* or *unjust :* secondly, when a man judges about
matters wherein he has no authority, and this is called
judgment *by usurpation :* thirdly, when the reason lacks
certainty, as when a man, without any solid motive, forms a
judgment on some doubtful or hidden matter, and then it
is called judgment by *suspicion* or *rash* judgment.

*Reply Obj.* 1. In these words Our Lord forbids rash judgment which is about the inward intention, or other uncertain
things, as Augustine states (*De Serm. Dom. in Monte* ii. 18).
Or else He forbids judgment about Divine things, which we
ought not to judge, but simply believe, since they are above
us, as Hilary declares in his commentary on Matth. v.
Or again according to Chrysostom* He forbids the judgment which proceeds not from benevolence but from
bitterness of heart.

*Reply Obj.* 2. A judge is appointed as God's servant;
wherefore it is written (Deut. i. 16): *Judge that which is just,*
and further on (*verse* 17), *because it is the judgment of God.*

---

* *Hom.* xvii. *in Matth.* in the *Opus Imperfectum* falsely ascribed
to S. John Chrysostom.

*Reply Obj.* 3. Those who stand guilty of grievous sins should not judge those who are guilty of the same or lesser sins, as Chrysostom* says on the words of Matth. vii. 1, *Judge not.* Above all does this hold when such sins are public, because there would be an occasion of scandal arising in the hearts of others. If however they are not public but hidden, and there be an urgent necessity for the judge to pronounce judgment, because it is his duty, he can reprove or judge with humility and fear. Hence Augustine says (*De Serm. Dom. in Monte,* ii. 19): *If we find that we are guilty of the same sin as another man, we should groan together with him, and invite him to strive against it together with us.* And yet it is not through acting thus that a man *condemns* himself so as to deserve to be condemned once again, but when, in condemning another, he shows himself to be equally deserving of condemnation on account of another or a like sin.

### Third Article.

#### WHETHER IT IS UNLAWFUL TO FORM A JUDGMENT FROM SUSPICIONS ?

*We proceed thus to the Third Article :—*

*Objection* 1. It would seem that it is not unlawful to form a judgment from suspicions. For suspicion is seemingly an uncertain opinion about an evil, wherefore the Philosopher states (*Ethic.* vi. 3) that suspicion is about both the true and the false. Now it is impossible to have any but an uncertain opinion about contingent singulars. Since then human judgment is about human acts, which are about singular and contingent matters, it seems that no judgment would be lawful, if it were not lawful to judge from suspicions.

*Obj.* 2. Further, A man does his neighbour an injury by judging him unlawfully. But an evil suspicion consists in nothing more than a man's opinion, and consequently does not seem to pertain to the injury of another man. Therefore judgment based on suspicion is not unlawful.

* *Hom.* xxiv.

*Obj*. 3. Further, If it is unlawful, it must needs be reducible to an injustice, since judgment is an act of justice, as stated above (A. 1).   Now an injustice is always a mortal sin according to its genus, as stated above (Q. LIX., A. 4). Therefore a judgment based on suspicion would always be a mortal sin, if it were unlawful.   But this is false, because *we cannot avoid suspicions*, according to a gloss of Augustine (*Tract*. xc. *in Joan.*) on 1 Cor. iv. 5, *Judge not before the time*.   Therefore a judgment based on suspicion would seem not to be unlawful.

*On the contrary*, Chrysostom* in commenting on the words of Matth. vii. 1, *Judge not*, etc., says: *By this commandment Our Lord does not forbid Christians to reprove others from kindly motives, but that Christian should despise Christian by boasting his own righteousness, by hating and condemning others for the most part on mere suspicion.*

*I answer that*, As Tully says (*De Invent. Rhet.* ii.), suspicion denotes evil thinking based on slight indications, and this is due to three causes.   First, from a man being evil in himself, and from this very fact, as though conscious of his own wickedness, he is prone to think evil of others, according to Eccles. x. 3, *The fool when he walketh in the way, whereas he himself is a fool, esteemeth all men fools.* Secondly, this is due to a man being ill disposed towards another: for when a man hates or despises another, or is angry with or envious of him, he is led by slight indications to think evil of him, because everyone easily believes what he desires.   Thirdly, this is due to long experience: wherefore the Philosopher says (*Rhet.* ii. 13) that *old people are very suspicious, for they have often experienced the faults of others*. The first two causes of suspicion evidently connote perversity of the affections, while the third diminishes the nature of suspicion, in as much as experience leads to certainty which is contrary to the nature of suspicion.   Consequently suspicion denotes a certain amount of vice, and the further it goes, the more vicious it is.

* *Hom*. xvii. *in Matth*. in the *Opus Imperfectum* falsely ascribed to S. John Chrysostom.

Now there are three degrees of suspicion. The first degree is when a man begins to doubt of another's goodness from slight indications. This is a venial and a light sin; for *it belongs to human temptation without which no man can go through this life*, according to a gloss on 1 Cor. iv. 5, *Judge not before the time*. The second degree is when a man, from slight indications, esteems another man's wickedness as certain. This is a mortal sin, if it be about a grave matter, since it cannot be without contempt of one's neighbour. Hence the same gloss goes on to say: *If then we cannot avoid suspicions, because we are human, we must nevertheless restrain our judgment, and refrain from forming a definite and fixed opinion*. The third degree is when a judge goes so far as to condemn a man on suspicion: this pertains directly to injustice, and consequently is a mortal sin.

*Reply Obj.* 1. Some kind of certainty is found in human acts, not indeed the certainty of a demonstration, but such as is befitting the matter in point, for instance when a thing is proved by suitable witnesses.

*Reply Obj.* 2. From the very fact that a man thinks evil of another without sufficient cause, he despises him unduly, and therefore does him an injury.

*Reply Obj.* 3. Since justice and injustice are about external operations, as stated above (Q. LVIII., AA. 8, 10, 11: Q. LIX., A. 1, *ad* 3), the judgment of suspicion pertains directly to injustice when it is betrayed by external action, and then it is a mortal sin, as stated above. The internal judgment pertains to justice, in so far as it is related to the external judgment, even as the internal to the external act, for instance as desire is related to fornication, or anger to murder.

### Fourth Article.

#### WHETHER DOUBTS SHOULD BE INTERPRETED FOR THE BEST ?

*We proceed thus to the Fourth Article :—*

*Objection* 1. It would seem that doubts should not be interpreted for the best. Because we should judge from what happens for the most part. But it happens for the most part that evil is done, since *the number of fools is infinite* (Eccles. i. 15), *for the imagination and thought of man's heart are prone to evil from his youth* (Gen. viii. 21). Therefore doubts should be interpreted for the worst rather than for the best.

*Obj.* 2. Further, Augustine says (*De Doctr. Christ.* i. 27) that *he leads a godly and just life who is sound in his estimate of things, and turns neither to this side nor to that.* Now he who interprets a doubtful point for the best, turns to one side. Therefore this should not be done.

*Obj.* 3. Further, Man should love his neighbour as himself. Now with regard to himself, a man should interpret doubtful matters for the worst, according to Job ix. 28, *I feared all my works.* Therefore it seems that doubtful matters affecting one's neighbour should be interpreted for the worst.

*On the contrary,* A gloss on Rom. xiv. 3, *He that eateth not, let him not judge him that eateth,* says: *Doubts should be interpreted in the best sense.*

*I answer that,* As stated above (A. 3, *ad* 2), from the very fact that a man thinks ill of another without sufficient cause, he injures and despises him. Now no man ought to despise or in any way injure another man without urgent cause: and, consequently, unless we have evident indications of a person's wickedness, we ought to deem him good, by interpreting for the best whatever is doubtful about him.

*Reply Obj.* 1. He who interprets doubtful matters for the best, may happen to be deceived more often than not; yet it is better to err frequently through thinking well of a wicked man, than to err less frequently through having an evil opinion of a good man, because in the latter case an injury is inflicted, but not in the former.

*Reply Obj.* 2. It is one thing to judge of things and another to judge of men. For when we judge of things, there is no question of the good or evil of the thing about which we are judging, since it will take no harm no matter what kind of judgment we form about it; but there is question of the good of the person who judges, if he judge truly, and of his evil if he judge falsely because *the true is the good of the intellect, and the false is its evil,* as stated in *Ethic.* vi. 2, wherefore everyone should strive to make his judgment accord with things as they are.   On the other hand when we judge of men, the good and evil in our judgment is considered chiefly on the part of the person about whom judgment is being formed; for he is deemed worthy of honour from the very fact that he is judged to be good, and deserving of contempt if he is judged to be evil.   For this reason we ought, in this kind of judgment, to aim at judging a man good, unless there is evident proof of the contrary.   And though we may judge falsely, our judgment in thinking well of another pertains to our good feeling and not to the evil of the intellect, even as neither does it pertain to the intellect's perfection to know the truth of contingent singulars in themselves.

*Reply Obj.* 3. One may interpret something for the worst or for the best in two ways.   First, by a kind of supposition; and thus, when we have to apply a remedy to some evil, whether our own or another's, in order for the remedy to be applied with greater certainty of a cure, it is expedient to take the worst for granted, since if a remedy be efficacious against a worse evil, much more is it efficacious against a lesser evil.   Secondly we may interpret something for the best or for the worst, by deciding or determining, and in this case when judging of things we should try to interpret each thing according as it is, and when judging of persons, to interpret things for the best as stated above.

## FIFTH ARTICLE.

### WHETHER WE SHOULD ALWAYS JUDGE ACCORDING TO THE WRITTEN LAW ?

*We proceed thus to the Fifth Article :—*

*Objection* 1. It would seem that we ought not always to judge according to the written law.   For we ought always to avoid judging unjustly.   But written laws sometimes contain injustice, according to Isa. x. 1, *Wo to them that make wicked laws, and when they write, write injustice.*

Therefore we ought not always to judge according to the written law.

*Obj.* 2. Further, Judgment has to be formed about individual happenings. But no written law can cover each and every individual happening, as the Philosopher declares (*Ethic.* v. 10). Therefore it seems that we are not always bound to judge according to the written law.

*Obj.* 3. Further, A law is written in order that the lawgiver's intention may be made clear. But it happens sometimes that even if the lawgiver himself were present he would judge otherwise. Therefore we ought not always to judge according to the written law.

*On the contrary*, Augustine says (*De Vera Relig.* xxxi.): *In these earthly laws, though men judge about them when they are making them, when once they are established and passed, the judges may judge no longer of them, but according to them.*

*I answer that*, As stated above (A. 1), judgment is nothing else but a decision or determination of what is just. Now a thing becomes just in two ways: first by the very nature of the case, and this is called *natural right*, secondly by some agreement between men, and this is called *positive right*, as stated above (Q. LVII., A. 2). Now laws are written for the purpose of manifesting both these rights, but in different ways. For the written law does indeed contain natural right, but it does not establish it, for the latter derives its force, not from the law but from nature: whereas the written law both contains positive right, and establishes it by giving it force of authority.

Hence it is necessary to judge according to the written law, else judgment would fall short either of the natural or of the positive right.

*Reply Obj.* 1. Just as the written law does not give force to the natural right, so neither can it diminish or annul its force, because neither can man's will change nature. Hence if the written law contains anything contrary to the natural right, it is unjust and has no binding force. For positive right has no place except where *it matters not*, according to the natural right, *whether a thing be done in one way or in another ;* as stated above (Q. LVII., A. 2, *ad* 2). Wherefore such documents are to be called, not laws, but rather corruptions of law, as stated above (I.-II., Q. XCV., A. 2): and consequently judgment should not be delivered according to them.

*Reply Obj.* 2. Even as unjust laws by their very nature are, either always or for the most part, contrary to the natural right, so too laws that are rightly established, fail in some cases, when if they were observed they would be contrary to the natural right. Wherefore in such cases judgment should be delivered, not according to the letter of the law, but according to equity which the lawgiver has in view. Hence the jurist says:* *By no reason of law, or favour of equity, is it allowable for us to interpret harshly, and render burdensome, those useful measures which have been enacted for the welfare of man.* In such cases even the lawgiver himself would decide otherwise; and if he had foreseen the case, he might have provided for it by law.

This suffices for the *Reply* to the *Third Objection.*

## SIXTH ARTICLE.

### WHETHER JUDGMENT IS RENDERED PERVERSE BY BEING USURPED ?

*We proceed thus to the Sixth Article :—*

*Objection* 1. It would seem that judgment is not rendered perverse by being usurped. For justice is rectitude in matters of action. Now truth is not impaired, no matter who tells it, but it may suffer from the person who ought to accept it. Therefore again justice loses nothing, no matter who declares what is just, and this is what is meant by judgment.

*Obj.* 2. Further, It belongs to judgment to punish sins. Now it is related to the praise of some that they punished sins without having authority over those whom they punished; such as Moses in slaying the Egyptian (Exod. ii. 12), and Phinees the son of Eleazar in slaying Zambri the son of Salu (Num. xxv. 7-14), and *it was reputed to him unto*

* Digest. i. 3; *De leg. senatusque consult.,* 25.

*justice* (Ps. cv. 31). Therefore usurpation of judgment pertains not to injustice.

*Obj.* 3. Further, Spiritual power is distinct from temporal. Now prelates having spiritual power sometimes interfere in matters concerning the secular power. Therefore usurped judgment is not unlawful.

*Obj.* 4. Further, Even as the judge requires authority in order to judge aright, so also does he need justice and knowledge, as shown above (A. 1, *ad* 1, 3; A. 2). But a judgment is not described as unjust, if he who judges lacks the habit of justice or the knowledge of the law. Neither therefore is it always unjust to judge by usurpation, i.e. without authority.

*On the contrary,* It is written (Rom. xiv. 4): *Who art thou that judgest another man's servant ?*

*I answer that,* Since judgment should be pronounced according to the written law, as stated above (A. 5), he that pronounces judgment, interprets, in a way, the letter of the law, by applying it to some particular case. Now since it belongs to the same authority to interpret and to make a law, just as a law cannot be made save by public authority, so neither can a judgment be pronounced except by public authority, which extends over those who are subject to the community. Wherefore even as it would be unjust for one man to force another to observe a law that was not approved by public authority, so too it is unjust, if a man compels another to submit to a judgment that is pronounced by other than the public authority.

*Reply Obj.* 1. When the truth is declared there is no obligation to accept it, and each one is free to receive it or not, as he wishes. On the other hand judgment implies an obligation, wherefore it is unjust for anyone to be judged by one who has no public authority.

*Reply Obj.* 2. Moses seems to have slain the Egyptian by authority received as it were, by divine inspiration; this seems to follow from Acts vii. 24, 25, where it is said that *striking the Egyptian . . . he thought that his brethren understood that God by his hand would save Israel* (Vulg.—

*them*).   Or it may be replied that Moses slew the Egyptian
in order to defend the man who was unjustly attacked,
without himself exceeding the limits of a blameless defence.
Wherefore Ambrose says (*De Offic*. i. 36) that *whoever does
not ward off a blow from a fellow man when he can, is as much
in fault as the striker;* and he quotes the example of Moses.
Again we may reply with Augustine (*QQ. Exod*. qu. 2)*
that just as *the soil gives proof of its fertility by producing
useless herbs before the useful seeds have grown, so this deed
of Moses was sinful although it gave a sign of great fertility*,
in so far, to wit, as it was a sign of the power whereby he
was to deliver his people.

With regard to Phinees the reply is that he did this out of
zeal for God by Divine inspiration; or because though not
as yet high-priest, he was nevertheless the high-priest's
son, and this judgment was his concern as of the other
judges, to whom this was commanded.†

*Reply Obj*. 3. The secular power is subject to the spiritual,
even as the body is subject to the soul.  Consequently the
judgment is not usurped if the spiritual authority interferes
in those temporal matters that are subject to the spiritual
authority or which have been committed to the spiritual
by the temporal authority.

*Reply Obj*. 4. The habits of knowledge and justice are
perfections of the individual, and consequently their absence
does not make a judgment to be usurped, as in the absence
of public authority which gives a judgment its coercive
force.

* Cf. *Contra Faust*. xxii. 70.
† Exod. xxii. 20; Levit. xx.; Deut. xiii., xvii.

# QUESTION LXI.

## OF THE PARTS OF JUSTICE.

### (*In Four Articles.*)

WE must now consider the parts of justice; (1) the subjective parts, which are the species of justice, i.e. distributive and commutative justice: (2) the quasi-integral parts:
(3) the quasi-potential parts, i.e. the virtues connected with
justice. The first consideration will be twofold: (1) The
parts of justice: (2) their opposite vices. And since restitution would seem to be an act of commutative justice, we
must consider (1) the distinction between commutative
and distributive justice, (2) restitution.

Under the first head there are four points of inquiry:
(1) Whether there are two species of justice, viz. distributive
and commutative ? (2) Whether in either case the mean
is taken in the same way ? (3) Whether their matter is
uniform or manifold ? (4) Whether in any of these species
the just is the same as counterpassion ?

## FIRST ARTICLE.

### WHETHER TWO SPECIES OF JUSTICE ARE SUITABLY ASSIGNED, VIZ. COMMUTATIVE AND DISTRIBUTIVE ?

*We proceed thus to the First Article :—*

*Objection* 1. It would seem that the two species of justice
are unsuitably assigned, viz. distributive and commutative.
That which is hurtful to the many cannot be a species
of justice, since justice is directed to the common good.
Now it is hurtful to the common good of the many, if the
goods of the community are distributed among many,

both because the goods of the community would be exhausted, and because the morals of men would be corrupted. For Tully says (*De Offic.* ii. 15): *He who receives becomes worse, and the more ready to expect that he will receive again.* Therefore distribution does not belong to any species of justice.

*Obj.* 2. Further, The act of justice is to render to each one what is his own, as stated above (Q. LVIII., A. 2). But when things are distributed, a man does not receive what was his, but becomes possessed of something which belonged to the community. Therefore this does not pertain to justice.

*Obj.* 3. Further, Justice is not only in the sovereign, but also in the subject, as stated above (Q. LVIII., A. 6). But it belongs exclusively to the sovereign to distribute. Therefore distribution does not always belong to justice.

*Obj.* 4. Further, *Distributive justice regards common goods* (*Ethic.* v. 4). Now matters regarding the community pertain to legal justice. Therefore distributive justice is a part, not of particular, but of legal justice.

*Obj.* 5. Further, Unity or multitude do not change the species of a virtue. Now commutative justice consists in rendering something to one person, while distributive justice consists in giving something to many. Therefore they are not different species of justice.

*On the contrary,* The Philosopher assigns two parts to justice and says (*Ethic.* v. 2) that *one directs distributions, the other, commutations.*

*I answer that,* As stated above (Q. LVIII., AA. 7, 8), particular justice is directed to the private individual, who is compared to the community as a part to the whole. Now a twofold order may be considered in relation to a part. In the first place there is the order of one part to another, to which corresponds the order of one private individual to another. This order is directed by commutative justice, which is concerned about the mutual dealings between two persons. In the second place there is the order of the whole towards the parts, to which corresponds the order of that which belongs to the community in relation to each single person. This order is directed by distributive justice, which distributes common goods proportionately. Hence there are two species of justice, distributive and commutative.

*Reply Obj.* 1. Just as a private individual is praised for moderation in his bounty, and blamed for excess therein, so too ought moderation to be observed in the distribution of common goods, wherein distributive justice directs.

*Reply Obj.* 2. Even as part and whole are somewhat the same, so too that which pertains to the whole, pertains somewhat to the part also: so that when the goods of the community are distributed among a number of individuals each one receives that which, in a way, is his own.

*Reply Obj.* 3. The act of distributing the goods of the community, belongs to none but those who exercise authority over those goods; and yet distributive justice is also in the subjects to whom those goods are distributed in so far as they are contented by a just distribution. Moreover distribution of common goods is sometimes made not to the state but to the members of a family, and such distribution can be made by authority of a private individual.

*Reply Obj.* 4. Movement takes its species from the term *whereunto*. Hence it belongs to legal justice to direct to the common good those matters which concern private individuals: whereas on the contrary it belongs to particular justice to direct the common good to particular individuals by way of distribution.

*Reply Obj.* 5. Distributive and commutative justice differ not only in respect of unity and multitude, but also in respect of different kinds of due: because common property is due to an individual in one way, and his personal property in another way.

### SECOND ARTICLE.

#### WHETHER THE MEAN IS TO BE OBSERVED IN THE SAME WAY IN DISTRIBUTIVE AS IN COMMUTATIVE JUSTICE ?

*We proceed thus to the Second Article :—*

*Objection* 1. It would seem that the mean in distributive justice is to be observed in the same way as in commutative justice. For each of these is a kind of particular justice, as stated above (A. 1). Now the mean is taken in the same way in all the parts of temperance or fortitude. Therefore the mean should also be observed in the same way in both distributive and commutative justice.

*Obj.* 2. Further, The form of a moral virtue consists in observing the mean which is determined in accordance with reason. Since, then, one virtue has one form, it seems that the mean for both should be the same.

*Obj.* 3. Further, In order to observe the mean in distributive justice we have to consider the various deserts of persons. Now a person's deserts are considered also in commutative justice, for instance, in punishments; thus a man who strikes a prince is punished more than one who strikes a private individual. Therefore the mean is observed in the same way in both kinds of justice.

*On the contrary,* The Philosopher says (*Ethic.* v. 3, 4) that the mean in distributive justice is observed according to *geometrical proportion,* whereas in commutative justice it follows *arithmetical proportion.*

*I answer that,* As stated above (A. 1), in distributive justice something is given to a private individual, in so far as what belongs to the whole is due to the part, and in a quantity that is proportionate to the importance of the position of that part in respect of the whole. Consequently in distributive justice a person receives all the more of the common goods, according as he holds a more prominent position in the community. This prominence in an aristocratic community is gauged according to virtue, in an oligarchy according to wealth, in a democracy according

to liberty, and in various ways according to various forms
of community. Hence in distributive justice the mean
is observed, not according to equality between thing and
thing, but according to proportion between things and
persons: in such a way that even as one person surpasses
another, so that which is given to one person surpasses
that which is allotted to another. Hence the Philosopher
says (*Ethic.* v. 3, 4) that the mean in the latter case follows
*geometrical proportion*, wherein equality depends not on
quantity but on proportion. For example we say that
6 is to 4 as 3 is to 2, because in either case the proportion
equals $1\frac{1}{2}$; since the greater number is the sum of the lesser
plus its half: whereas the equality of excess is not one of
quantity, because 6 exceeds 4 by 2, while 3 exceeds 2
by 1.

On the other hand in commutations something is paid
to an individual on account of something of his that has
been received, as may be seen chiefly in selling and buying,
where the notion of commutation is found primarily.
Hence it is necessary to equalize thing with thing, so that
the one person should pay back to the other just so much
as he has become richer out of that which belonged to the
other. The result of this will be equality according to the
*arithmetical mean* which is gauged according to equal excess
in quantity. Thus 5 is the mean between 6 and 4, since it
exceeds the latter and is exceeded by the former, by 1.
Accordingly if, at the start, both persons have 5, and one
of them receives 1 out of the other's belongings, the one
that is the receiver, will have 6, and the other will be left
with 4: and so there will be justice if both be brought back
to the mean, 1 being taken from him that has 6, and given
to him that has 4, for then both will have 5 which is the
mean.

*Reply Obj.* 1. In the other moral virtues the rational, not
the real mean, is to be followed: but justice follows the real
mean; wherefore the mean, in justice, depends on the
diversity of things.

*Reply Obj.* 2. Equality is the general form of justice,

wherein distributive and commutative justice agree: but in one we find equality of geometrical proportion, whereas in the other we find equality of arithmetical proportion.

*Reply Obj.* 3. In actions and passions a person's station affects the quantity of a thing: for it is a greater injury to strike a prince than a private person.   Hence in distributive justice a person's station is considered in itself, whereas in commutative justice it is considered in so far as it causes a diversity of things.

### Third Article.

#### WHETHER THERE IS A DIFFERENT MATTER FOR BOTH KINDS OF JUSTICE ?

*We proceed thus to the Third Article :—*

*Objection* 1. It would seem that there is not a different matter for both kinds of justice.   Diversity of matter causes diversity of virtue, as in the case of fortitude and temperance.   Therefore, if distributive and commutative justice have different matters, it would seem that they are not comprised under the same virtue, viz. justice.

*Obj.* 2. Further, The distribution that has to do with distributive justice is one of *wealth or of honours, or of whatever can be distributed among the members of the community* (*Ethic.* v. 2), which very things are the subject matter of commutations between one person and another, and this belongs to commutative justice.   Therefore the matters of distributive and commutative justice are not distinct.

*Obj.* 3. Further, If the matter of distributive justice differs from that of commutative justice, for the reason that they differ specifically, where there is no specific difference, there ought to be no diversity of matter.   Now the Philosopher (*loc. cit.*) reckons commutative justice as one species, and yet this has many kinds of matter.   Therefore the matter of these species of justice is, seemingly, not of many kinds.

*On the contrary*, It is stated in *Ethic.* v. 2 that *one kind of justice directs distributions, and another commutations.*

*I answer that,* As stated above (Q. LVII., AA. 8, 10), justice is about certain external operations, namely distribution and commutation. These consist in the use of certain externals, whether things, persons or even works: of things, as when one man takes from or restores to another that which is his; of persons, as when a man does an injury to the very person of another, for instance by striking or insulting him, or even by showing respect for him; and of works, as when a man justly exacts a work of another, or does a work for him. Accordingly, if we take for the matter of each kind of justice the things themselves of which the operations are the use, the matter of distributive and commutative justice is the same, since things can be distributed out of the common property to individuals, and be the subject of commutation between one person and another; and again there is a certain distribution and payment of laborious works.

If, however, we take for the matter of both kinds of justice the principal actions themselves, whereby we make use of persons, things, and works, there is then a difference of matter between them. For distributive justice directs distributions, while commutative justice directs commutations that can take place between two persons. Of these some are involuntary, some voluntary. They are involuntary when anyone uses another man's chattel, person, or work against his will, and this may be done secretly by fraud, or openly by violence. In either case the offence may be committed against the other man's chattel or person, or against a person connected with him. If the offence is against his chattel and this be taken secretly, it is called *theft*, if openly, it is called *robbery*. If it be against another man's person, it may affect either the very substance of his person, or his dignity. If it be against the substance of his person, a man is injured secretly if he is treacherously slain, struck or poisoned, and openly, if he is publicly slain, imprisoned, struck or maimed. If it be against his personal dignity, a man is injured secretly by false witness, detractions and so forth, whereby he is deprived of his good name, and openly, by being accused in a court of law, or by public insult. If it be against a personal connexion, a man is injured in the person of his wife, secretly (for the most part) by adultery, in the person of his slave, if the latter be induced to leave his master: which things can also be done openly. The same applies to other personal connexions, and whatever injury may be committed against the principal, may be committed against them also. Adultery, however, and inducing a slave to leave his master are properly injuries against the person; yet the latter, since a slave is his master's chattel, is referred to theft.

Voluntary commutations are when a man voluntarily transfers his chattel to another person. And if he transfer it simply so that the recipient incurs no debt, as in the case of gifts, it is an act, not of justice but of liberality. A voluntary transfer belongs to justice in so far as it includes the notion of debt, and this may occur in many ways. First when one man simply transfers his thing to another in exchange for another thing, as happens in selling and buying. Secondly when a man transfers his thing to another, that the latter may have the use of it with the obligation of returning it to its owner. If he grant the use of a thing gratuituously, it is called *usufruct* in things that bear fruit; and simply *borrowing* on *loan* in things that bear no fruit, such as money, pottery etc.; but if not even the use is granted gratis, it is called *letting* or *hiring*. Thirdly, a man transfers his thing with the intention of recovering it, not for the purpose of its use, but that it may be kept safe, as in a *deposit*, or under some obligation, as when a man pledges his property, or when one man stands security for another. In all these actions, whether voluntary or involuntary, the mean is taken in the same way according to the equality of repayment. Hence all these actions belong to the one same species of justice, namely commutative justice. And this suffices for the *Replies* to the *Objections*.

## FOURTH ARTICLE.

### WHETHER THE JUST IS ABSOLUTELY THE SAME AS RETALIATION?

*We proceed thus to the Fourth Article :—*

*Objection* 1. It would seem that the just is absolutely the same as retaliation. For the judgment of God is absolutely just. Now the judgment of God is such that a man has to suffer in proportion with his deeds, according to Matth. vii. 2: *With what measure you judge, you shall be judged : and with what measure you mete, it shall be measured to you again.* Therefore the just is absolutely the same as retaliation.

*Obj.* 2. Further, In either kind of justice something is given to someone according to a kind of equality. In distributive justice this equality regards personal dignity, which would seem to depend chiefly on what a person has done for the good of the community; while in commutative justice it regards the thing in which a person has suffered loss. Now in respect of either equality there is retaliation in respect of the deed committed. Therefore it would seem that the just is absolutely the same as retaliation.

*Obj.* 3. Further, The chief argument against retaliation is based on the difference between the voluntary and the involuntary; for he who does an injury involuntarily is less severely punished. Now voluntary and involuntary taken in relation to ourselves, do not diversify the mean of justice since this is the real mean and does not depend on us. Therefore it would seem that the just is absolutely the same as retaliation.

*On the contrary,* The Philosopher proves (*Ethic.* v. 5) that the just is not always the same as retaliation.

*I answer that,* Retaliation (*contrapassum*) denotes equal passion repaid for previous action; and the expression applies most properly to injurious passions and actions, whereby a man harms the person of his neighbour; for instance if a man strike, that he be struck back. This kind of just is laid down in the Law (Exod. xxi. 23, 24): *He shall render life for life, eye for eye*, etc. And since also to take away what belongs to another is to do an unjust thing, it follows that secondly retaliation consists in this also, that whosoever causes loss to another, should suffer loss in his belongings. This just loss is also found in the Law (Exod. xxii. 1): *If any man steal an ox or a sheep, and kill or sell it, he shall restore five oxen for one ox and four sheep for one sheep.* Thirdly retaliation is transferred to voluntary commutations, where action and passion are on both sides, although voluntariness detracts from the nature of passion, as stated above (Q. LIX., A. 3).

In all these cases, however, repayment must be made on a basis of equality according to the requirements of commutative justice, namely that the meed of passion be equal to the action. Now there would not always be equality if passion were in the same species as the action. Because, in the first place, when a person injures the person of one who is greater, the action surpasses any passion of the same species that he might undergo, wherefore he that strikes a prince, is not only struck back, but is much more severely punished. In like manner when a man despoils another of his property against the latter's will, the action surpasses the passion if he be merely deprived of that thing, because the man who caused another's loss, himself would lose nothing, and so he is punished by making restitution several times over, because not only did he injure a private individual, but also the common weal, the security of whose protection he has infringed. Nor again would there be equality of passion in voluntary commutations, were one always to exchange one's chattel for another man's, because it might happen that the other man's chattel is much greater than our own: so that it becomes necessary to equalize passion and action in commutations according to a certain proportionate commensuration, for which purpose money was invented. Hence retaliation is in accordance with commutative justice: but there is no place for it in distributive justice, because in distributive justice we do not consider the equality between thing and thing or between passion and action (whence the expression *contrapassum*), but according to proportion between things and persons, as stated above (A. 2).

*Reply Obj.* 1. This form of the Divine judgment is in accordance with the conditions of commutative justice, in so far as rewards are apportioned to merits, and punishments to sins.

*Reply Obj.* 2. When a man who has served the community is paid for his services, this is to be referred to commutative, not distributive, justice. Because distributive justice considers the equality, not between the thing received and the thing done, but between the thing received by one person and the thing received by another according to the respective conditions of those persons.

*Reply Obj.* 3. When the injurious action is voluntary, the injury is aggravated and consequently is considered as a greater thing. Hence it requires a greater punishment in repayment, by reason of a difference, not on our part, but on the part of the thing.

# QUESTION LXII.

## OF RESTITUTION.

### (*In Eight Articles.*)

WE must now consider restitution, under which head there are eight points of inquiry: (1) Of what is it an act ? (2) Whether it is always of necessity for salvation to restore what one has taken away ?   (3) Whether it is necessary to restore more than has been taken away ?   (4) Whether it is necessary to restore what one has not taken away ? (5) Whether it is necessary to make restitution to the person from whom something has been taken ?   (6) Whether the person who has taken something away is bound to restore it ?   (7) Whether any other person is bound to restitution ? (8) Whether one is bound to restore at once ?

## FIRST ARTICLE.

### WHETHER RESTITUTION IS AN ACT OF COMMUTATIVE JUSTICE ?

*We proceed thus to the First Article :—*

*Objection* 1. It would seem that restitution is not an act of commutative justice.   For justice regards the notion of what is due.   Now one may restore, even as one may give, that which is not due.   Therefore restitution is not the act of any part of justice.

*Obj.* 2. Further, That which has passed away and is no more cannot be restored.   Now justice and injustice are about certain actions and passions, which are unenduring and transitory.   Therefore restitution would not seem to be the act of a part of justice.

*Obj.* 3. Further, Restitution is repayment of something taken away. Now something may be taken away from a man not only in commutation, but also in distribution, as when, in distributing, one gives a man less than his due. Therefore restitution is not more an act of commutative than of distributive justice.

*On the contrary,* Restitution is opposed to taking away. Now it is an act of commutative injustice to take away what belongs to another. Therefore to restore it is an act of that justice which directs commutations.

*I answer that,* To restore is seemingly the same as to reinstate a person in the possession or dominion of his thing, so that in restitution we consider the equality of justice attending the payment of one thing for another, and this belongs to commutative justice. Hence restitution is an act of commutative justice, occasioned by one person having what belongs to another, either with his consent, for instance on loan or deposit, or against his will, as in robbery or theft.

*Reply Obj.* 1. That which is not due to another is not his properly speaking, although it may have been his at some time: wherefore it is a mere gift rather than a restitution, when anyone renders to another what is not due to him. It is however somewhat like a restitution, since the thing itself is materially the same; yet it is not the same in respect of the formal aspect of justice, which considers that thing as belonging to this particular man: and so it is not restitution properly so called.

*Reply Obj.* 2. In so far as the word restitution denotes something done over again, it implies identity of object. Hence it would seem originally to have applied chiefly to external things, which can pass from one person to another, since they remain the same both substantially and in respect of the right of dominion. But, even as the term *commutation* has passed from suchlike things to those actions and passions which confer reverence or injury, harm or profit on another person, so too the term *restitution* is applied, to things which though they be transitory in reality, yet remain in their effect; whether this touch his body, as when the body is hurt by being struck, or his reputation, as when a man remains defamed or dishonoured by injurious words.

*Reply Obj.* 3. Compensation is made by the distributor to the man to whom less was given than his due, by comparison of thing with thing, when the latter receives so much the more according as he received less than his due: and consequently it pertains to commutative justice.

## Second Article.

### WHETHER RESTITUTION OF WHAT HAS BEEN TAKEN AWAY IS NECESSARY FOR SALVATION ?

*We proceed thus to the Second Article :—*

*Objection* 1. It would seem that it is not necessary to restore what has been taken away. For that which is impossible is not necessary for salvation. But sometimes it is impossible to restore what has been taken, as when a man has taken limb or life. Therefore it does not seem necessary for salvation to restore what one has taken from another.

*Obj.* 2. Further, The commission of a sin is not necessary for salvation, for then a man would be in a dilemma. But sometimes it is impossible, without sin, to restore what has been taken, as when one has taken away another's good name by telling the truth. Therefore it is not necessary for salvation to restore what one has taken from another.

*Obj.* 3. Further, What is done cannot be undone. Now sometimes a man loses his personal honour by being unjustly insulted. Therefore that which has been taken from him cannot be restored to him: so that it is not necessary for salvation to restore what one has taken.

*Obj.* 4. Further, To prevent a person from obtaining a good thing is seemingly the same as to take it away from him, since *to lack little is almost the same as to lack nothing at all*, as the Philosopher says (*Phys.* ii. 5). Now when anyone prevents a man from obtaining a benefice or the like, seemingly he is not bound to restore the benefice, since this would be sometimes impossible. Therefore it is not necessary for salvation to restore what one has taken.

*On the contrary*, Augustine says (*Ep. ad Maced.* cxliii.): *Unless a man restore what he has purloined, his sin is not forgiven.*

*I answer that*, Restitution as stated above (A. 1) is an act of commutative justice, and this demands a certain equality. Wherefore restitution denotes the return of the thing unjustly taken; since it is by giving it back that equality is re-established. If, however, it be taken away justly, there will be equality, and so there will be no need for restitution, for justice consists in equality. Since therefore the safeguarding of justice is necessary for salvation, it follows that it is necessary for salvation to restore what has been taken unjustly.

*Reply Obj.* 1. When it is impossible to repay the equivalent, it suffices to repay what one can, as in the case of honour due to God and our parents, as the Philosopher states (*Ethic.* viii. 14). Wherefore when that which has been taken cannot be restored in equivalent, compensation should be made as far as possible: for instance if one man has deprived another of a limb, he must make compensation either in money or in honour, the condition of either party being duly considered according to the judgment of a good man.

*Reply Obj.* 2. There are three ways in which one may take away another's good name. First, by saying what is true, and this justly, as when a man reveals another's sin, while observing the right order of so doing, and then he is not bound to restitution. Secondly, by saying what is untrue and unjustly, and then he is bound to restore that man's good name, by confessing that he told an untruth. Thirdly, by saying what is true, but unjustly, as when a man reveals another's sin contrarily to the right order of so doing, and then he is bound to restore his good name as far as he can, and yet without telling an untruth; for instance by saying that he spoke ill, or that he defamed him unjustly; or if he be unable to restore his good name, he must compensate him otherwise, the same as in other cases, as stated above (*ad* 1).

*Reply Obj.* 3. The action of the man who has defamed another cannot be undone, but it is possible, by showing him deference, to undo its effect, viz. the lowering of the other man's personal dignity in the opinion of other men.

*Reply Obj.* 4. There are several ways of preventing a man from obtaining a benefice.  First, justly: for instance, if having in view the honour of God or the good of the Church, one procures its being conferred on a more worthy subject, and then there is no obligation whatever to make restitution or compensation.   Secondly, unjustly, if the intention is to injure the person whom one hinders, through hatred, revenge or the like.   In this case, if before the benefice has been definitely assigned to anyone, one prevents its being conferred on a worthy subject by counselling that it be not conferred on him, one is bound to make some compensation, after taking account of the circumstances of persons and things according to the judgment of a prudent person: but one is not bound in equivalent, because that man had not obtained the benefice and might have been prevented in many ways from obtaining it.   If, on the other hand, the benefice had already been assigned to a certain person, and someone, for some undue cause procures its revocation, it is the same as though he had deprived a man of what he already possessed, and consequently he would be bound to compensation in equivalent, in proportion, however, to his means.

## THIRD ARTICLE.

### WHETHER IT SUFFICES TO RESTORE THE EXACT AMOUNT TAKEN ?

*We proceed thus to the Third Article :—*

*Objection* 1. It would seem that it is not sufficient to restore the exact amount taken.  For it is written (Exod. xxii. 1): *If a man shall steal an ox or a sheep and kill or sell it, he shall*

*restore five oxen for one ox, and four sheep for one sheep.*
Now everyone is bound to keep the commandments of the
Divine law. Therefore a thief is bound to restore four
or fivefold.

*Obj.* 2. Further, *What things soever were written, were
written for our learning* (Rom. xv. 4). Now Zachæus said
(Luke xix. 8) to Our Lord: *If I have wronged any man of
any thing, I restore him fourfold.* Therefore a man is bound
to restore several times over the amount he has taken
unjustly.

*Obj.* 3. Further, No one can be unjustly deprived of what
he is not bound to give. Now a judge justly deprives a
thief of more than the amount of his theft, under the head
of damages. Therefore a man is bound to pay it, and
consequently it is not sufficient to restore the exact amount.

*On the contrary,* Restitution re-establishes equality where
an unjust taking has caused inequality. Now equality
is restored by repaying the exact amount taken. Therefore
there is no obligation to restore more than the exact amount
taken.

*I answer that,* When a man takes another's thing unjustly,
two things must be considered. One is the inequality on
the part of the thing, which inequality is sometimes void of
injustice, as is the case in loans. The other is the sin of
injustice, which is consistent with equality on the part of
the thing, as when a person intends to use violence but
fails.

As regards the first, the remedy is applied by making
restitution, since thereby equality is re-established; and for
this it is enough that a man restore just so much as he has
belonging to another. But as regards the sin, the remedy
is applied by punishment, the infliction of which belongs
to the judge: and so, until a man is condemned by the
judge, he is not bound to restore more than he took, but when
once he is condemned, he is bound to pay the penalty.

Hence it is clear how to answer the *First Objection :*
because this law fixes the punishment to be inflicted by the
judge. Nor is this commandment to be kept now, because

since the coming of Christ no man is bound to keep the judicial
precepts, as stated above (I.-II., Q. CIV., A. 3).    Nevertheless the same might be determined by human law, and then
the same answer would apply.

*Reply Obj.* 2. Zachæus said this being willing to do more
than he was bound to do; hence he had said already: *Behold,*
. . . *the half of my goods I give to the poor.*

*Reply Obj.* 3. By condemning the man justly, the judge
can exact more by way of damages; and yet this was not
due before the sentence.

## FOURTH ARTICLE.

### WHETHER A MAN IS BOUND TO RESTORE WHAT HE HAS NOT TAKEN ?

*We proceed thus to the Fourth Article :—*

*Objection* 1. It would seem that a man is bound to restore
what he has not taken.   For he that has inflicted a loss
on a man is bound to remove that loss.   Now it happens
sometimes that the loss sustained is greater than the thing
taken: for instance, if you dig up a man's seeds, you inflict
on the sower a loss equal to the coming harvest, and thus
you would seem to be bound to make restitution accordingly.   Therefore a man is bound to restore what he has
not taken.

*Obj.* 2. Further, He who retains his creditor's money
beyond the stated time, would seem to occasion his loss
of all his possible profits from that money, and yet he does
not really take them.   Therefore it seems that a man is
bound to restore what he did not take.

*Obj.* 3. Further, Human justice is derived from Divine
justice.   Now a man is bound to restore to God more than
he has received from Him, according to Matth. xxv. 26,
*Thou knewest that I reap where I sow not, and gather where
I have not strewed.*   Therefore it is just that one should
restore to a man also, something that one has not taken.

*On the contrary,* Restitution belongs to justice, because
it re-establishes equality.    But if one were to restore

what one did not take, there would not be equality. There-fore it is not just to make such a restitution.

*I answer that*, Whoever brings a loss upon another person, seemingly, takes from him the amount of the loss, since, according to the Philosopher (*Ethic.* v. 4) *loss* is so-called from a man having *less** than his due. Therefore a man is bound to make restitution according to the loss he has brought upon another.

Now a man suffers a loss in two ways. First, by being deprived of what he actually has; and a loss of this kind is always to be made good by repayment in equivalent: for instance if a man damnifies another by destroying his house he is bound to pay him the value of the house. Secondly, a man may damnify another by preventing him from obtaining what he was on the way to obtain. A loss of this kind need not be made good in equivalent; because to have a thing virtually is less than to have it actually, and to be on the way to obtain a thing is to have it merely virtually or potentially, and so were he to be indemnified by receiving the thing actually, he would be paid, not the exact value taken from him, but more, and this is not necessary for salvation, as stated above. However he is bound to make some compensation, according to the condition of persons and things.

From this we see how to answer the *First* and *Second Objections :* because the sower of the seed in the field, has the harvest, not actually but only virtually. In like manner he that has money has the profit not yet actually but only virtually: and both may be hindered in many ways.

*Reply Obj.* 3. God requires nothing from us but what He Himself has sown in us. Hence this saying is to be under-stood as expressing either the shameful thought of the lazy servant, who deemed that he had received nothing from the other, or the fact that God expects from us

* The derivation is more apparent in English than in Latin, where *damnum* stands for *loss*, and *minus* for *less*. Aristotle merely says that to have more than your own is called *gain*, and to have less than you started with is called *loss*.

the fruit of His gifts, which fruit is from Him and from us, although the gifts themselves are from God without us.

## FIFTH ARTICLE.

### WHETHER RESTITUTION MUST ALWAYS BE MADE TO THE PERSON FROM WHOM A THING HAS BEEN TAKEN ?

*We proceed thus to the Fifth Article :—*

*Objection* 1. It would seem that restitution need not always be made to the person from whom a thing has been taken. For it is not lawful to injure anyone. Now it would sometimes be injurious to the man himself, or to others, were one to restore to him what has been taken from him; if, for instance, one were to return a madman his sword. Therefore restitution need not always be made to the person from whom a thing has been taken.

*Obj.* 2. Further, If a man has given a thing unlawfully, he does not deserve to recover it. Now sometimes a man gives unlawfully that which another accepts unlawfully, as in the case of the giver and receiver who are guilty of simony. Therefore it is not always necessary to make restitution to the person from whom one has taken something.

*Obj.* 3. Further, No man is bound to do what is impossible. Now it is sometimes impossible to make restitution to the person from whom a thing has been taken, either because he is dead, or because he is too far away, or because he is unknown to us. Therefore restitution need not always be made to the person from whom a thing has been taken.

*Obj.* 4. Further, We owe more compensation to one from whom we have received a greater favour. Now we have received greater favours from others (our parents for instance) than from a lender or depositor. Therefore sometimes we ought to succour some other person rather than make restitution to one from whom we have taken something.

*Obj.* 5. Further, It is useless to restore a thing which reverts to the restorer by being restored. Now if a prelate has unjustly taken something from the Church and makes restitution to the Church, it reverts into his hands, since he is the guardian of the Church's property. Therefore he ought not to restore to the Church from whom he has taken: and so restitution should not always be made to the person from whom something has been taken away.

*On the contrary*, It is written (Rom. xiii. 7): *Render . . . to all men their dues ; tribute to whom tribute is due, custom to whom custom.*

*I answer that*, Restitution re-establishes the equality of commutative justice, which equality consists in the equalizing of thing to thing, as stated above (A. 2: Q. LVIII., A. 10). Now this equalizing of things is impossible, unless he that has less than his due receive what is lacking to him: and for this to be done, restitution must be made to the person from whom a thing has been taken.

*Reply Obj.* 1. When the thing to be restored appears to be grievously injurious to the person to whom it is to be restored, or to some other, it should not be restored to him there and then, because restitution is directed to the good of the person to whom it is made, since all possessions come under the head of the useful. Yet he who retains another's property must not appropriate it, but must either reserve it, that he may restore it at a fitting time, or hand it over to another to keep it more securely.

*Reply Obj.* 2. A person may give a thing unlawfully in two ways. First through the giving itself being illicit and against the law, as is the case when a man gives a thing simoniacally. Such a man deserves to lose what he gave, wherefore restitution should not be made to him: and, since the receiver acted against the law in receiving, he must not retain the price, but must use it for some pious object. Secondly a man gives unlawfully, through giving for an unlawful purpose, albeit the giving itself is not unlawful, as when a woman receives payment for fornication: wherefore she may keep what she has received. If, however, she has extorted overmuch by fraud or deceit, she would be bound to restitution.

*Reply Obj.* 3. If the person to whom restitution is due is unknown altogether, restitution must be made as far as possible, for instance by giving an alms for his spiritual welfare (whether he be dead or living): but not without previously making a careful inquiry about his person. If the person to whom restitution is due be dead, restitution should be made to his heir, who is looked upon as one with him. If he be very far away, what is due to him should be sent to him, especially if it be of great value and can easily be sent: else it should be deposited in a safe place to be kept for him, and the owner should be advised of the fact.

*Reply Obj.* 4. A man is bound, out of his own property, to succour his parents, or those from whom he has received greater benefits; but he ought not to compensate a benefactor out of what belongs to others; and he would be doing this if he were to compensate one with what is due to another. Exception must be made in cases of extreme need, for then he could and should even take what belongs to another in order to succour a parent.

*Reply Obj.* 5. There are three ways in which a prelate can rob the Church of her property. First by laying hands on Church property which is committed, not to him but to another; for instance, if a bishop appropriates the property of the chapter. In such a case it is clear that he is bound to restitution, by handing it over to those who are its lawful owners. Secondly by transferring to another person (for instance a relation or a friend) Church property committed to himself: in which case he must make restitution to the Church, and have it under his own care, so as to hand it over to his successor. Thirdly, a prelate may lay hands on Church property, merely in intention, when, to wit, he begins to have a mind to hold it as his own and not in the name of the Church: in which case he must make restitution by renouncing his intention.

## Sixth Article.

### WHETHER HE THAT HAS TAKEN A THING IS ALWAYS BOUND TO RESTITUTION ?

*We proceed thus to the Sixth Article :—*

*Objection* 1. It would seem that he who has taken a thing is not always bound to restore it. Restitution re-establishes the equality of justice, by taking away from him that has more and giving to him that has less. Now it happens sometimes that he who has taken that which belongs to another, no longer has it, through its having passed into another's hands. Therefore it should be restored, not by the person that took it, but by the one that has it.

*Obj.* 2. Further, No man is bound to reveal his own crime. But by making restitution a man would sometimes reveal his crime, as in the case of theft. Therefore he that has taken a thing is not always bound to restitution.

*Obj.* 3. Further, The same thing should not be restored several times. Now sometimes several persons take a thing at the same time, and one of them restores it in its entirety. Therefore he that takes a thing is not always bound to restitution.

*On the contrary*, He that has sinned is bound to satisfaction. Now restitution belongs to satisfaction. Therefore he that has taken a thing is bound to restore it.

*I answer that*, With regard to a man who has taken another's property, two points must be considered: the thing taken, and the taking. By reason of the thing taken, he is bound to restore it as long as he has it in his possession, since the thing that he has in addition to what is his, should be taken away from him, and given to him who lacks it according to the form of commutative justice. On the other hand, the taking of the thing that is another's property, may be threefold. For sometimes it is injurious, i.e. against the will of the owner, as in theft and robbery: in which case the thief is bound to restitution not only by reason of the thing, but also by reason of the injurious action, even though the thing is no longer in his possession.   For just as a man who strikes another, though he gain nothing thereby, is bound to compensate the injured person, so too he that is guilty of theft or robbery, is bound to make compensation for the loss incurred, although he be no better off; and in addition he must be punished for the injustice committed. Secondly, a man takes another's property for his own profit but without committing an injury, i.e. with the consent of the owner, as in the case of a loan: and then, the taker is bound to restitution, not only by reason of the thing, but also by reason of the taking, even if he has lost the thing: for he is bound to compensate the person who has done him a favour, and he would not be doing so if the latter were to lose thereby.   Thirdly, a man takes another's property without injury to the latter or profit to himself, as in the case of a deposit; wherefore he that takes a thing thus, incurs no obligation on account of the taking, in fact by taking he grants a favour; but he is bound to restitution on account of the thing taken.   Consequently if this thing be taken from him without any fault on his part, he is not bound to restitution, although he would be, if he were to lose the thing through a grievous fault on his part.

*Reply Obj.* 1. The chief end of restitution is, not that he who has more than his due may cease to have it, but that he who has less than his due may be compensated.   Wherefore there is no place for restitution in those things which one man may receive from another without loss to the latter, as when a person takes a light from another's candle. Consequently although he that has taken something from another, may have ceased to have what he took, through having transferred it to another, yet since that other is deprived of what is his, both are bound to restitution, he that took the thing, on account of the injurious taking, and he that has it, on account of the thing.

*Reply Obj.* 2. Although a man is not bound to reveal his crime to other men, yet is he bound to reveal it to God in confession; and so he may make restitution of another's property through the priest to whom he confesses.

*Reply Obj.* 3. Since restitution is chiefly directed to the compensation for the loss incurred by the person from whom a thing has been taken unjustly, it stands to reason that when he has received sufficient compensation from one, the others are not bound to any further restitution in his regard: rather ought they to refund the person who has made restitution, who, nevertheless, may excuse them from so doing.

## SEVENTH ARTICLE.

### WHETHER RESTITUTION IS BINDING ON THOSE WHO HAVE NOT TAKEN ?

*We proceed thus to the Seventh Article :—*

*Objection* 1. It would seem that restitution is not binding on those who have not taken. For restitution is a punishment of the taker. Now none should be punished except the one who sinned. Therefore none are bound to restitution save the one who has taken.

*Obj.* 2. Further, Justice does not bind one to increase another's property. Now if restitution were binding not only on the man who takes a thing but also on all those who co-operate with him in any way whatever, the person from whom the thing was taken would be the gainer, both because he would receive restitution many times over, and because sometimes a person co-operates towards a thing being taken away from someone, without its being taken away in effect. Therefore the others are not bound to restitution.

*Obj.* 3. Further, No man is bound to expose himself to danger, in order to safeguard another's property. Now sometimes a man would expose himself to the danger of death, were he to betray a thief, or withstand him. Therefore one is not bound to restitution, through not betraying or withstanding a thief.

*On the contrary,* It is written (Rom. i. 32): *They who do such things are worthy of death, and not only they that do them, but also they that consent to them that do them.* Therefore in like manner they that consent are bound to restitution.

*I answer that,* As stated above (A. 6), a person is bound to

restitution not only on account of someone else's property
which he has taken, but also on account of the injurious
taking.   Hence whoever is cause of an unjust taking is
bound to restitution.   This happens in two ways, directly
and indirectly.   Directly, when a man induces another to
take, and this in three ways.   First, on the part of the taking,
by moving a man to take, either by express command,
counsel, or consent, or by praising a man for his courage
in thieving.   Secondly, on the part of the taker, by giving
him shelter or any other kind of assistance.   Thirdly, on
the part of the thing taken, by taking part in the theft or
robbery, as a fellow evil-doer.   Indirectly, when a man does
not prevent another from evil-doing (provided he be able
and bound to prevent him), either by omitting the command or counsel which would hinder him from thieving or
robbing, or by omitting to do what would have hindered
him, or by sheltering him after the deed.   All these are
expressed as follows:

*By command, by counsel, by consent, by flattery, by
receiving, by participation, by silence, by not preventing,
by not denouncing.*

It must be observed, however, that in five of these cases
the co-operator is always bound to restitution.   First, in
the case of command: because he that commands is the
chief mover, wherefore he is bound to restitution principally.
Secondly, in the case of consent; namely of one without
whose consent the robbery cannot take place.   Thirdly, in the
case of receiving; when, to wit, a man is a receiver of thieves,
and gives them assistance.   Fourthly, in the case of participation; when a man takes part in the theft and in the booty.
Fifthly, he who does not prevent the theft, whereas he is
bound to do so; for instance, persons in authority who are
bound to safeguard justice on earth, are bound to restitution,
if by their neglect thieves prosper, because their salary is
given to them in payment of their preserving justice here
below.

In the other cases mentioned above, a man is not always
bound to restitution: because counsel and flattery are not

always the efficacious cause of robbery. Hence the counsellor or flatterer is bound to restitution, only when it may be judged with probability that the unjust taking resulted from such causes.

*Reply Obj.* 1. Not only is he bound to restitution who commits the sin, but also he who is in any way cause of the sin, whether by counselling, or by commanding, or in any other way whatever.

*Reply Obj.* 2. He is bound chiefly to restitution, who is the principal in the deed; first of all, the *commander ;* secondly, the *executor,* and in due sequence, the others: yet so that, if one of them make restitution, another is not bound to make restitution to the same person. Yet those who are principals in the deed, and who took possession of the thing, are bound to compensate those who have already made restitution. When a man commands an unjust taking that does not follow, no restitution has to be made, since its end is chiefly to restore the property of the person who has been unjustly injured.

*Reply Obj.* 3. He that fails to denounce a thief or does not withstand or reprehend him is not always bound to restitution, but only when he is obliged, in virtue of his office, to do so: as in the case of earthly princes who do not incur any greater danger thereby; for they are invested with public authority, in order that they may maintain justice.

EIGHTH ARTICLE.

WHETHER A MAN IS BOUND TO IMMEDIATE RESTITUTION, OR MAY HE PUT IT OFF ?

*We proceed thus to the Eighth Article :—*

*Objection* 1. It would seem that a man is not bound to immediate restitution, and can lawfully delay to restore. For affirmative precepts do not bind for always. Now the necessity of making restitution is binding through an affirmative precept. Therefore a man is not bound to immediate restitution.

*Obj.* 2. Further, No man is bound to do what is impossible.

But it is sometimes impossible to make restitution at once. Therefore no man is bound to immediate restitution.

*Obj.* 3. Further, Restitution is an act of virtue, viz. of justice. Now time is one of the circumstances requisite for virtuous acts. Since then the other circumstances are not determinate for acts of virtue, but are determinable according to the dictate of prudence, it seems that neither in restitution is there any fixed time, so that a man be bound to restore at once.

*On the contrary*, All matters of restitution seem to come under one head. Now a man who hires the services of a wage-earner, must not delay compensation, as appears from Levit. xix. 13, *The wages of him that hath been hired by thee shall not abide with thee until the morning.* Therefore neither is it lawful, in other cases of restitution, to delay, and restitution should be made at once.

*I answer that,* Even as it is a sin against justice to take another's property, so also is it to withhold it, since, to withhold the property of another against the owner's will, is to deprive him of the use of what belongs to him, and to do him an injury. Now it is clear that it is wrong to remain in sin even for a short time; and one is bound to renounce one's sin at once, according to Ecclus. xxi. 2, *Flee from sin as from the face of a serpent.* Consequently one is bound to immediate restitution, if possible, or to ask for a respite from the person who is empowered to grant the use of the thing.

*Reply. Obj.* 1. Although the precept about the making of restitution is affirmative in form, it implies a negative precept forbidding us to withhold another's property.

*Reply Obj.* 2. When one is unable to restore at once, this very inability excuses one from immediate restitution: even as a person is altogether excused from making restitution if he is altogether unable to make it. He is, however, bound either himself or through another to ask the person to whom he owes compensation to grant him a remission or a respite.

*Reply Obj.* 3. Whenever the omission of a circumstance is

contrary to virtue that circumstance must be looked upon as determinate, and we are bound to observe it: and since delay of restitution involves a sin of unjust detention which is opposed to just detention, it stands to reason that the time is determinate in the point of restitution being immediate.

# QUESTION LXIII

## OF RESPECT OF PERSONS.

### (*In Four Articles.*)

WE must now consider the vices opposed to the aforesaid parts of justice. First we shall consider respect of persons which is opposed to distributive justice: secondly we shall consider the vices opposed to commutative justice.

Under the first head there are four points of inquiry: (1) Whether respect of persons is a sin? (2) Whether it takes place in the dispensation of spiritualities? (3) Whether it takes place in showing honour? (4) Whether it takes place in judicial sentences?

### First Article.

#### WHETHER RESPECT OF PERSONS IS A SIN?

*We proceed thus to the First Article :—*

*Objection* 1. It would seem that respect of persons is not a sin. For the word *person* includes a reference to personal dignity.* Now it belongs to distributive justice to consider personal dignity. Therefore respect of persons is not a sin.

*Obj.* 2. Further, In human affairs persons are of more importance than things, since things are for the benefit of persons and not conversely. But respect of things is not a sin. Much less, therefore, is respect of persons.

*Obj.* 3. Further, No injustice or sin can be in God. Yet God seems to respect persons, since of two men circumstanced alike He sometimes upraises one by grace, and leaves the other in sin, according to Matth. xxiv. 40: *Two shall be in*

* Cf. P. I., Q. XXIX., A. 3, *ad* 2.

*a bed* (Vulg.,—*field\**), *one shall be taken, and one shall be left.* Therefore respect of persons is not a sin.

*On the contrary,* Nothing but sin is forbidden in the Divine law. Now respect of persons is forbidden, Deut. i. 17: *Neither shall you respect any man's person.* Therefore respect of persons is a sin.

*I answer that,* Respect of persons is opposed to distributive justice. For the equality of distributive justice consists in allotting various things to various persons in proportion to their personal dignity. Accordingly, if one considers that personal property by reason of which the thing allotted to a particular person is due to him, this is respect not of the person but of the cause. Hence a gloss on Eph. vi. 9, *There is no respect of persons with God* (Vulg.,—*Him*), says that *a just judge regards causes, not persons.* For instance if you promote a man to a professorship on account of his having sufficient knowledge, you consider the due cause, not the person; but if, in conferring something on someone, you consider in him not the fact that what you give him is proportionate or due to him, but the fact that he is this particular man (e.g. Peter or Martin), then there is respect of the person, since you give him something not for some cause that renders him worthy of it, but simply because he is this person. And any circumstance that does not amount to a reason why this man be worthy of this gift, is to be referred to his person: for instance if a man promote someone to a prelacy or a professorship, because he is rich or because he is a relation of his, it is respect of persons. It may happen, however, that a circumstance of person makes a man worthy as regards one thing, but not as regards another: thus consanguinity makes a man worthy to be appointed heir to an estate, but not to be chosen for a position of ecclesiastical authority: wherefore consideration of the same circumstance of person will amount to respect of persons in one matter and not in another. It follows, accordingly, that respect of persons is opposed to distributive justice in that it fails to observe due proportion.

* *Bed* is the reading of Luke xvii. 34.

Now nothing but sin is opposed to virtue: and therefore respect of persons is a sin.

*Reply Obj.* 1. In distributive justice we consider those circumstances of a person which result in dignity or right, whereas in respect of persons we consider circumstances that do not so result.

*Reply Obj.* 2. Persons are rendered proportionate to and worthy of things which are distributed among them, by reason of certain things pertaining to circumstances of person, wherefore such conditions ought to be considered as the proper cause. But when we consider the persons themselves, that which is not a cause is considered as though it were; and so it is clear that although persons are more worthy, absolutely speaking, yet they are not more worthy in this regard.

*Reply Obj.* 3. There is a twofold giving. One belongs to justice, and occurs when we give a man his due: in suchlike givings respect of persons takes place. The other giving belongs to liberality, when one gives gratis that which is not a man's due: such is the bestowal of the gifts of grace, whereby sinners are chosen by God. In such a giving there is no place for respect of persons, because anyone may, without injustice, give of his own as much as he will, and to whom he will, according to Matth. xx. 14, 15, *Is it not lawful for me to do what I will? . . . Take what is thine, and go thy way.*

## Second Article.

### WHETHER RESPECT OF PERSONS TAKES PLACE IN THE DISPENSATION OF SPIRITUAL GOODS ?

*We proceed thus to the Second Article :—*

*Objection* 1. It would seem that respect of persons does not take place in the dispensation of spiritual goods. For it would seem to savour of respect of persons if a man confers ecclesiastical dignity or benefice on account of consanguinity, since consanguinity is not a cause whereby a man is rendered worthy of an ecclesiastical benefice. Yet this apparently is not a sin, for ecclesiastical prelates are wont to do so.

Therefore the sin of respect of persons does not take place in the conferring of spiritual goods.

*Obj.* 2. Further, To give preference to a rich man rather than to a poor man seems to pertain to respect of persons, according to James ii. 2, 3. Nevertheless dispensations to marry within forbidden degrees are more readily granted to the rich and powerful than to others. Therefore the sin of respect of persons seems not to take place in the dispensation of spiritual goods.

*Obj.* 3. Further, According to jurists* it suffices to choose a good man, and it is not requisite that one choose the better man. But it would seem to savour of respect of persons to choose one who is less good for a higher position. Therefore respect of persons is not a sin in spiritual matters.

*Obj.* 4. Further, According to the law of the Church (*ibid.*) the person to be chosen should be *a member of the flock*. Now this would seem to imply respect of persons, since sometimes more competent persons would be found elsewhere. Therefore respect of persons is not a sin in spiritual matters.

*On the contrary,* It is written (James ii. 1): *Have not the faith of Our Lord Jesus Christ . . . with respect of persons.* On these words a gloss of Augustine says: *Who is there that would tolerate the promotion of a rich man to a position of honour in the Church, to the exclusion of a poor man more learned and holier ?*†

*I answer that,* As stated above (A. 1), respect of persons is a sin, in so far as it is contrary to justice. Now the graver the matter in which justice is transgressed, the more grievous the sin: so that, spiritual things being of greater import than temporal, respect of persons is a more grievous sin in dispensing spiritualities than in dispensing temporalities. And since it is respect of persons when something is allotted to a person out of proportion to his deserts, it must be observed that a person's worthiness may be considered in two ways. First, simply and absolutely: and in this way the man who abounds the more in the spiritual gifts of grace

---

* Cap. *Cum dilectus.*          † Augustine, *Ep. ad Hieron.* clxvii.

is the more worthy. Secondly, in relation to the common good; for it happens at times that the less holy and less learned man may conduce more to the common good, on account of worldly authority or activity, or something of the kind. And since the dispensation of spiritualities is directed chiefly to the common good, according to 1 Cor. xii. 7, *The manifestation of the Spirit is given to every man unto profit*, it follows that in the dispensation of spiritualities the simply less good are sometimes preferred to the better, without respect of persons, just as God sometimes bestows gratuitous graces on the less worthy.

*Reply Obj.* 1. We must make a distinction with regard to a prelate's kinsfolk: for sometimes they are less worthy, both absolutely speaking, and in relation to the common good: and then if they are preferred to the more worthy, there is a sin of respect of persons in the dispensation of spiritual goods, whereof the ecclesiastical superior is not the owner, with power to give them away as he will, but the dispenser, according to 1 Cor. iv. 1, *Let a man so account of us as of the ministers of Christ, and the dispensers of the mysteries of God*. Sometimes however the prelate's kinsfolk are as worthy as others, and then without respect of persons he can lawfully give preference to his kindred since there is at least this advantage, that he can trust the more in their being of one mind with him in conducting the business of the Church. Yet he would have to forego so doing for fear of scandal, if anyone might take an example from him and give the goods of the Church to their kindred without regard to their deserts.

*Reply Obj.* 2. Dispensations for contracting marriage came into use for the purpose of strengthening treaties of peace: and this is more necessary for the common good in relation to persons of standing, so that there is no respect of persons in granting dispensations more readily to such persons.

*Reply Obj.* 3. In order that an election be not rebutted in a court of law, it suffices to elect a good man, nor is it necessary to elect the better man, because otherwise every election might have a flaw. But as regards the conscience of an elector, it is necessary to elect one who is better, either absolutely speaking, or in relation to the common good.   For if it is possible to have one who is more competent for a post, and yet another be preferred, it is necessary to have some cause for this.   If this cause have anything to do with the matter in point, he who is elected will, in this respect, be more competent; and if that which is taken for cause have nothing to do with the matter, it will clearly be respect of persons.

*Reply Obj.* 4. The man who is taken from among the members of a particular Church, is generally speaking more useful as regards the common good, since he loves more the Church wherein he was brought up.   For this reason it was commanded (Deut. xvii. 15): *Thou mayest not make a man of another nation king, who is not thy brother.*

### THIRD ARTICLE.

#### WHETHER RESPECT OF PERSONS TAKES PLACE IN SHOWING HONOUR AND RESPECT?

*We proceed thus to the Third Article :—*

*Objection* 1. It would seem that respect of persons does not take place in showing honour and respect.   For honour is apparently nothing else than *reverence shown to a person in recognition of his virtue,* as the Philosopher states (*Ethic.* i. 5). Now prelates and princes should be honoured although they be wicked, even as our parents, of whom it is written (Exod. xx. 12): *Honour thy father and thy mother.*   Again masters, though they be wicked, should be honoured by their servants, according to 1 Tim. vi. 1: *Whoever are servants under the yoke, let them count their masters worthy of all honour.*   Therefore it seems that it is not a sin to respect persons in showing honour.

*Obj.* 2. Further, It is commanded (Lev. xix. 32): *Rise up before the hoary head, and honour the person of the aged man.* But this seems to savour of respect of persons, since sometimes old men are not virtuous; according to Dan. xiii. 5:

*Iniquity came out from the ancients of the people.*\* Therefore
it is not a sin to respect persons in showing honour.

*Obj.* 3. Further, On the words of James ii. 1, *Have not
the faith . . . with respect of persons,* a gloss† of Augustine
says: *If the saying of James, ' If there shall come into your
assembly a man having a golden ring,' etc., refer to our daily
meetings, who sins not here, if however he sin at all ?* Yet it
is respect of persons to honour the rich for their riches, for
Gregory says in a homily (xxviii. *in Ev.*): *Our pride is blunted,
since in men we honour, not the nature wherein they are made
to God's image, but wealth,* so that, wealth not being a due
cause of honour, this will savour of respect of persons.
Therefore it is not a sin to respect persons in showing
honour.

*On the contrary,* A gloss on James ii. 1, says: *Whoever
honours the rich for their riches, sins,* and in like manner,
if a man be honoured for other causes that do not render
him worthy of honour. Now this savours of respect of persons.
Therefore it is a sin to respect persons in showing honour.

*I answer that,* To honour a person is to recognize him as
having virtue, wherefore virtue alone is the due cause of
a person being honoured. Now it is to be observed that
a person may be honoured not only for his own virtue, but
also for another's: thus princes and prelates, although they
be wicked, are honoured as standing in God's place, and as
representing the community over which they are placed,
according to Prov. xxvi. 8, *As he that casteth a stone into
the heap of Mercury, so is he that giveth honour to a fool.*
For, since the gentiles ascribed the keeping of accounts to
Mercury, *the heap of Mercury* signifies the casting up of an
account, when a merchant sometimes substitutes a pebble‡
for one hundred marks. So too, is a fool honoured if he
stand in God's place or represent the whole community:
and in the same way parents and masters should be honoured,
on account of their having a share of the dignity of God

---

\* Vulg.,—*Iniquity came out from Babylon from the ancient judges,
that seemed to govern the people.*

† See p. 189, footnote †.

‡ *Lapillus* or *calculus* whence the English word *calculate.*

Who is the Father and Lord of all. The aged should be honoured, because old age is a sign of virtue, though this sign fail at times: wherefore, according to Wis. iv. 8, 9, *venerable old age is not that of long time, nor counted by the number of years; but the understanding of a man is grey hairs, and a spotless life is old age.* The rich ought to be honoured by reason of their occupying a higher position in the community: but if they be honoured merely for their wealth, it will be the sin of respect of persons.

Hence the *Replies* to the *Objections* are clear.

## Fourth Article.

### WHETHER THE SIN OF RESPECT OF PERSONS TAKES PLACE IN JUDICIAL SENTENCES ?

*We proceed thus to the Fourth Article :—*

*Objection* 1. It would seem that the sin of respect of persons does not take place in judicial sentences. For respect of persons is opposed to distributive justice, as stated above (A. 1): whereas judicial sentences seem to pertain chiefly to commutative justice. Therefore respect of persons does not take place in judicial sentences.

*Obj.* 2. Further, Penalties are inflicted according to a sentence. Now it is not a sin to respect persons in pronouncing penalties, since a heavier punishment is inflicted on one who injures the person of a prince than on one who injures the person of others. Therefore respect of persons does not take place in judicial sentences.

*Obj.* 3. Further, It is written (Ecclus. iv. 10): *In judging be merciful to the fatherless.* But this seems to imply respect of the person of the needy. Therefore in judicial sentences respect of persons is not a sin.

*On the contrary,* It is written (Prov. xviii. 5): *It is not good to accept the person in judgment.**

*I answer that,* As stated above (Q. LX., A. 1), judgment is an act of justice, in as much as the judge restores to the

* Vulg.,—*It is not good to accept the person of the wicked, to decline from the truth of judgment.*

equality of justice, those things which may cause an opposite inequality. Now respect of persons involves a certain inequality, in so far as something is allotted to a person out of that proportion to him in which the equality of justice consists. Wherefore it is evident that judgment is rendered corrupt by respect of persons.

*Reply Obj.* 1. A judgment may be looked at in two ways. First, in view of the thing judged, and in this way judgment is common to commutative and distributive justice: because it may be decided by judgment how some common good is to be distributed among many, and how one person is to restore to another what he has taken from him. Secondly, it may be considered in view of the form of judgment, in as much as, even in commutative justice, the judge takes from one and gives to another, and this belongs to distributive justice. In this way respect of persons may take place in any judgment.

*Reply Obj.* 2. When a person is more severely punished on account of a crime committed against a greater person, there is no respect of persons, because the very difference of persons causes, in that case, a diversity of things, as stated above (Q. LVIII., A. 10, *ad* 3: Q. LXI., A.2, *ad* 3).

*Reply Obj.* 3. In pronouncing judgment one ought to succour the needy as far as possible, yet without prejudice to justice: else the saying of Exod. xxiii. 3 would apply: *Neither shalt thou favour a poor man in judgment.*

# QUESTION LXIV.

## OF MURDER.

### (*In Eight Articles.*)

IN due sequence we must consider the vices opposed to commutative justice. We must consider (1) those sins that are committed in relation to involuntary commutations: (2) those that are committed with regard to voluntary commutations. Sins are committed in relation to involuntary commutations by doing an injury to one's neighbour against his will: and this can be done in two ways, namely by deed or by word. By deed when one's neighbour is injured either in his own person, or in a person connected with him, or in his possessions.

We must therefore consider these points in due order, and in the first place we shall consider murder whereby a man inflicts the greatest injury on his neighbour. Under this head there are eight points of inquiry: (1) Whether it is a sin to kill dumb animals or even plants ? (2) Whether it is lawful to kill a sinner ? (3) Whether this is lawful to a private individual, or to a public person only ? (4) Whether this is lawful to a cleric ? (5) Whether it is lawful to kill oneself ? (6) Whether it is lawful to kill a just man ? (7) Whether it is lawful to kill a man in self-defence ? (8) Whether accidental homicide is a mortal sin ?

### FIRST ARTICLE.

#### WHETHER IT IS UNLAWFUL TO KILL ANY LIVING THING ?

*We proceed thus to the First Article :—*

*Objection* 1. It would seem unlawful to kill any living thing. For the Apostle says (Rom. xiii. 2): *They that resist*

*the ordinance of God purchase to themselves damnation.**
Now Divine providence has ordained that all living things
should be preserved, according to Ps. cxlvi. 8, 9, *Who maketh
grass to grow on the mountains . . ., Who giveth to beasts
their food.*  Therefore it seems unlawful to take the life of
any living thing.

*Obj.* 2. Further, Murder is a sin because it deprives a
man of life.  Now life is common to all animals and plants.
Hence for the same reason it is apparently a sin to slay
dumb animals and plants.

*Obj.* 3. Further, In the Divine law a special punishment is
not appointed save for a sin.  Now a special punishment
had to be inflicted, according to the Divine law, on one who
killed another man's ox or sheep (Exod. xxii. 1).  Therefore
the slaying of dumb animals is a sin.

*On the contrary,* Augustine says (*De Civ. Dei* i. 20): *When
we hear it said, ' Thou shalt not kill,' we do not take it as
referring to trees, for they have no sense, nor to irrational
animals, because they have no fellowship with us.  Hence it
follows that the words, ' Thou shalt not kill ' refer to the killing
of a man.*

*I answer that,* There is no sin in using a thing for the
purpose for which it is.  Now the order of things is such
that the imperfect are for the perfect, even as in the process
of generation nature proceeds from imperfection to perfection.
Hence it is that just as in the generation of a man there is
first a living thing, then an animal, and lastly a man, so
too things, like the plants, which merely have life, are all
alike for animals, and all animals are for man.  Wherefore
it is not unlawful if man use plants for the good of animals,
and animals for the good of man, as the Philosopher states
(*Polit.* i. 3).

Now the most necessary use would seem to consist in
the fact that animals use plants, and men use animals, for
food, and this cannot be done unless these be deprived
of life: wherefore it is lawful both to take life from plants

* Vulg.,—*He that resisteth the power, resisteth the ordinance of
God: and they that resist, purchase to themselves damnation.*

for the use of animals, and from animals for the use of men. In fact this is in keeping with the commandment of God Himself: for it is written (Gen. i. 29, 30): *Behold I have given you every herb . . . and all trees . . . to be your meat, and to all beasts of the earth :* and again (*ibid.* ix. 3): *Everything that moveth and liveth shall be meat to you.*

*Reply Obj.* 1. According to the Divine ordinance the life of animals and plants is preserved not for themselves but for man. Hence, as Augustine says (*De Civ. Dei* i. 20), *by a most just ordinance of the Creator, both their life and their death are subject to our use.*

*Reply Obj.* 2. Dumb animals and plants are devoid of the life of reason whereby to set themselves in motion; they are moved, as it were by another, by a kind of natural impulse, a sign of which is that they are naturally enslaved and accommodated to the uses of others.

*Reply Obj.* 3. He that kills another's ox, sins, not through killing the ox, but through injuring another man in his property. Wherefore this is not a species of the sin of murder but of the sin of theft or robbery.

## SECOND ARTICLE.

### WHETHER IT IS LAWFUL TO KILL SINNERS ?

*We proceed thus to the Second Article :—*

*Objection* 1. It would seem unlawful to kill men who have sinned. For Our Lord in the parable (Matth. xiii.) forbade the uprooting of the cockle which denotes wicked men according to a gloss. Now whatever is forbidden by God is a sin. Therefore it is a sin to kill a sinner.

*Obj.* 2. Further, Human justice is conformed to Divine justice. Now according to Divine justice sinners are kept back for repentance, according to Ezech. xxxiii. 11, *I desire not the death of the wicked, but that the wicked turn from his way and live.* Therefore it seems altogether unjust to kill sinners.

*Obj.* 3. Further, It is not lawful, for any good end

whatever, to do that which is evil in itself, according to
Augustine (*Contra Mendac.* vii.) and the Philosopher
(*Ethic.* ii. 6). Now to kill a man is evil in itself, since we
are bound to have charity towards all men, and *we wish
our friends to live and to exist*, according to *Ethic.* ix. 4.
Therefore it is nowise lawful to kill a man who has sinned.

*On the contrary*, It is written (Exod. xxii. 18): *Wizards
thou shalt not suffer to live ;* and (Ps. c. 8): *In the morning
I put to death all the wicked of the land.*

*I answer that*, As stated above (A. 1), it is lawful to kill
dumb animals, in so far as they are naturally directed to
man's use, as the imperfect is directed to the perfect. Now
every part is directed to the whole, as imperfect to perfect,
wherefore every part is naturally for the sake of the whole.
For this reason we observe that if the health of the whole
body demands the excision of a member, through its being
decayed or infectious to the other members, it will be both
praiseworthy and advantageous to have it cut away. Now
every individual person is compared to the whole community,
as part to whole. Therefore if a man be dangerous and
infectious to the community, on account of some sin, it
is praiseworthy and advantageous that he be killed in order
to safeguard the common good, since *a little leaven corrupteth
the whole lump* (1 Cor. v. 6).

*Reply Obj.* 1. Our Lord commanded them to forbear from
uprooting the cockle in order to spare the wheat, i.e. the
good. This occurs when the wicked cannot be slain without
the good being killed with them, either because the wicked
lie hidden among the good, or because they have many
followers, so that they cannot be killed without danger to
the good, as Augustine says (*Contra Parmen.* iii. 2). Wherefore Our Lord teaches that we should rather allow the wicked
to live, and that vengeance is to be delayed until the last
judgment, rather than that the good be put to death together
with the wicked. When, however, the good incur no danger,
but rather are protected and saved by the slaying of the
wicked, then the latter may be lawfully put to death.

*Reply Obj.* 2. According to the order of His wisdom,

God sometimes slays sinners forthwith in order to deliver the good, whereas sometimes He allows them time to repent, according as He knows what is expedient for His elect. This also does human justice imitate according to its powers; for it puts to death those who are dangerous to others, while it allows time for repentance to those who sin without grievously harming others.

*Reply Obj.* 3. By sinning man departs from the order of reason, and consequently falls away from the dignity of his manhood, in so far as he is naturally free, and exists for himself, and he falls into the slavish state of the beasts, by being disposed of according as he is useful to others. This is expressed in Ps. xlviii. 21: *Man, when he was in honour, did not understand ; he hath been compared to senseless beasts, and made like to them,* and Prov. xi. 29: *The fool shall serve the wise.* Hence, although it be evil in itself to kill a man so long as he preserve his dignity, yet it may be good to kill a man who has sinned, even as it is to kill a beast. For a bad man is worse than a beast, and is more harmful, as the Philosopher states (*Polit.* i. 1 and *Ethic.* vii. 6).

## THIRD ARTICLE.

### WHETHER IT IS LAWFUL FOR A PRIVATE INDIVIDUAL TO KILL A MAN WHO HAS SINNED ?

*We proceed thus to the Third Article :—*

*Objection* 1. It would seem lawful for a private individual to kill a man who has sinned. For nothing unlawful is commanded in the Divine law. Yet, on account of the sin of the molten calf, Moses commanded (Exod. xxxii. 27): *Let every man kill his brother, and friend, and neighbour.* Therefore it is lawful for private individuals to kill a sinner.

*Obj.* 2. Further, As stated above (A. 2, *ad* 3), man, on account of sin, is compared to the beasts. Now it is lawful for any private individual to kill a wild beast, especially if it be harmful. Therefore for the same reason, it is lawful for any private individual to kill a man who has sinned.

*Obj*. 3. Further, A man, though a private individual, deserves praise for doing what is useful for the common good. Now the slaying of evildoers is useful for the common good, as stated above (A. 2). Therefore it is deserving of praise if even private individuals kill evildoers.

*On the contrary*, Augustine says (*De Civ. Dei* i.):* *A man who, without exercising public authority, kills an evildoer, shall be judged guilty of murder, and all the more, since he has dared to usurp a power which God has not given him.*

*I answer that*, As stated above (A. 2), it is lawful to kill an evildoer in so far as it is directed to the welfare of the whole community, so that it belongs to him alone who has charge of the community's welfare. Thus it belongs to a physician to cut off a decayed limb, when he has been entrusted with the care of the health of the whole body. Now the care of the common good is entrusted to persons of rank having public authority: wherefore they alone, and not private individuals, can lawfully put evildoors to death.

*Reply Obj*. 1. The person by whose authority a thing is done really does the thing, as Dionysius declares (*Coel. Hier*. iii.). Hence according to Augustine (*De Civ. Dei* i. 21), *He slays not who owes his service to one who commands him, even as a sword is merely the instrument to him that wields it.* Wherefore those who, at the Lord's command, slew their neighbours and friends, would seem not to have done this themselves, but rather He by whose authority they acted thus: just as a soldier slays the foe by the authority of his sovereign, and the executioner slays the robber by the authority of the judge.

*Reply Obj*. 2. A beast is by nature distinct from man, wherefore in the case of a wild beast, there is no need for an authority to kill it; whereas, in the case of domestic animals, such authority is required, not for their sake, but on account of the owner's loss. On the other hand a man who has sinned is not by nature distinct from good men; hence a public authority is requisite in order to condemn him to death for the common good.

* Can. *Quicumque percutit*, caus. xxiii., qu. 8.

*Reply Obj.* 3. It is lawful for any private individual to do anything for the common good, provided it harm nobody: but if it be harmful to some other, it cannot be done, except by virtue of the judgment of the person to whom it pertains to decide what is to be taken from the parts for the welfare of the whole.

### Fourth Article.

#### Whether it is lawful for clerics to kill evildoers?

*We proceed thus to the Fourth Article :—*

*Objection* 1. It would seem lawful for clerics to kill evildoers. For clerics especially should fulfil the precept of the Apostle (1 Cor. iv. 16): *Be ye followers of me as I also am of Christ*, whereby we are called upon to imitate God and His saints. Now the very God Whom we worship puts evildoers to death, according to Ps. cxxxv. 10, *Who smote Egypt with their firstborn.* Again Moses made the Levites slay twenty-three thousand men on account of the worship of the calf (Exod. xxxii.), the priest Phinees slew the Israelite who went in to the woman of Madian (Num. xxv.), Samuel killed Agag king of Amalec (1 Kings xv.), Elias slew the priests of Baal (3 Kings xviii.), Mathathias killed the man who went up to the altar to sacrifice (1 Mach. ii.); and, in the New Testament, Peter killed Ananias and Saphira (Acts v.). Therefore it seems that even clerics may kill evildoers.

*Obj.* 2. Further, Spiritual power is greater than the secular and is more united to God. Now the secular power as *God's minister* lawfully puts evildoers to death, according to Rom. xiii. 4. Much more therefore may clerics, who are God's ministers and have spiritual power, put evildoers to death.

*Obj.* 3. Further, Whosoever lawfully accepts an office, may lawfully exercise the functions of that office. Now it belongs to the princely office to slay evildoers, as stated above (A. 3). Therefore those clerics who are earthly princes may lawfully slay malefactors.

*On the contrary*, It is written (1 Tim. iii. 2, 3): *It behoveth
. . . a bishop to be without crime\* . . . not given to wine,
no striker.*

*I answer that*, It is unlawful for clerics to kill, for two
reasons. First, because they are chosen for the ministry
of the altar, whereon is represented the Passion of Christ
slain *Who, when He was struck did not strike†* (1 Pet. ii. 23).
Therefore it becomes not clerics to strike or kill : for ministers
should imitate their master, according to Ecclus. x. 2, *As
the judge of the people is himself, so also are his ministers.*
The other reason is because clerics are entrusted with the
ministry of the New Law, wherein no punishment of death
or of bodily maiming is appointed : wherefore they should
abstain from such things in order that they may be fitting
ministers of the New Testament.

*Reply Obj.* 1. God works in all things without exception
whatever is right, yet in each one according to its mode.
Wherefore everyone should imitate God in that which is
specially becoming to him. Hence, though God slays evildoers even corporally, it does not follow that all should
imitate Him in this. As regards Peter, he did not put
Ananias and Saphira to death by his own authority or with
his own hand, but published their death sentence pronounced by God. The priests or Levites of the Old Testament were the ministers of the Old Law, which appointed
corporal penalties, so that it was fitting for them to slay
with their own hands.

*Reply Obj.* 2. The ministry of clerics is concerned with
better things than corporal slayings, namely with things
pertaining to spiritual welfare, and so it is not fitting for
them to meddle with minor matters.

*Reply Obj.* 3. Ecclesiastical prelates accept the office of
earthly princes, not that they may inflict capital punishment themselves, but that this may be carried into effect
by others in virtue of their authority.

---

\* Vulg.,—*Blameless. Without crime* is the reading in Tit. i. 7.
† Vulg.,—*When He suffered, He threatened not.*

## FIFTH ARTICLE.

### WHETHER IT IS LAWFUL TO KILL ONESELF?

*We proceed thus to the Fifth Article :—*

*Objection* 1. It would seem lawful for a man to kill himself. For murder is a sin in so far as it is contrary to justice. But no man can do an injustice to himself, as is proved in *Ethic.* v. 11. Therefore no man sins by killing himself.

*Obj.* 2. Further, It is lawful, for one who exercises public authority, to kill evildoers. Now he who exercises public authority is sometimes an evildoer. Therefore he may lawfully kill himself.

*Obj.* 3. Further, It is lawful for a man to suffer spontaneously a lesser danger that he may avoid a greater: thus it is lawful for a man to cut off a decayed limb even from himself, that he may save his whole body. Now sometimes a man, by killing himself, avoids a greater evil, for example an unhappy life, or the shame of sin. Therefore a man may kill himself.

*Obj.* 4. Further, Samson killed himself, as related in Judges xvi., and yet he is numbered among the saints (Heb. xi.). Therefore it is lawful for a man to kill himself.

*Obj.* 5. Further, It is related (2 Mach. xiv. 42) that a certain Razias killed himself, *choosing to die nobly rather than to fall into the hands of the wicked, and to suffer abuses unbecoming his noble birth.* Now nothing that is done nobly and bravely is unlawful. Therefore suicide is not unlawful.

*On the contrary,* Augustine says (*De Civ. Dei* i. 20): *Hence it follows that the words ' Thou shalt not kill ' refer to the killing of a man ;—not another man ; therefore, not even thyself. For he who kills himself, kills nothing else than a man.*

*I answer that,* It is altogether unlawful to kill oneself, for three reasons. First, because everything naturally loves itself, the result being that everything naturally keeps itself in being, and resists corruptions so far as it can. Wherefore suicide is contrary to the inclination of nature, and to charity whereby every man should love himself.   Hence suicide is always a mortal sin, as being contrary to the natural law and to charity.

Secondly, because every part, as such, belongs to the whole. Now every man is part of the community, and so, as such, he belongs to the community.   Hence by killing himself he injures the community, as the Philosopher declares (*Ethic.* v. 11).

Thirdly, because life is God's gift to man, and is subject to His power, Who kills and makes to live.   Hence whoever takes his own life, sins against God, even as he who kills another's slave, sins against that slave's master, and as he who usurps to himself judgment of a matter not entrusted to him.   For it belongs to God alone to pronounce sentence of death and life, according to Deut. xxxii. 39, *I will kill and I will make to live*.

*Reply Obj*. 1. Murder is a sin, not only because it is contrary to justice, but also because it is opposed to charity which a man should have towards himself: in this respect suicide is a sin in relation to oneself.   In relation to the community and to God, it is sinful, by reason also of its opposition to justice.

*Reply Obj*. 2. One who exercises public authority may lawfully put to death an evildoer, since he can pass judgment on him.   But no man is judge of himself.   Wherefore it is not lawful for one who exercises public authority to put himself to death for any sin whatever: although he may lawfully commit himself to the judgment of others.

*Reply Obj*. 3. Man is made master of himself through his free-will: wherefore he can lawfully dispose of himself as to those matters which pertain to this life which is ruled by man's free-will.   But the passage from this life to another and happier one is subject not to man's free-will but to the power of God.   Hence it is not lawful for man to take his own life that he may pass to a happier life, nor that he may escape any unhappiness whatsoever of the present life, because the ultimate and most fearsome evil of this life is death, as the Philosopher states (*Ethic*. iii. 6). Therefore to bring death upon oneself in order to escape the other afflictions of this life, is to adopt a greater evil in order to avoid a lesser. In like manner it is unlawful to take one's own life on account of one's having committed a sin, both because by so doing one does oneself a very great injury, by depriving oneself of the time needful for repentance, and because it is not lawful to slay an evildoer except by the sentence of the public authority. Again it is unlawful for a woman to kill herself lest she be violated, because she ought not to commit on herself the very great sin of suicide, to avoid the lesser sin of another. For she commits no sin in being violated by force, provided she does not consent, since *without consent of the mind there is no stain on the body*, as the Blessed Lucy declared. Now it is evident that fornication and adultery are less grievous sins than taking a man's, especially one's own, life: since the latter is most grievous, because one injures oneself, to whom one owes the greatest love. Moreover it is most dangerous since no time is left wherein to expiate it by repentance. Again it is not lawful for anyone to take his own life for fear he should consent to sin, because *evil must not be done that good may come* (Rom. iii. 8) or that evil may be avoided, especially if the evil be of small account and an uncertain event, for it is uncertain whether one will at some future time consent to a sin, since God is able to deliver man from sin under any temptation whatever.

*Reply Obj.* 4. As Augustine says (*De Civ. Dei* i. 21), *not even Samson is to be excused that he crushed himself together with his enemies under the ruins of the house, except the Holy Ghost, Who had wrought many wonders through him, had secretly commanded him to do this*. He assigns the same reason in the case of certain holy women, who at the time of persecution took their own lives, and who are commemorated by the Church.

*Reply Obj.* 5. It belongs to fortitude that a man does not shrink from being slain by another, for the sake of the good of virtue, and that he may avoid sin. But that a man take his own life in order to avoid penal evils has indeed an appearance of fortitude (for which reason some, among whom was Razias, have killed themselves thinking to act from fortitude), yet it is not true fortitude, but rather a weakness of soul unable to bear penal evils, as the Philosopher (*Ethic.* iii. 7) and Augustine (*De Civ. Dei* i. 22, 23) declare.

## SIXTH ARTICLE.

### WHETHER IT IS EVER LAWFUL TO KILL THE INNOCENT ?

*We proceed thus to the Sixth Article :—*

*Objection* 1. It would seem that in some cases it is lawful to kill the innocent. The fear of God is never manifested by sin, since on the contrary *the fear of the Lord driveth out sin* (Ecclus. i. 27). Now Abraham was commended in that he feared the Lord, since he was willing to slay his innocent son. Therefore one may, without sin, kill an innocent person.

*Obj.* 2. Further, Among those sins that are committed against one's neighbour, the more grievous seem to be those whereby a more grievous injury is inflicted on the person sinned against. Now to be killed is a greater injury to a sinful than to an innocent person, because the latter, by death, passes forthwith from the unhappiness of this life to the glory of heaven. Since then it is lawful in certain cases to kill a sinful man, much more is it lawful to slay an innocent or a righteous person.

*Obj.* 3. Further, What is done in keeping with the order of justice is not a sin. But sometimes a man is forced, according to the order of justice, to slay an innocent person: for instance, when a judge, who is bound to judge according to the evidence, condemns to death a man whom he knows to be innocent, but who is convicted by false witnesses; and again the executioner, who in obedience to the judge puts to death the man who has been unjustly sentenced.

*On the contrary*, It is written (Exod. xxiii. 7): *The innocent and just person thou shalt not put to death.*

*I answer that*, An individual man may be considered in

two ways: first, in himself; secondly, in relation to something else. If we consider a man in himself, it is unlawful to kill any man, since in every man though he be sinful, we ought to love the nature which God has made, and which is destroyed by slaying him. Nevertheless, as stated above (A. 2) the slaying of a sinner becomes lawful in relation to the common good, which is corrupted by sin. On the other hand the life of righteous men preserves and forwards the common good, since they are the chief part of the community. Therefore it is in no way lawful to slay the innocent.

*Reply Obj*. 1. God is Lord of death and life, for by His decree both the sinful and the righteous die. Hence he who at God's command kills an innocent man does not sin, as neither does God Whose behest he executes: indeed his obedience to God's commands is a proof that he fears Him.

*Reply Obj*. 2. In weighing the gravity of a sin we must consider the essential rather than the accidental. Wherefore he who kills a just man, sins more grievously than he who slays a sinful man: first, because he injures one whom he should love more, and so acts more in opposition to charity: secondly, because he inflicts an injury on a man who is less deserving of one, and so acts more in opposition to justice: thirdly, because he deprives the community of a greater good: fourthly, because he despises God more, according to Luke x. 16, *He that despiseth you despiseth Me*. On the other hand it is accidental to the slaying that the just man whose life is taken be received by God into glory.

*Reply Obj*. 3. If the judge knows that a man who has been convicted by false witnesses, is innocent he must, like Daniel, examine the witnesses with great care, so as to find a motive for acquitting the innocent: but if he cannot do this he should remit him for judgment by a higher tribunal. If even this is impossible, he does not sin if he pronounce sentence in accordance with the evidence, for it is not he that puts the innocent man to death, but they who necessary for salvation that a man omit the act of moderate self-defence in order to avoid killing the other man, since one is bound to take more care of one's own life than of another's. But as it is unlawful to take a man's life, except for the public authority acting for the common good, as stated above (A. 3), it is not lawful for a man to intend killing a man in self-defence, except for such as have public authority, who while intending to kill a man in self-defence, refer this to the public good, as in the case of a soldier fighting against the foe, and in the minister of the judge struggling with robbers, although even these sin if they be moved by private animosity.

*Reply Obj.* 1. The words quoted from Augustine refer to the case when one man intends to kill another to save himself from death. The passage quoted in the *Second Objection* is to be understood in the same sense. Hence he says pointedly, *for the sake of these things*, whereby he indicates the intention. This suffices for the *Reply* to the *Second Objection*.

*Reply Obj.* 3. Irregularity results from the act though sinless of taking a man's life, as appears in the case of a judge who justly condemns a man to death. For this reason a cleric, though he kill a man in self-defence, is irregular, albeit he intends not to kill him, but to defend himself.

*Reply Obj.* 4. The act of fornication or adultery is not necessarily directed to the preservation of one's own life, as is the act whence sometimes results the taking of a man's life.

*Reply Obj.* 5. The defence forbidden in this passage is that which comes from revengeful spite. Hence a gloss says: *Not defending yourselves,—that is, not striking your enemy back.*

## Eighth Article.

### WHETHER ONE IS GUILTY OF MURDER THROUGH KILLING SOMEONE BY CHANCE ?

*We proceed thus to the Eighth Article :—*

*Objection* 1. It would seem that one is guilty of murder through killing someone by chance. For we read (Gen. iv.

23, 24) that Lamech slew a man in mistake for a wild beast,\* and that he was accounted guilty of murder. Therefore one incurs the guilt of murder through killing a man by chance.

*Obj.* 2. Further, It is written (Exod. xxi. 22): *If . . . one strike a woman with child, and she miscarry indeed . . ., if her death ensue thereupon, he shall render life for life.* Yet this may happen without any intention of causing her death. Therefore one is guilty of murder through killing someone by chance.

*Obj.* 3. Further, The Decretals† contain several canons prescribing penalties for unintentional homicide. Now penalty is not due save for guilt. Therefore he who kills a man by chance, incurs the guilt of murder.

*On the contrary,* Augustine says to Publicola (*Ep.* xlvii.): *When we do a thing for a good and lawful purpose, if thereby we unintentionally cause harm to anyone, it should by no means be imputed to us.* Now it sometimes happens by chance that a person is killed as a result of something done for a good purpose. Therefore the person who did it is not accounted guilty.

*I answer that,* According to the Philosopher (*Phys.* ii. 6) *chance is a cause that acts beside one's intention.* Hence chance happenings, strictly speaking, are neither intended nor voluntary. And since every sin is voluntary, according to Augustine (*De Vera Relig.* xiv.) it follows that chance happenings, as such, are not sins.

Nevertheless it happens that what is not actually and directly voluntary and intended, is voluntary and intended accidentally, according as that which removes an obstacle is called an accidental cause. Wherefore he who does not remove something whence homicide results whereas he ought to remove it, is in a sense guilty of voluntary homicide. This happens in two ways: first when a man causes another's death through occupying himself with unlawful things which he ought to avoid: secondly, when he does not take sufficient care. Hence, according to jurists, if a man

---

\* The text of the Bible does not say so, but this was the Jewish traditional commentary on Gen. iv. 23.      † Dist. l.

pursue a lawful occupation and take due care, the result being that a person loses his life, he is not guilty of that person's death: whereas if he be occupied with something unlawful, or even with something lawful, but without due care, he does not escape being guilty of murder, if his action results in someone's death.

*Reply Obj.* 1. Lamech did not take sufficient care to avoid taking a man's life: and so he was not excused from being guilty of homicide.

*Reply Obj.* 2. He that strikes a woman with child does something unlawful: wherefore if there results the death either of the woman or of the animated fœtus, he will not be excused from homicide, especially seeing that death is the natural result of such a blow.

*Reply Obj.* 3. According to the canons a penalty is inflicted on those who cause death unintentionally, through doing something unlawful, or failing to take sufficient care.

# QUESTION LXV.

## OF OTHER INJURIES COMMITTED ON THE PERSON

### (*In Four Articles*).

WE must now consider other sinful injuries committed on the person. Under this head there are four points of inquiry: (1) The mutilation of members: (2) Blows: (3) Imprisonment: (4) Whether the sins that consist in inflicting suchlike injuries are aggravated through being perpetrated on persons connected with others ?

## FIRST ARTICLE.

### WHETHER IN SOME CASES IT MAY BE LAWFUL TO MAIM ANYONE ?

*We proceed thus to the First Article :—*

*Objection* 1. It would seem that in no case can it be lawful to maim anyone. For Damascene says (*De Fide Orth*. iv. 20) that *sin consists in departing from what is according to nature, towards that which is contrary to nature*. Now according to nature it is appointed by God that a man's body should be entire in its members, and it is contrary to nature that it should be deprived of a member. Therefore it seems that it is always a sin to maim a person.

*Obj*. 2. Further, As the whole soul is to the whole body, so are the parts of the soul to the parts of the body (*De Amima* ii. 1). But it is unlawful to deprive a man of his soul by killing him, except by public authority. Therefore neither is it lawful to maim anyone, except perhaps by public authority.

*Obj*. 3. Further, The welfare of the soul is to be preferred

to the welfare of the body.   Now it is not lawful for a man
to maim himself for the sake of the soul's welfare: since the
council of Nicea* punished those who castrated themselves
that they might preserve chastity.   Therefore it is not
lawful for any other reason to maim a person.

*On the contrary*, It is written (Exod. xxi. 24): *Eye for eye,
tooth for tooth, hand for hand, foot for foot.*

*I answer that*, Since a member is part of the whole human
body, it is for the sake of the whole, as the imperfect for
the perfect.   Hence a member of the human body is to be
disposed of according as it is expedient for the body.   Now
a member of the human body is of itself useful to the good
of the whole body, yet, accidentally it may happen to be
hurtful, as when a decayed member is a source of corruption
to the whole body.   Accordingly so long as a member is
healthy and retains its natural disposition, it cannot be
cut off without injury to the whole body.   But as the whole
of man is directed as to his end to the whole of the community of which he is a part, as stated above (Q. LXI., A. 1:
Q. LXIV., AA. 2, 5), it may happen that although the
removal of a member may be detrimental to the whole
body, it may nevertheless be directed to the good of the
community, in so far as it is applied to a person as a punishment for the purpose of restraining sin.   Hence just as by
public authority a person is lawfully deprived of life altogether
on account of certain more heinous sins, so is he deprived
of a member on account of certain lesser sins.   But this is
not lawful for a private individual, even with the consent
of the owner of the member, because this would involve an
injury to the community, to whom the man and all his
parts belong.   If, however, the member be decayed and
therefore a source of corruption to the whole body, then it
is lawful with the consent of the owner of the member, to
cut away the member for the welfare of the whole body,
since each one is entrusted with the care of his own welfare.
The same applies if it be done with the consent of the person
whose business it is to care for the welfare of the person

* P. I., sect. 4, can. i.

who has a decayed member: otherwise it is altogether unlawful to maim anyone.

*Reply Obj.* 1. Nothing prevents that which is contrary to a particular nature from being in harmony with universal nature: thus death and corruption, in the physical order, are contrary to the particular nature of the thing corrupted, although they are in keeping with universal nature. In like manner to maim anyone, though contrary to the particular nature of the body of the person maimed, is nevertheless in keeping with natural reason in relation to the common good.

*Reply Obj.* 2. The life of the entire man is not directed to something belonging to man; on the contrary whatever belongs to man is directed to his life. Hence in no case does it pertain to a person to take anyone's life, except to the public authority to whom is entrusted the procuring of the common good. But the removal of a member can be directed to the good of one man, and consequently in certain cases can pertain to him.

*Reply Obj.* 3. A member should not be removed for the sake of the bodily health of the whole, unless otherwise nothing can be done to further the good of the whole. Now it is always possible to further one's spiritual welfare otherwise than by cutting off a member, because sin is always subject to the will: and consequently in no case is it allowable to maim oneself, even to avoid any sin whatever. Hence Chrysostom, in his exposition on Matth. xix. 12 (*Hom.* lxii. *in Matth.*), *There are eunuchs who have made themselves eunuchs for the kingdom of heaven,* says: *Not by maiming themselves, but by destroying evil thoughts, for a man is accursed who maims himself, since they are murderers who do such things.* And further on he says: *Nor is lust tamed thereby, on the contrary it becomes more importunate, for the seed springs in us from other sources, and chiefly from an incontinent purpose and a careless mind: and temptation is curbed not so much by cutting off a member as by curbing one's thoughts.*

### Sᴇᴄᴏɴᴅ Aʀᴛɪᴄʟᴇ.

#### Wʜᴇᴛʜᴇʀ ɪᴛ ɪs ʟᴀᴡꜰᴜʟ ꜰᴏʀ ᴘᴀʀᴇɴᴛs ᴛᴏ sᴛʀɪᴋᴇ ᴛʜᴇɪʀ ᴄʜɪʟᴅʀᴇɴ, ᴏʀ ᴍᴀsᴛᴇʀs ᴛʜᴇɪʀ sʟᴀᴠᴇs ?

*We proceed thus to the Second Article :—*

*Objection* 1. It would seem unlawful for parents to strike their children, or masters their slaves. For the Apostle says (Eph. vi. 4): *You, fathers, provoke not your children to anger ;* and further on (*verse* 9): *And you, masters, do the same thing to your slaves* (Vulg.,—*to them*) *forbearing threatenings.* Now some are provoked to anger by blows, and become more troublesome when threatened. Therefore neither should parents strike their children, nor masters their slaves.

*Obj.* 2. Further, The Philosopher says (*Ethic.* x. 9) that *a father's words are admonitory and not coercive.* Now blows are a kind of coercion. Therefore it is unlawful for parents to strike their children.

*Obj.* 3. Further, Everyone is allowed to impart correction, for this belongs to the spiritual almsdeeds, as stated above (Q. XXXII., A. 2). If, therefore, it is lawful for parents to strike their children for the sake of correction, for the same reason it will be lawful for any person to strike anyone, which is clearly false. Therefore the same conclusion follows.

*On the contrary,* It is written (Prov. xiii. 24): *He that spareth the rod hateth his son* and further on (xxiii. 13): *Withhold not correction from a child, for if thou strike him with the rod, he shall not die. Thou shalt beat him with the rod, and deliver his soul from hell.* Again it is written (Ecclus. xxxiii. 28): *Torture and fetters are for a malicious slave.*

*I answer that,* Harm is done a body by striking it, yet not so as when it is maimed: since maiming destroys the body's integrity, while a blow merely affects the sense with pain, wherefore it causes much less harm than cutting off a member. Now it is unlawful to do a person a harm, except by way of punishment in the cause of justice. Again, no man justly punishes another, except one who is subject to his jurisdiction. Therefore it is not lawful for a man to strike another, unless he have some power over the one whom he strikes. And since the child is subject to the power of the parent, and the slave to the power of his master, a parent can lawfully strike his child, and a master his slave that instruction may be enforced by correction.

*Reply Obj.* 1. Since anger is a desire for vengeance, it is aroused chiefly when a man deems himself unjustly injured, as the Philosopher states (*Rhet.* ii.). Hence when parents are forbidden to provoke their children to anger, they are not prohibited from striking their children for the purpose of correction, but from inflicting blows on them without moderation. The command that masters should forbear from threatening their slaves may be understood in two ways. First that they should be slow to threaten, and this pertains to the moderation of correction; secondly, that they should not always carry out their threats, that is that they should sometimes by a merciful forgiveness temper the judgment whereby they threatened punishment.

*Reply Obj.* 2. The greater power should exercise the greater coercion. Now just as a city is a perfect community, so the governor of a city has perfect coercive power: wherefore he can inflict irreparable punishments such as death and mutilation. On the other hand the father and the master who preside over the family household, which is an imperfect community, have imperfect coercive power, which is exercised by inflicting lesser punishments, for instance by blows, which do not inflict irreparable harm.

*Reply Obj.* 3. It is lawful for anyone to impart correction to a willing subject. But to impart it to an unwilling subject belongs to those only who have charge over him. To this pertains chastisement by blows.

## THIRD ARTICLE.

### WHETHER IT IS LAWFUL TO IMPRISON A MAN?

*We proceed thus to the Third Article :—*

*Objection* 1. It would seem unlawful to imprison a man. An act which deals with undue matter is evil in its genus, as stated above (I.-II., Q. XVIII., A. 2). Now man, having a free-will, is undue matter for imprisonment which is inconsistent with free-will. Therefore it is unlawful to imprison a man.

*Obj.* 2. Further, Human justice should be ruled by Divine justice. Now according to Ecclus. xv. 14, *God left man in the hand of his own counsel.* Therefore it seems that a man ought not to be coerced by chains or prisons.

*Obj.* 3. Further, No man should be forcibly prevented except from doing an evil deed; and any man can lawfully prevent another from doing this. If, therefore, it were lawful to imprison a man, in order to restrain him from evil deeds, it would be lawful for anyone to put a man in prison; and this is clearly false. Therefore the same conclusion follows.

*On the contrary*, We read in Lev. xxiv. that a man was imprisoned for the sin of blasphemy.

*I answer that*, In the goods of the body three things may be considered in due order. First, the substantial integrity of the body, and this is injured by death or maiming. Secondly, pleasure or rest of the senses, and to this striking or anything causing a sense of pain is opposed. Thirdly, the movement or use of the members, and this is hindered by binding or imprisoning or any kind of detention.

Therefore it is unlawful to imprison or in any way detain a man, unless it be done according to the order of justice, either in punishment, or as a measure of precaution against some evil.

*Reply Obj.* 1. A man who abuses the power entrusted to him deserves to lose it, and therefore when a man by sinning abuses the free use of his members, he becomes a fitting matter for imprisonment.

*Reply Obj.* 2. According to the order of His wisdom God sometimes restrains a sinner from accomplishing a sin, according to Job v. 12: *Who bringeth to nought the designs of the malignant, so that their hand cannot accomplish what they had begun,* while sometimes He allows them to do what they will. In like manner, according to human justice, men are imprisoned, not for every sin but for certain ones.

*Reply Obj.* 3. It is lawful for anyone to restrain a man for a time from doing some unlawful deed there and then: as when a man prevents another from throwing himself over a precipice, or from striking another. But to him alone who has the right of disposing in general of the actions and of the life of another does it belong primarily to imprison or fetter, because by so doing he hinders him from doing not only evil but also good deeds.

### FOURTH ARTICLE.

#### WHETHER THE SIN IS AGGRAVATED BY THE FACT THAT THE AFORESAID INJURIES ARE PERPETRATED ON THOSE WHO ARE CONNECTED WITH OTHERS ?

*We proceed thus to the Fourth Article :—*

*Objection* 1. It would seem that the sin is not aggravated by the fact that the aforesaid injuries are perpetrated on those who are connected with others. Suchlike injuries take their sinful character from inflicting an injury on another against his will. Now the evil inflicted on a man's own person is more against his will than that which is inflicted on a person connected with him. Therefore an injury inflicted on a person connected with another is less grievous.

*Obj.* 2. Further, Holy Writ reproves those especially who do injuries to orphans and widows: hence it is written (Ecclus. xxxv. 17): *He will not despise the prayers of the fatherless, nor the widow when she poureth out her complaint.* Now the widow and the orphan are not connected with other persons. Therefore the sin is not aggravated through an injury being inflicted on one who is connected with others.

*Obj.* 3. Further, The person who is connected has a will of his own just as the principal person has, so that something may be voluntary for him and yet against the will of the principal person, as in the case of adultery which pleases the woman but not the husband. Now these injuries are sinful in so far as they consist in an involuntary commutation. Therefore suchlike injuries are of a less sinful nature.

*On the contrary,* It is written (Deut. xxviii. 32) as though indicating an aggravating circumstance: *Thy sons and thy daughters shall be given to another people, thy eyes looking on.* *

*I answer that,* Other things being equal, an injury is a more grievous sin according as it affects more persons; and hence it is that it is a more grievous sin to strike or injure a person in authority than a private individual, because it conduces to the injury of the whole community, as stated above (I.-II., Q. LXXIII., A. 9). Now when an injury is inflicted on one who is connected in any way with another, that injury affects two persons, so that, other things being equal, the sin is aggravated by this very fact. It may happen, however, that in view of certain circumstances, a sin committed against one who is not connected with any other person, is more grievous, on account of either the dignity of the person, or the greatness of the injury.

*Reply Obj.* 1. An injury inflicted on a person connected with others is less harmful to the persons with whom he is connected, than if it were perpetrated immediately on them, and from this point of view it is a less grievous sin. But all that belongs to the injury of the person with whom he is connected, is added to the sin of which a man is guilty through injuring the other one in himself.

*Reply Obj.* 2. Injuries done to widows and orphans are more insisted upon both through being more opposed to mercy, and because the same injury done to such persons is more grievous to them since they have no one to turn to for relief.

*Reply Obj.* 3. The fact that the wife voluntarily consents to the adultery, lessens the sin and injury, so far as the woman is concerned, for it would be more grievous, if the adulterer oppressed her by violence. But this does not remove the injury as affecting her husband, since *the wife hath not power of her own body; but the husband* (1 Cor. vii. 4). The same applies to similar cases. Of adultery, however, as it is opposed not only to justice but also to chastity, we shall speak in the treatise on Temperance (Q. CLIV., A. 8).

* Vulg.,—*May thy sons and thy daughters be given,* etc.

# QUESTION LXVI.

## OF THEFT AND ROBBERY.

### (*In Nine Articles.*)

WE must now consider the sins opposed to justice, whereby a man injures his neighbour in his belongings; namely theft and robbery.

Under this head there are nine points of inquiry: (1) Whether it is natural to man to possess external things? (2) Whether it is lawful for a man to possess something as his own? (3) Whether theft is the secret taking of another's property? (4) Whether robbery is a species of sin distinct from theft? (5) Whether every theft is a sin? (6) Whether theft is a mortal sin? (7) Whether it is lawful to thieve in a case of necessity? (8) Whether every robbery is a mortal sin? (9) Whether robbery is a more grievous sin than theft?

### FIRST ARTICLE.

#### WHETHER IT IS NATURAL FOR MAN TO POSSESS EXTERNAL THINGS?

*We proceed thus to the First Article :—*

*Objection* 1. It would seem that it is not natural for man to possess external things. For no man should ascribe to himself that which is God's. Now the dominion over all creatures is proper to God, according to Ps. xxiii. 1, *The earth is the Lord's*, etc. Therefore it is not natural for man to possess external things.

*Obj.* 2. Further, Basil in expounding the words of the rich man (Luke xii. 18), *I will gather all things that are grown* *to me, and my goods,* says:* *Tell me : which are thine ? where did you take them from and bring them into being ?* Now whatever man possesses naturally, he can fittingly call his own. Therefore man does not naturally possess external things.

*Obj.* 3. Further, According to Ambrose (*De Trin.* i.†) *dominion denotes power.* But man has no power over external things, since he can work no change in their nature. Therefore the possession of external things is not natural to man.

*On the contrary,* It is written (Ps. viii. 8): *Thou hast subjected all things under his feet.*

*I answer that,* External things can be considered in two ways. First, as regards their nature, and this is not subject to the power of man, but only to the power of God Whose mere will all things obey. Secondly, as regards their use, and in this way, man has a natural dominion over external things, because, by his reason and will, he is able to use them for his own profit, as they were made on his account: for the imperfect is always for the sake of the perfect, as stated above (Q. LXIV., A. 1). It is by this argument that the Philosopher proves (*Polit.* i. 3) that the possession of external things is natural to man. Moreover, this natural dominion of man over other creatures, which is competent to man in respect of his reason wherein God's image resides, is shown forth in man's creation (Gen. i. 26) by the words: *Let us make man to Our image and likeness : and let him have dominion over the fishes of the sea,* etc.

*Reply Obj.* 1. God has sovereign dominion over all things: and He, according to His providence, directed certain things to the sustenance of man's body. For this reason man has a natural dominion over things, as regards the power to make use of them.

*Reply Obj.* 2. The rich man is reproved for deeming external things to belong to him principally, as though he had not received them from another, namely from God.

* *Hom. in Luc* xii. 18.        † *De Fide, ad Gratianum,* i. 1.

*Reply Obj.* 3. This argument considers the dominion over external things as regards their nature. Such a dominion belongs to God alone, as stated above.

## SECOND ARTICLE.

### WHETHER IT IS LAWFUL FOR A MAN TO POSSESS A THING AS HIS OWN ?

*We proceed thus to the Second Article :—*

*Objection* 1. It would seem unlawful for a man to possess a thing as his own. For whatever is contrary to the natural law is unlawful. Now according to the natural law all things are common property: and the possession of property is contrary to this community of goods. Therefore it is unlawful for any man to appropriate any external thing to himself.

*Obj.* 2. Further, Basil in expounding the words of the rich man quoted above (A. 1, *Obj.* 2), says: *The rich who deem as their own property the common goods they have seized upon, are like to those who by going beforehand to the play prevent others from coming, and appropriate to themselves what is intended for common use.* Now it would be unlawful to prevent others from obtaining possession of common goods. Therefore it is unlawful to appropriate to oneself what belongs to the community.

*Obj.* 3. Further, Ambrose says,* and his words are quoted in the Decretals:† *Let no man call his own that which is common property:* and by *common* he means external things, as is clear from the context. Therefore it seems unlawful for a man to appropriate an external thing to himself.

*On the contrary*, Augustine says (*De Hæres.*, hær. 40): *The 'Apostolici' are those who with extreme arrogance have given themselves that name, because they do not admit into their communion persons who are married or possess anything of their own, such as both monks and clerics who in considerable number are to be found in the Catholic Church.* Now the reason why these people are heretics was because, severing themselves from the Church, they think that those who enjoy

* *Serm.* lxiv., *de temp.*     † Dist. xlvii., Can. *Sicut hi.*

the use of the above things, which they themselves lack, have no hope of salvation. Therefore it is erroneous to maintain that it is unlawful for a man to possess property.

*I answer that,* Two things are competent to man in respect of exterior things. One is the power to procure and dispense them, and in this regard it is lawful for man to possess property. Moreover this is necessary to human life for three reasons. First because every man is more careful to procure what is for himself alone than that which is common to many or to all: since each one would shirk the labour and leave to another that which concerns the community, as happens where there is a great number of servants. Secondly, because human affairs are conducted in more orderly fashion if each man is charged with taking care of some particular thing himself, whereas there would be confusion if everyone had to look after any one thing indeterminately. Thirdly, because a more peaceful state is ensured to man if each one is contented with his own. Hence it is to be observed that quarrels arise more frequently where there is no division of the things possessed.

The second thing that is competent to man with regard to external things is their use. In this respect man ought to possess external things, not as his own, but as common, so that, to wit, he is ready to communicate them to others in their need. Hence the Apostle says (1 Tim. vi. 17, 18): *Charge the rich of this world . . . to give easily, to communicate to others,* etc.

*Reply Obj.* 1. Community of goods is ascribed to the natural law, not that the natural law dictates that all things should be possessed in common, and that nothing should be possessed as one's own: but because the division of possessions is not according to the natural law, but rather arose from human agreement which belongs to positive law, as stated above (Q. LVII., AA. 2, 3). Hence the ownership of possessions is not contrary to the natural law, but an addition thereto devised by human reason.

*Reply Obj.* 2. A man would not act unlawfully if by going beforehand to the play he prepared the way for others:

but he acts unlawfully if by so doing he hinders others from going. In like manner a rich man does not act unlawfully if he anticipates someone in taking possession of something which at first was common property, and gives others a share: but he sins if he excludes others indiscriminately from using it. Hence Basil says (*ibid.*): *Why are you rich while another is poor, unless it be that you may have the merit of a good stewardship, and he the reward of patience?*

*Reply Obj.* 3. When Ambrose says: *Let no man call his own that which is common*, he is speaking of ownership as regards use, wherefore he adds: *He who spends too much is a robber.*

### THIRD ARTICLE.

#### WHETHER THE ESSENCE OF THEFT CONSISTS IN TAKING ANOTHER'S THING SECRETLY?

*We proceed thus to the Third Article :—*

*Objection* 1. It would seem that it is not essential to theft to take another's thing secretly. For that which diminishes a sin, does not, apparently, belong to the essence of a sin. Now to sin secretly tends to diminish a sin, just as, on the contrary, it is written as indicating an aggravating circumstance of the sin of some (Isa. iii. 9): *They have proclaimed abroad their sin as Sodom, and they have not hid it.* Therefore it is not essential to theft that it should consist in taking another's thing secretly.

*Obj.* 2. Further, Ambrose says,* and his words are embodied in the Decretals:† *It is no less a crime to take from him that has, than to refuse to succour the needy when you can and are well off.* Therefore just as theft consists in taking another's thing, so does it consist in keeping it back.

*Obj.* 3. Further, A man may take by stealth from another, even that which is his own, for instance a thing that he has deposited with another, or that has been taken away from him unjustly. Therefore it is not essential to theft that it should consist in taking another's thing secretly.

*On the contrary*, Isidore says (*Etym.* x.): ' *Fur* ' (*thief*) *is derived from ' furvus ' and so from ' fuscus ' (dark), because he takes advantage of the night.*

* *Loc. cit.*, A. 2, *obj.* 3, Can. *Sicut hi.*     † Dist. xlvii.

*I answer that,* Three things combine together to constitute theft. The first belongs to theft as being contrary to justice, which gives to each one that which is his, so that it belongs to theft to take possession of what is another's. The second thing belongs to theft as distinct from those sins which are committed against the person, such as murder and adultery, and in this respect it belongs to theft to be about a thing possessed: for if a man takes what is another's not as a possession but as a part (for instance, if he amputates a limb), or as a person connected with him (for instance, if he carry off his daughter or his wife), it is not strictly speaking a case of theft. The third difference is that which completes the nature of theft, and consists in a thing being taken secretly: and in this respect it belongs properly to theft that it consists in *taking another's thing secretly*.

*Reply Obj.* 1. Secrecy is sometimes a cause of sin, as when a man employs secrecy in order to commit a sin, for instance in fraud and guile. In this way it does not diminish sin, but constitutes a species of sin: and thus it is in theft. In another way secrecy is merely a circumstance of sin, and thus it diminishes sin, both because it is a sign of shame, and because it removes scandal.

*Reply Obj.* 2. To keep back what is due to another, inflicts the same kind of injury as taking a thing unjustly: wherefore an unjust detention is included in an unjust taking.

*Reply Obj.* 3. Nothing prevents that which belongs to one person simply, from belonging to another in some respect: thus a deposit belongs simply to the depositor, but with regard to its custody it is the depositary's, and the thing stolen is the thief's, not simply, but as regards its custody.

## FOURTH ARTICLE.

### WHETHER THEFT AND ROBBERY ARE SINS OF DIFFERENT SPECIES ?

*We proceed thus to the Fourth Article :—*

*Objection* 1. It would seem that theft and robbery are not sins of different species. For theft and robbery differ as *secret* and *manifest:* because theft is taking something secretly, while robbery is to take something violently and openly. Now in the other kinds of sins, the secret and the manifest do not differ specifically. Therefore theft and robbery are not different species of sin.

*Obj.* 2. Further, Moral actions take their species from the end, as stated above (I.-II., Q. I., A. 3: Q. XVIII., A. 6). Now theft and robbery are directed to the same end, viz. the possession of another's property. Therefore they do not differ specifically.

*Obj.* 3. Further, Just as a thing is taken by force for the sake of possession, so is a woman taken by force for pleasure: wherefore Isidore says (*Etym.* x.) that *he who commits a rape is called a corrupter, and the victim of the rape is said to be corrupted.* Now it is a case of rape whether the woman be carried off publicly or secretly. Therefore the thing appropriated is said to be taken by force, whether it be done secretly or publicly. Therefore theft and robbery do not differ.

*On the contrary,* The Philosopher (*Ethic.* v. 2) distinguishes theft from robbery, and states that theft is done in secret, but that robbery is done openly.

*I answer that,* Theft and robbery are vices contrary to justice, in as much as one man does another an injustice. Now *no man suffers an injustice willingly,* as stated in *Ethic.* v. 9. Wherefore theft and robbery derive their sinful nature, through the taking being involuntary on the part of the person from whom something is taken. Now the involuntary is twofold, namely, through violence and through ignorance, as stated in *Ethic.* iii. I. Therefore the sinful aspect of robbery differs from that of theft: and consequently they differ specifically.

*Reply Obj.* I. In the other kinds of sin the sinful nature is not derived from something involuntary, as in the sins opposed to justice: and so where there is a different kind of involuntary, there is a different species of sin.

*Reply Obj.* 2. The remote end of robbery and theft is the same. But this is not enough for identity of species, because there is a difference of proximate ends, since the robber wishes to take a thing by his own power, but the thief, by cunning.

*Reply Obj.* 3. The robbery of a woman cannot be secret on the part of the woman who is taken: wherefore even if it be secret as regards the others from whom she is taken, the nature of robbery remains on the part of the woman to whom violence is done.

### FIFTH ARTICLE.

#### WHETHER THEFT IS ALWAYS A SIN ?

*We proceed thus to the Fifth Article :—*

*Objection* 1. It would seem that theft is not always a sin. For no sin is commanded by God, since it is written (Ecclus. xv. 21): *He hath commanded no man to do wickedly.*   Yet we find that God commanded theft, for it is written (Exod. xii. 35, 36): *And the children of Israel did as the Lord had commanded Moses* (Vulg.,—*as Moses had commanded*) ... *and they stripped the Egyptians.*   Therefore theft is not always a sin.

*Obj.* 2. Further, If a man finds a thing that is not his and takes it, he seems to commit a theft, for he takes another's property.   Yet this seems lawful according to natural equity, as the jurists hold.*   Therefore it seems that theft is not always a sin.

*Obj.* 3. Further, He that takes what is his own does not seem to sin, because he does not act against justice, since he does not destroy its equality.   Yet a man commits a theft even if he secretly take his own property that is detained by or in the safe-keeping of another.   Therefore it seems that theft is not always a sin.

*On the contrary*, It is written (Exod. xx. 15): *Thou shalt not steal.*

*I answer that*, If anyone consider what is meant by theft, he will find that it is sinful on two counts.   First, because of its opposition to justice, which gives to each one what is his, so that for this reason theft is contrary to justice, through being a taking of what belongs to another.   Secondly, because of the guile or fraud committed by the thief, by

* See *loc. cit.* in *Reply*.

laying hands on another's property secretly and cunningly. Wherefore it is evident that every theft is a sin.

*Reply Obj.* 1. It is no theft for a man to take another's property either secretly or openly by order of a judge who has commanded him to do so, because it becomes his due by the very fact that it is adjudicated to him by the sentence of the court. Hence still less was it a theft for the Israelites to take away the spoils of the Egyptians at the command of the Lord Who ordered this to be done on account of the ill-treatment accorded to them by the Egyptians without any cause: wherefore it is written significantly (Wis. x. 19): *The just took the spoils of the wicked.*

*Reply Obj.* 2. With regard to treasure-trove a distinction must be made. For some there are that were never in anyone's possession, for instance precious stones and jewels, found on the sea-shore, and such the finder is allowed to keep.\* The same applies to treasure hidden underground long since and belonging to no man, except that according to civil law the finder is bound to give half to the owner of the land, if the treasure trove be in the land of another person.† Hence in the parable of the gospel (Matth. xiii. 44) it is said of the finder of the treasure hidden in a field that he bought the field, as though he purposed thus to acquire the right of possessing the whole treasure. On the other hand the treasure-trove may be nearly in someone's possession: and then if anyone take it with the intention, not of keeping it but of returning it to the owner who does not look upon such things as unappropriated, he is not guilty of theft. In like manner if the thing found appears to be unappropriated, and if the finder believes it to be so, although he keep it, he does not commit a theft.‡ In any other case the sin of theft is committed:§ wherefore Augustine says in a homily (*Serm.* clxxviii. *De Verb. Apost.*): *If thou hast found a thing and not returned it, thou hast stolen it* (Dig. xiv. 5, can. *Si quid invenisti*).

---

\* Dig., I. viii., *De divis. rerum:* Inst., II. i., *De rerum divis.*
† Inst., *loc. cit.,* 39 : Cod. X. xv., *De Thesauris.*
‡ Inst., *loc. cit.,* 47.
§ Dig., XLI. i., *De acquirend. rerum dominio,* 9 : Inst., *loc. cit.,* 48.

*Reply Obj*. 3. He who by stealth takes his own property which is deposited with another man burdens the depositary, who is bound either to restitution, or to prove himself innocent.   Hence he is clearly guilty of sin, and is bound to ease the depositary of his burden.   On the other hand he who, by stealth, takes his own property, if this be unjustly detained by another, he sins indeed; yet not because he burdens the retainer, and so he is not bound to restitution or compensation: but he sins against general justice by disregarding the order of justice and usurping judgment concerning his own property.   Hence he must make satisfaction to God and endeavour to allay whatever scandal he may have given his neighbour by acting in this way.

## SIXTH ARTICLE.

### WHETHER THEFT IS A MORTAL SIN?

*We proceed thus to the Sixth Article :—*

*Objection* 1. It would seem that theft is not a mortal sin. For it is written (Prov. vi. 30): *The fault is not so great when a man hath stolen*.   But every mortal sin is a great fault. Therefore theft is not a mortal sin.

*Obj*. 2. Further, Mortal sin deserves to be punished with death.   But in the Law theft is punished not by death but by indemnity, according to Exod. xxii. 1, *If any man steal an ox or a sheep . . . he shall restore five oxen for one ox, and four sheep for one sheep*.   Therefore theft is not a mortal sin.

*Obj*. 3. Further, Theft can be committed in small even as in great things.   But it seems unreasonable for a man to be punished with eternal death for the theft of a small thing such as a needle or a quill.   Therefore theft is not a mortal sin.

*On the contrary*, No man is comdemned by the Divine judgment save for a mortal sin.   Yet a man is condemned for theft, according to Zach. v. 3, *This is the curse that goeth forth over the face of the earth ; for every thief shall be judged as is there written*.   Therefore theft is a mortal sin.

*I answer that*, As stated above (Q. LIX., A. 4: I.-II., Q. LXXII., A. 5), a mortal sin is one that is contrary to charity as the spiritual life of the soul. Now charity consists principally in the love of God, and secondarily in the love of our neighbour, which is shown in our wishing and doing him well. But theft is a means of doing harm to our neighbour in his belongings; and if men were to rob one another habitually, human society would be undone. Therefore theft, as being opposed to charity, is a mortal sin.

*Reply Obj.* 1. The statement that theft is not a great fault is in view of two cases. First, when a person is led to thieve through necessity. This necessity diminishes or entirely removes sin, as we shall show further on (A. 7). Hence the text continues: *For he stealeth to fill his hungry soul.* Secondly, theft is stated not to be a great fault in comparison with the guilt of adultery, which is punished with death. Hence the text goes on to say of the thief that *if he be taken, he shall restore sevenfold . . . but he that is an adulterer . . . shall destroy his own soul.*

*Reply Obj.* 2. The punishments of this life are medicinal rather than retributive. For retribution is reserved to the Divine judgment which is pronounced against sinners *according to truth* (Rom. ii. 2). Wherefore, according to the judgment of the present life the death punishment is inflicted, not for every mortal sin, but only for such as inflict an irreparable harm, or again for such as contain some horrible deformity. Hence according to the present judgment the pain of death is not inflicted for theft which does not inflict an irreparable harm, except when it is aggravated by some grave circumstance, as in the case of sacrilege which is the theft of a sacred thing, of peculation, which is theft of common property, as Augustine states (*Tract. 1., super Joan.*), and of kidnapping which is stealing a man, for which the pain of death is inflicted (Exod. xxi. 16).

*Reply Obj.* 3. Reason accounts as nothing that which is little: so that a man does not consider himself injured in very little matters: and the person who takes such things can presume that this is not against the will of the owner. And if a person take suchlike very little things, he may be

proportionately excused from mortal sin.   Yet if his intention is to rob and injure his neighbour, there may be a mortal
sin even in these very little things, even as there may be
through consent in a mere thought.

### Seventh Article.

#### WHETHER IT IS LAWFUL TO STEAL THROUGH STRESS OF NEED ?

*We proceed thus to the Seventh Article :—*

*Objection* 1. It would seem unlawful to steal through
stress of need.   For penance is not imposed except on one
who has sinned.   Now it is stated (Extra, *De furtis*, Cap.
*Si quis*): *If anyone, through stress of hunger or nakedness,
steal food, clothing or beast, he shall do penance for three weeks.*
Therefore it is not lawful to steal through stress of need.

*Obj.* 2. Further, The Philosopher says (*Ethic.* ii. 6) that
*there are some actions whose very name implies wickedness,* and
among these he reckons theft.   Now that which is wicked in
itself may not be done for a good end.   Therefore a man
cannot lawfully steal in order to remedy a need.

*Obj.* 3. Further, A man should love his neighbour as
himself.   Now, according to Augustine (*Contra Mendac.* vii.),
it is unlawful to steal in order to succour one's neighbour
by giving him an alms.   Therefore neither is it lawful to
steal in order to remedy one's own needs.

*On the contrary,* In cases of need all things are common
property, so that there would seem to be no sin in taking
another's property, for need has made it common.

*I answer that,* Things which are of human right cannot
derogate from natural right or Divine right.   Now according
to the natural order established by Divine providence,
inferior things are ordained for the purpose of succouring
man's needs by their means.   Wherefore the division and
appropriation of things which are based on human law, do
not preclude the fact that man's needs have to be remedied
by means of these very things.   Hence whatever certain
people have in superabundance is due, by natural law, to the

purpose of succouring the poor. For this reason Ambrose* says, and his words are embodied in the Decretals (Dist. xlvii., can. *Sicut* ii.): *It is the hungry man's bread that you withhold, the naked man's cloak that you store away, the money that you bury in the earth is the price of the poor man's ransom and freedom.*

Since, however, there are many who are in need, while it is impossible for all to be succoured by means of the same thing, each one is entrusted with the stewardship of his own things, so that out of them he may come to the aid of those who are in need. Nevertheless, if the need be so manifest and urgent, that it is evident that the present need must be remedied by whatever means be at hand (for instance when a person is in some imminent danger, and there is no other possible remedy), then it is lawful for a man to succour his own need by means of another's property, by taking it either openly or secretly: nor is this properly speaking theft or robbery.

*Reply Obj.* 1. This decretal considers cases where there is no urgent need.

*Reply Obj.* 2. It is not theft, properly speaking, to take secretly and use another's property in a case of extreme need: because that which he takes for the support of his life becomes his own property by reason of that need.

*Reply Obj.* 3. In a case of a like need a man may also take secretly another's property in order to succour his neighbour in need.

## EIGHTH ARTICLE.

### WHETHER ROBBERY MAY BE COMMITTED WITHOUT SIN?

*We proceed thus to the Eighth Article :—*

*Objection* 1. It would seem that robbery may be committed without sin. For spoils are taken by violence, and this seems to belong to the essence of robbery, according to what has been said (A. 4). Now it is lawful to take spoils from the enemy; for Ambrose says (*De Patriarch.* 4)*: *When the conqueror has taken possession of the spoils, military discipline demands that all should be reserved for the sovereign,*

* *Loc. cit.,* A. 2, *obj.* 3.        † *De Abraham* i. 3.

in order, to wit, that he may distribute them.   Therefore in certain cases robbery is lawful.

*Obj.* 2. Further, It is lawful to take from a man what is not his.   Now the things which unbelievers have are not theirs, for Augustine says (*Ep. ad Vincent. Donat.* xciii.): *You falsely call things your own, for you do not possess them justly, and according to the laws of earthly kings you are commanded to forfeit them.*   Therefore it seems that one may lawfully rob unbelievers.

*Obj.* 3. Further, Earthly princes violently extort many things from their subjects: and this seems to savour of robbery.   Now it would seem a grievous matter to say that they sin in acting thus, for in that case nearly every prince would be damned.   Therefore in some cases robbery is lawful.

*On the contrary,* Whatever is taken lawfully may be offered to God in sacrifice and oblation.   Now this cannot be done with the proceeds of robbery, according to Isa. lxi. 8, *I am the Lord that love judgment, and hate robbery in a holocaust* Therefore it is not lawful to take anything by robbery.

*I answer that,* Robbery implies a certain violence and coercion employed in taking unjustly from a man that which is his.   Now in human society no man can exercise coercion except through public authority: and, consequently, if a private individual not having public authority takes another's property by violence, he acts unlawfully and commits a robbery, as burglars do.   As regards princes, the public power is entrusted to them that they may be the guardians of justice: hence it is unlawful for them to use violence or coercion, save within the bounds of justice:—either by fighting against the enemy, or against the citizens, by punishing evil-doers: and whatever is taken by violence of this kind is not the spoils of robbery, since it is not contrary to justice.   On the other hand to take other people's property violently and against justice, in the exercise of public authority, is to act unlawfully and to be guilty of robbery; and whoever does so is bound to restitution.

*Reply Obj.* 1. A distinction must be made in the matter

of spoils.   For if they who take spoils from the enemy, are waging a just war, such things as they seize in the war become their own property.   This is no robbery, so that they are not bound to restitution.   Nevertheless even they who are engaged in a just war may sin in taking spoils through cupidity arising from an evil intention, if, to wit, they fight chiefly not for justice but for spoil.   For Augustine says (*De Verb. Dom.* xix; *Serm.* lxxxii.) that *it is a sin to fight for booty*.   If, however, those who take the spoil, are waging an unjust war, they are guilty of robbery, and are bound to restitution.

*Reply Obj.* 2. Unbelievers possess their goods unjustly in so far as they are ordered by the laws of earthly princes to forfeit those goods.   Hence these may be taken violently from them, not by private but by public authority.

*Reply Obj.* 3. It is no robbery if princes exact from their subjects that which is due to them for the safe-guarding of the common good, even if they use violence in so doing: but if they extort something unduly by means of violence, it is robbery even as burglary is.   Hence Augustine says (*De Civ. Dei* iv. 4): *If justice be disregarded what is a king but a mighty robber ? since what is a robber but a little king ?* And it is written (Ezech. xxii. 27): *Her princes in the midst of her, are like wolves ravening the prey*.   Wherefore they are bound to restitution, just as robbers are, and by so much do they sin more grievously than robbers, as their actions are fraught with greater and more universal danger to public justice whose wardens they are.

## Ninth Article.

### WHETHER THEFT IS A MORE GRIEVOUS SIN THAN ROBBERY ?

*We proceed thus to the Ninth Article :—*

*Objection* 1. It would seem that theft is a more grievous sin than robbery.   For theft adds fraud and guile to the taking of another's property: and these things are not found in robbery.   Now fraud and guile are sinful in themselves, as stated above (Q. LV., AA. 4, 5).   Therefore theft is a more grievous sin than robbery.

*Obj*. 2. Further, Shame is fear about a wicked deed, as stated in *Ethic*. iv. 9.   Now men are more ashamed of theft than of robbery.   Therefore theft is more wicked than robbery.

*Obj*. 3. Further, The more persons a sin injures the more grievous it would seem to be.   Now the great and the lowly may be injured by theft: whereas only the weak can be injured by robbery, since it is possible to use violence towards them.   Therefore the sin of theft seems to be more grievous than the sin of robbery.

*On the contrary*, According to the laws robbery is more severely punished than theft.

*I answer that*, Robbery and theft are sinful, as stated above (AA. 4, 6), on account of the involuntariness on the part of the person from whom something is taken: yet so that in theft the involuntariness is due to ignorance, whereas in robbery it is due to violence.   Now a thing is more involuntary through violence than through ignorance, because violence is more directly opposed to the will than ignorance.   Therefore robbery is a more grievous sin than theft.   There is also another reason, since robbery not only inflicts a loss on a person in his things, but also conduces to the ignominy and injury of his person, and this is of graver import than fraud or guile which belong to theft.   Hence the *Reply* to the *First Objection* is evident.

*Reply Obj*. 2. Men who adhere to sensible things think more of external strength which is evidenced in robbery, than of internal virtue which is forfeit through sin: wherefore they are less ashamed of robbery than of theft.

*Reply Obj*. 3. Although more persons may be injured by theft than by robbery, yet more grievous injuries may be inflicted by robbery than by theft: for which reason also robbery is more odious.

# QUESTION LXVII.

## OF THE INJUSTICE OF A JUDGE, IN JUDGING.

### (*In Four Articles.*)

WE must now consider those vices opposed to commutative justice, that consist in words injurious to our neighbours. We shall consider (1) those which are connected with judicial proceedings, and (2) injurious words uttered extra-judicially.

Under the first head five points occur for our consideration: (1) The injustice of a judge in judging: (2) The injustice of the prosecutor in accusing: (3) The injustice of the defendant in defending himself: (4) The injustice of the witnesses in giving evidence: (5) The injustice of the advocate in defending.

Under the first head there are four points of inquiry: (1) Whether a man can justly judge one who is not his subject? (2) Whether it is lawful for a judge, on account of the evidence, to deliver judgment in opposition to the truth which is known to him? (3) Whether a judge can justly sentence a man who is not accused? (4) Whether he can justly remit the punishment?

### FIRST ARTICLE.

#### WHETHER A MAN CAN JUSTLY JUDGE ONE WHO IS NOT SUBJECT TO HIS JURISDICTION?

*We proceed thus to the First Article :—*

*Objection* 1. It would seem that a man can justly judge one who is not subject to his jurisdiction. For it is stated

237

(Dan. xiii.) that Daniel sentenced the ancients who were convicted of bearing false witness. But these ancients were not subject to Daniel; indeed they were judges of the people. Therefore a man may lawfully judge one that is not subject to his jurisdiction.

*Obj.* 2. Further, Christ was no man's subject, indeed He was *King of kings and Lord of lords* (Apoc. xix. 16). Yet He submitted to the judgment of a man. Therefore it seems that a man may lawfully judge one that is not subject to his jurisdiction.

*Obj.* 3. Further, According to the law\* a man is tried in this or that court according to his kind of offence. Now sometimes the defendant is not the subject of the man whose business it is to judge in that particular place, for instance when the defendant belongs to another diocese or is exempt. Therefore it seems that a man may judge one that is not his subject.

*On the contrary*, Gregory† in commenting on Deut. xxiii. 25, *If thou go into thy friend's corn*, etc., says: *Thou mayest not put the sickle of judgment to the corn that is entrusted to another.*

*I answer that*, A judge's sentence is like a particular law regarding some particular fact. Wherefore just as a general law should have coercive power, as the Philosopher states (*Ethic*. x. 9), so too the sentence of a judge should have coercive power, whereby either party is compelled to comply with the judge's sentence; else the judgment would be of no effect. Now coercive power is not exercised in human affairs, save by those who hold public authority: and those who have this authority are accounted the superiors of those over whom they preside whether by ordinary or by delegated authority. Hence it is evident that no man can judge others than his subjects and this in virtue either of delegated or of ordinary authority.

*Reply Obj.* 1. In judging those ancients Daniel exercised an authority delegated to him by Divine instinct. This is indicated where it is said (*verse* 45) that *the Lord raised up the ... spirit of a young boy.*

---

\* Cap. *Licet ratione, de Foro Comp.*              † *Regist.* xi. epist. 64.

*Reply Obj.* 2. In human affairs a man may submit of his own accord to the judgment of others although these be not his superiors, an example of which is when parties agree to a settlement by arbitrators. Wherefore it is necessary that the arbitrator should be upheld by a penalty, since the arbitrators through not exercising authority in the case, have not of themselves full power of coercion. Accordingly in this way did Christ of his own accord submit to human judgment: and thus too did Pope Leo* submit to the judgment of the emperor.†

*Reply Obj.* 3. The bishop of the defendant's diocese becomes the latter's superior as regards the fault committed, even though he be exempt: unless perchance the defendant offend in a matter exempt from the bishop's authority, for instance in administering the property of an exempt monastery. But if an exempt person commits a theft, or a murder or the like, he may be justly condemned by the ordinary.

### SECOND ARTICLE.

#### WHETHER IT IS LAWFUL FOR A JUDGE TO PRONOUNCE JUDGMENT AGAINST THE TRUTH THAT HE KNOWS, ON ACCOUNT OF EVIDENCE TO THE CONTRARY ?

*We proceed thus to the Second Article :—*

*Objection* 1. It would seem unlawful for a judge to pronounce judgment against the truth that he knows, on account of evidence to the contrary. For it is written (Deut. xvii. 9): *Thou shalt come to the priests of the Levitical race, and to the judge that shall be at that time; and thou shalt ask of them, and they shall show thee the truth of the judgment.* Now sometimes certain things are alleged against the truth, as when something is proved by means of false witnesses. Therefore it is unlawful for a judge to pronounce judgment according to what is alleged and proved in opposition to the truth which he knows.

*Obj.* 2. Further, In pronouncing judgment a man should conform to the Divine judgment, since *it is the judgment*

---

* Leo IV.         † Can. *Nos si incompetenter*, caus. ii., qu. 7.

*of God* (Deut. i. 17). Now *the judgment of God is according
to the truth* (Rom. ii. 2), and it was foretold of Christ (Isa.
xi. 3, 4): *He shall not judge according to the sight of the eyes,
nor reprove according to the hearing of the ears. But He
shall judge the poor with justice, and shall reprove with equity
for the meek of the earth.* Therefore the judge ought not to
pronounce judgment according to the evidence before him
if it be contrary to what he knows himself.

*Obj.* 3. Further, The reason why evidence is required in
a court of law, is that the judge may have a faithful record
of the truth of the matter, wherefore in matters of common
knowledge there is no need of judicial procedure, according
to 1 Tim. v. 24, *Some men's sins are manifest, going before
to judgment.* . . . Consequently, if the judge by his personal
knowledge is aware of the truth, he should pay no heed to
the evidence, but should pronounce sentence according to
the truth which he knows.

*Obj.* 4. Further, The word *conscience* denotes application
of knowledge to a matter of action as stated in the First
Part (Q. LXXIX., A. 13). Now it is a sin to act contrary
to one's knowledge. Therefore a judge sins if he pronounces
sentence according to the evidence but against his conscience
of the truth.

*On the contrary*, Augustine* says in his commentary on
the Psalter: *A good judge does nothing according to his
private opinion, but pronounces sentence according to the
law and the right.* Now this is to pronounce judgment
according to what is alleged and proved in court. Therefore a judge ought to pronounce judgment in accordance
with these things, and not according to his private opinion.

*I answer that*, As stated above (A. 1: Q. LX., AA. 2, 6)
it is the duty of a judge to pronounce judgment in as much
as he exercises public authority, wherefore his judgment
should be based on information acquired by him, not from
his knowledge as a private individual, but from what he
knows as a public person. Now the latter knowledge comes
to him both in general and in particular:—in general through
the public laws, whether Divine or human, and he should

* Ambrose, *Super Ps.* cxviii. serm. 20.

admit no evidence that conflicts therewith:—in some particular matter, through documents and witnesses, and other legal means of information, which in pronouncing his sentence, he ought to follow rather than the information he has acquired as a private individual. And yet this same information may be of use to him, so that he can more rigorously sift the evidence brought forward, and discover its weak points. If, however, he is unable to reject that evidence juridically, he must, as stated above, follow it in pronouncing sentence.

*Reply Obj.* 1. The reason why, in the passage quoted, it is stated that the judges should first of all be asked their reasons, is to make it clear that the judges ought to judge the truth in accordance with the evidence.

*Reply Obj.* 2. To judge belongs to God in virtue of His own power: wherefore His judgment is based on the truth which He Himself knows, and not on knowledge imparted by others: the same is to be said of Christ, Who is true God and true man: whereas other judges do not judge in virtue of their own power, so that there is no comparison.

*Reply Obj.* 3. The Apostle refers to the case where something is well known not to the judge alone, but both to him and to others, so that the guilty party can by no means deny his guilt (as in the case of notorious criminals), and is convicted at once from the evidence of the fact. If, on the other hand, it be well known to the judge, but not to others, or to others, but not to the judge, then it is necessary for the judge to sift the evidence.

*Reply Obj.* 4. In matters touching his own person, a man must form his conscience from his own knowledge, but in matters concerning the public authority, he must form his conscience in accordance with the knowledge attainable in the public judicial procedure.

### Third Article.

#### WHETHER A JUDGE MAY CONDEMN A MAN WHO IS NOT ACCUSED ?

*We proceed thus to the Third Article :—*

*Objection* 1. It would seem that a judge may pass sentence on a man who is not accused. For human justice is derived from Divine justice. Now God judges the sinner even though there be no accuser. Therefore it seems that a man may pass sentence of condemnation on a man even though there be no accuser.

*Obj.* 2. Further, An accuser is required in judicial procedure in order that he may relate the crime to the judge. Now sometimes the crime may come to the judge's knowledge otherwise than by accusation; for instance, by denunciation, or by evil report, or through the judge himself being an eye-witness. Therefore a judge may condemn a man without there being an accuser.

*Obj.* 3. Further, The deeds of holy persons are related in Holy Writ, as models of human conduct. Now Daniel was at the same time the accuser and the judge of the wicked ancients (Dan. xiii.). Therefore it is not contrary to justice for a man to condemn anyone as judge while being at the same time his accuser.

*On the contrary,* Ambrose in his commentary on 1 Cor. v. 2, expounding the Apostle's sentence on the fornicator, says that *a judge should not condemn without an accuser, since Our Lord did not banish Judas, who was a thief, yet was not accused.*

*I answer that,* A judge is an interpreter of justice. Wherefore, as the Philosopher says (*Ethic.* v. 4), *men have recourse to a judge as to one who is the personification of justice.* Now, as stated above (Q. LVIII., A. 2), justice is not between a man and himself but between one man and another. Hence a judge must needs judge between two parties, which is the case when one is the prosecutor, and the other the defendant. Therefore in criminal cases the judge cannot sentence a man unless the latter has an accuser, according to Acts

xxv. 16: *It is not the custom of the Romans to condemn any man, before that he who is accused have his accusers present, and have liberty to make his answer, to clear himself of the crimes* of which he is accused.

*Reply Obj.* 1. God, in judging man, takes the sinner's conscience as his accuser, according to Rom. ii. 15, *Their thoughts between themselves accusing, or also defending one another*; or again, He takes the evidence of the fact as regards the deed itself, according to Gen. iv. 10, *The voice of thy brother's blood crieth to Me from the earth.*

*Reply Obj.* 2. Public disgrace takes the place of an accuser. Hence a gloss on Gen. iv. 10, *The voice of they brother's blood*, etc. says: *There is no need of an accuser when the crime committed is notorious.* In a case of denunciation, as stated above (Q. XXXIII., A. 7), the amendment, not the punishment, of the sinner is intended: wherefore when a man is denounced for a sin, nothing is done against him, but for him, so that no accuser is required. The punishment that is inflicted is on account of his rebellion against the Church, and since this rebellion is manifest, it stands instead of an accuser. The fact that the judge himself was an eye-witness, does not authorize him to proceed to pass sentence, except according to the order of judicial procedure.

*Reply Obj.* 3. God, in judging man, proceeds from His own knowledge of the truth, whereas man does not, as stated above (A. 2). Hence a man cannot be accuser, witness and judge at the same time, as God is. Daniel was at once accuser and judge, because he was the executor of the sentence of God, by whose instinct he was moved, as stated above (A. 1, *ad* 1).

## FOURTH ARTICLE.

### WHETHER THE JUDGE CAN LAWFULLY REMIT THE PUNISHMENT?

*We proceed thus to the Fourth Article :—*

*Objection* 1. It would seem that the judge can lawfully remit the punishment. For it is written (James ii. 13):

*Judgment without mercy* shall be done *to him that hath not done mercy*. Now no man is punished for not doing what he cannot do lawfully. Therefore any judge can lawfully do mercy by remitting the punishment.

*Obj.* 2. Further, Human judgment should imitate the Divine judgment. Now God remits the punishment to sinners, because He desires not the death of the sinner, according to Ezech. xviii. 23. Therefore a human judge also may lawfully remit the punishment to one who repents.

*Obj.* 3. Further, It is lawful for anyone to do what is profitable to someone and harmful to none. Now the remission of his punishment profits the guilty man and harms nobody. Therefore the judge can lawfully loose a guilty man from his punishment.

*On the contrary*, It is written (Deut. xiii. 8, 9) concerning anyone who would persuade a man to serve strange gods: *Neither let thy eye spare him to pity and conceal him, but thou shalt presently put him to death :* and of the murderer it is written (Deut. xix. 12, 13): *He shall die. Thou shalt not pity him.*

*I answer that*, As may be gathered from what has been said (AA. 2, 3), with regard to the question in point, two things may be observed in connection with a judge. One is that he has to judge between accuser and defendant, while the other is that he pronounces the judicial sentence, in virtue of his power, not as a private individual but as a public person. Accordingly on two counts a judge is hindered from loosing a guilty person from his punishment. First on the part of the accuser, whose right it sometimes is that the guilty party should be punished,—for instance on account of some injury committed against the accuser,— because it is not in the power of a judge to remit such punishment, since every judge is bound to give each man his right. Secondly, he finds a hindrance on the part of the commonwealth, whose power he exercises, and to whose good it belongs that evil-doers should be punished.

Nevertheless in this respect there is a difference between judges of lower degree and the supreme judge, i.e. the sovereign, to whom the entire public authority is entrusted. For the inferior judge has no power to exempt a guilty man from punishment against the laws imposed on him by his superior.    Wherefore Augustine in commenting on John xix. 11, *Thou shouldst not have any power against Me,* says (*Tract.* cxvi. *in Joan.*): *The power which God gave Pilate was such that he was under the power of Cæsar, so that he was by no means free to acquit the person accused.*   On the other hand the sovereign who has full authority in the commonwealth, can lawfully remit the punishment to a guilty person, provided the injured party consent to the remission, and that this do not seem detrimental to the public good.

*Reply Obj.* 1. There is a place for the judge's mercy in matters that are left to the judge's discretion, because in like matters a good man is slow to punish as the Philosopher states (*Ethic.* v. 10).   But in matters that are determined in accordance with Divine or human laws, it is not left to him to show mercy.

*Reply Obj.* 2. God has supreme power of judging, and it concerns Him whatever is done sinfully against anyone. Therefore He is free to remit the punishment, especially since punishment is due to sin chiefly because it is done against Him.   He does not, however, remit the punishment, except in so far as it becomes His goodness, which is the source of all laws.

*Reply Obj.* 3. If the judge were to remit punishment inordinately, he would inflict an injury on the community, for whose good it behoves ill-deeds to be punished, in order that men may avoid sin.   Hence the text, after appointing the punishment of the seducer, adds (Deut. xiii. 11): *That all Israel hearing may fear, and may do no more anything like this.*   He would also inflict harm on the injured person; who is compensated by having his honour restored in the punishment of the man who has injured him.

# QUESTION LXVIII.

## OF MATTERS CONCERNING UNJUST ACCUSATION.

### (*In Four Articles.*)

WE must now consider matters pertaining to unjust accusation. Under this head there are four points of inquiry: (1) Whether a man is bound to accuse ? (2) Whether the accusation should be made in writing ? (3) How is an accusation vitiated ? (4) How should those be punished who have accused a man wrongfully ?

### FIRST ARTICLE.

#### WHETHER A MAN IS BOUND TO ACCUSE ?

*We proceed thus to the First Article :—*

*Objection* 1. It would seem that a man is not bound to accuse. For no man is excused on account of sin from fulfilling a Divine precept, since he would thus profit by his sin. Yet on account of sin some are disqualified from accusing, such as those who are excommunicate or of evil fame, or who are accused of grievous crimes and are not yet proved to be innocent.\* Therefore a man is not bound by a Divine precept to accuse.

*Obj.* 2. Further, Every duty depends on charity which is *the end of the precept:*† wherefore it is written (Rom. xiii. 8): *Owe no man anything, but to love one another.* Now that which belongs to charity is a duty that man owes to all both of high and of low degree, both superiors and inferiors. Since therefore subjects should not accuse their superiors, nor persons of lower degree, those of a higher degree, as shown in several chapters (Decret. II., qu. vii.), it seems that it is no man's duty to accuse.

---

\* 1 Tim. i. 5.  † Can. *Definimus,* caus. iv., qu. 1; caus. vi., qu. 1.

*Obj.* 3. Further, No man is bound to act against the fidelity which he owes his friend; because he ought not to do to another what he would not have others do to him. Now to accuse anyone is sometimes contrary to the fidelity that one owes a friend; for it is written (Prov. xi. 13): *He that walketh deceitfully, revealeth secrets; but he that is faithful, concealeth the thing committed to him by his friend.* Therefore a man is not bound to accuse.

*On the contrary,* It is written (Lev. v. 1): *If any one sin, and hear the voice of one swearing, and is a witness either because he himself hath seen, or is privy to it: if he do not utter it, he shall bear his iniquity.*

*I answer that,* As stated above (Q. XXXIII., AA. 6, 7: Q. LXVII., A. 3, *ad* 2), the difference between denunciation and accusation is that in denunciation we aim at a brother's amendment, whereas in accusation we intend the punishment of his crime. Now the punishments of this life are sought, not for their own sake, because this is not the final time of retribution, but in their character of medicine, conducing either to the amendment of the sinner, or to the good of the commonwealth whose calm is ensured by the punishment of evil-doers. The former of these is intended in denunciation, as stated, whereas the second regards properly accusation. Hence in the case of a crime that conduces to the injury of the commonwealth, a man is bound to accusation, provided he can offer sufficient proof, since it is the accuser's duty to prove: as, for example, when anyone's sin conduces to the bodily or spiritual corruption of the community. If, however, the sin be not such as to affect the community, or if he cannot offer sufficient proof, a man is not bound to attempt to accuse, since no man is bound to do what he cannot duly accomplish.

*Reply Obj.* 1. Nothing prevents a man being debarred by sin from doing what men are under an obligation to do: for instance from meriting eternal life, and from receiving the sacraments of the Church. Nor does a man profit by this: indeed it is a most grievous fault to fail to do what one is bound to do, since virtuous acts are perfections of man.

*Reply Obj.* 2. Subjects are debarred from accusing their superiors, *if it is not the affection of charity but their own wickedness that leads them to defame and disparage the conduct of their superiors,*\*—or again if the subject who wishes to accuse his superior is himself guilty of crime.† Otherwise, provided they be in other respects qualified to accuse, it is lawful for subjects to accuse their superiors out of charity.

*Reply Obj.* 3. It is contrary to fidelity to make known secrets to the injury of a person; but not if they be revealed for the good of the community, which should always be preferred to a private good.   Hence it is unlawful to receive any secret in detriment to the common good: and yet a thing is scarcely a secret when there are sufficient witnesses to prove it.

## SECOND ARTICLE.

### WHETHER IT IS NECESSARY FOR THE ACCUSATION TO BE MADE IN WRITING ?

*We proceed thus to the Second Article :—*

*Objection* 1. It would seem unnecessary for the accusation to be made in writing.   For writing was devised as an aid to the human memory of the past.   But an accusation is made in the present.   Therefore the accusation needs not to be made in writing.

*Obj.* 2. Further, It is laid down (Decret. II., qu. viii., can. *Per scripta*) that *no man may accuse or be accused in his absence.*   Now writing seems to be useful in the fact that it is a means of notifying something to one who is absent, as Augustine declares (*De Trin.* x. 1).   Therefore the accusation need not be in writing: and all the more that the canon declares that *no accusation in writing should be accepted.*

*Obj.* 3. Further, A man's crime is made known by denunciation, even as by accusation.   Now writing is unnecessary in denunciation.   Therefore it is seemingly unnecessary in accusation.

*On the contrary,* It is laid down (Decret. II., qu. viii., can.

---

\* Append. Grat. ad can. *Sunt nonnulli*, caus. ii., qu. 7.
† Decret. II., qu. vii., can. *Præsumunt.*

*Accusatorum*) that *the role of accuser must never be sanctioned without the accusation be in writing*.

*I answer that*, As stated above (Q. LXVII., A. 3), when the process in a criminal case goes by way of accusation, the accuser is in the position of a party, so that the judge stands between the accuser and the accused for the purpose of the trial of justice, wherein it behoves one to proceed on certainties, as far as possible. Since however verbal utterances are apt to escape one's memory, the judge would be unable to know for certain what had been said and with what qualifications, when he comes to pronounce sentence, unless it were drawn up in writing. Hence it has with reason been established that the accusation, as well as other parts of the judicial procedure, should be put into writing.

*Reply Obj.* 1. Words are so many and so various that it is difficult to remember each one. A proof of this is the fact that if a number of people who have heard the same words be asked what was said, they will not agree in repeating them, even after a short time. And since a slight difference of words changes the sense, even though the judge's sentence may have to be pronounced soon afterwards, the certainty of judgment requires that the accusation be drawn up in writing.

*Reply Obj.* 2. Writing is needed not only on account of the absence of the person who has something to notify, or of the person to whom something is notified, but also on account of the delay of time as stated above (*ad* 1). Hence when the canon says, *Let no accusation be accepted in writing* it refers to the sending of an accusation by one who is absent: but it does not exclude the necessity of writing when the accuser is present.

*Reply Obj.* 3. The denouncer does not bind himself to give proofs: wherefore he is not punished if he is unable to prove. For this reason writing is unnecessary in a denunciation: and it suffices that the denunciation be made verbally to the Church, who will proceed, in virtue of her office, to the correction of the brother.

## Third Article.

### WHETHER AN ACCUSATION IS RENDERED UNJUST BY CALUMNY, COLLUSION OR EVASION ?

*We proceed thus to the Third Article :—*

*Objection* 1. It would seem that an accusation is not rendered unjust by calumny, collusion or evasion. For according to Decret. II., qu. iii.,* *calumny consists in falsely charging a person with a crime.* Now sometimes one man falsely accuses another of a crime through ignorance of fact which excuses him. Therefore it seems that an accusation is not always rendered unjust through being slanderous.

*Obj.* 2. Further, It is stated by the same authority that *collusion consists in hiding the truth about a crime.* But seemingly this is not unlawful, because one is not bound to disclose every crime, as stated above (A. 1: Q. XXXIII., A. 7). Therefore it seems that an accusation is not rendered unjust by collusion.

*Obj.* 3. Further, It is stated by the same authority that *evasion consists in withdrawing altogether from an accusation.* But thus can be done without injustice: for it is stated there also: *If a man repent of having made a wicked accusation and inscription†  in a matter which he cannot prove, and come to an understanding with the innocent party whom he has accused, let them acquit one another.* Therefore evasion does not render an accusation unjust.

*On the contrary,* It is stated by the same authority: *The rashness of accusers shows itself in three ways. For they are guilty either of calumny, or of collusion, or of evasion.*

*I answer that,* As stated above (A. 1), accusation is ordered for the common good which it aims at procuring by means of knowledge of the crime. Now no man ought to injure a person unjustly, in order to promote the common good. Wherefore a man may sin in two ways when making an accusation: first through acting unjustly against the accused, by charging him falsely with the commission of a crime,

* Append. Grat. ad can. *Si quem pœnituerit.*
† Cf. footnote on II.-II., Q. XXXIII., A. 7.

i.e. by calumniating him; secondly, on the part of the commonwealth, whose good is intended chiefly in an accusation, when anyone with wicked intent hinders a sin being punished. This again happens in two ways: first by having recourse to fraud in making the accusation. This belongs to collusion (*prævaricatio*) for *he that is guilty of collusion is like one who rides astraddle* (*varicator*), *because he helps the other party, and betrays his own side*.* Secondly by withdrawing altogether from the accusation. This is evasion (*tergiversatio*) for by desisting from what he had begun he seems to turn his back (*tergum vertere*).

*Reply Obj.* 1. A man ought not to proceed to accuse except of what he is quite certain about, wherein ignorance of fact has no place. Yet he who falsely charges another with a crime is not a calumniator unless he gives utterance to false accusations out of malice. For it happens sometimes that a man through levity of mind proceeds to accuse someone, because he believes too readily what he hears, and this pertains to rashness; while, on the other hand sometimes a man is led to make an accusation on account of an error for which he is not to blame. All these things must be weighed according to the judge's prudence, lest he should declare a man to have been guilty of calumny, who through levity of mind or an error for which he is not to be blamed has uttered a false accusation.

*Reply Obj.* 2. Not everyone who hides the truth about a crime is guilty of collusion, but only he who deceitfully hides the matter about which he makes the accusation, by collusion with the defendant, dissembling his proofs, and admitting false excuses.

*Reply Obj.* 3. Evasion consists in withdrawing altogether from the accusation, by renouncing the intention of accusing, not anyhow, but inordinately. There are two ways, however, in which a man may rightly desist from accusing without committing a sin:—in one way, in the very process of accusation, if it come to his knowledge that the matter of his accusation is false, and then by mutual consent the accuser and the defendant acquit one another:—in another

* Append. Grat., *loc. cit.*

way, if the accusation be quashed by the sovereign to whom belongs the care of the common good, which it is intended to procure by the accusation.

### FOURTH ARTICLE.

#### WHETHER AN ACCUSER WHO FAILS TO PROVE HIS INDICTMENT IS BOUND TO THE PUNISHMENT OF RETALIATION ?

*We proceed thus to the Fourth Article :—*

*Objection* 1. It would seem that the accuser who fails to prove his indictment is not bound to the punishment of retaliation. For sometimes a man is led by a just error to make an accusation, in which case the judge acquits the accuser, as stated in Decret. II., qu. iii.* Therefore the accuser who fails to prove his indictment is not bound to the punishment of retaliation.

*Obj.* 2. Further, If the punishment of retaliation ought to be inflicted on one who has accused unjustly, this will be on account of the injury he has done to someone:—but not on account of any injury done to the person of the accused, for in that case the sovereign could not remit this punishment; nor on account of an injury to the commonwealth, because then the accused could not acquit him. Therefore the punishment of retaliation is not due to one who has failed to prove his accusation.

*Obj.* 3. Further, The one same sin does not deserve a two-fold punishment, according to Nahum i. 9:† *God shall not judge the same thing a second time.* But he who fails to prove his accusation, incurs the punishment due to defamation,‡ which punishment even the Pope seemingly cannot remit, according to a statement of Pope Gelasius:§ *Although we are able to save souls by Penance, we are unable to remove the defamation.* Therefore he is not bound to suffer the punishment of retaliation.

*On the contrary,* Pope Hadrian I. says (Cap. lii.): *He that fails to prove his accusation, must himself suffer the punishment which his accusation inferred.*

---

\* Append. Grat., *loc. cit.*                    † Septuagint version.
‡ Can. *Infames*, caus. vi., qu. 1.
§ Callist. I., *Epist. ad omn. Gall. episc.*

*I answer that,* As stated above (A. 2), in a case, where the procedure is by way of accusation, the accuser holds the position of a party aiming at the punishment of the accused. Now the duty of the judge is to establish the equality of justice between them: and the equality of justice requires that a man should himself suffer whatever harm he has intended to be inflicted on another, according to Exod. xxi. 24, *Eye for eye, tooth for tooth.* Consequently it is just that he who by accusing a man has put him in danger of being punished severely, should himself suffer a like punishment.

*Reply Obj.* 1. As the Philosopher says (*Ethic.* v. 5) justice does not always require counterpassion, because it matters considerably whether a man injures another voluntarily or not. Voluntary injury deserves punishment, involuntary deserves forgiveness. Hence when the judge becomes aware that a man has made a false accusation, not with a mind to do harm, but involuntarily through ignorance or a just error, he does not impose the punishment of retaliation.

*Reply Obj.* 2. He who accuses wrongfully sins both against the person of the accused and against the commonwealth; wherefore he is punished on both counts. This is the meaning of what is written (Deut. xix. 18-20): *And when after most diligent inquisition, they shall find that the false witness hath told a lie against his brother : they shall render to him as he meant to do to his brother*, and this refers to the injury done to the person: and afterwards, referring to the injury done to the commonwealth, the text continues: *And thou shalt take away the evil out of the midst of thee, that others hearing may fear, and may not dare to do such things.* Specially, however, does he injure the person of the accused, if he accuse him falsely. Wherefore the accused, if innocent, may condone the injury done to himself, particularly if the accusation were made not calumniously but out of levity of mind. But if the accuser desist from accusing an innocent man, through collusion with the latter's adversary, he inflicts an injury on the commonwealth: and this cannot be condoned by the accused, although it can be remitted by the sovereign, who has charge of the commonwealth.

*Reply Obj.* 3. The accuser deserves the punishment of retaliation in compensation for the harm he attempts to inflict on his neighbour: but the punishment of disgrace is due to him for his wickedness in accusing another man calumniously. Sometimes the sovereign remits the punishment, and not the disgrace, and sometimes he removes the disgrace also: wherefore the Pope also can remove this disgrace. When Pope Gelasius says: *We cannot remove the disgrace*, he may mean either the disgrace attaching to the deed (*infamia facti*), or that sometimes it is not expedient to remove it, or again he may be referring to the disgrace inflicted by the civil judge, as Gratian states (*loc. cit.*).

# QUESTION LXIX.

## OF SINS COMMITTED AGAINST JUSTICE ON THE PART OF THE DEFENDANT.

### (*In Four Articles.*)

WE must now consider those sins which are committed against justice on the part of the defendant. Under this head there are four points of inquiry: (1) Whether it is a mortal sin to deny the truth which would lead to one's condemnation ? (2) Whether it is lawful to defend oneself with calumnies ? (3) Whether it is lawful to escape condemnation by appealing ? (4) Whether it is lawful for one who has been condemned to defend himself by violence if he be able to do so ?

## FIRST ARTICLE.

### WHETHER ONE CAN, WITHOUT A MORTAL SIN, DENY THE TRUTH WHICH WOULD LEAD TO ONE'S CONDEMNATION ?

*We proceed thus to the First Article :—*

*Objection* 1. It would seem that one can, without a mortal sin, deny the truth which would lead to one's condemnation. For Chrysostom says (*Hom.* xxxi. *super Ep. ad Heb.*): *I do not say that you should lay bare your guilt publicly, nor accuse yourself before others.* Now if the accused were to confess the truth in court, he would lay bare his guilt and be his own accuser. Therefore he is not bound to tell the truth: and so he does not sin mortally if he tell a lie in court.

*Obj.* 2. Further, Just as it is an officious lie when one tells a lie in order to rescue another man from death, so is it an officious lie when one tells a lie in order to free oneself from death, since one is more bound towards oneself than towards another. Now an officious lie is considered not a mortal but a venial sin. Therefore if the accused denies the truth in court, in order to escape death, he does not sin mortally.

*Obj.* 3. Further, Every mortal sin is contrary to charity, as stated above (Q. XXIV., A. 12). But that the accused lie by denying himself to be guilty of the crime laid to his charge is not contrary to charity, neither as regards the love we owe God, nor as to the love due to our neighbour. Therefore such a lie is not a mortal sin.

*On the contrary,* Whatever is opposed to the glory of God is a mortal sin, because we are bound by precept to *do all to the glory of God* (1 Cor. x. 31). Now it is to the glory of God that the accused confess that which is alleged against him, as appears from the words of Josue to Achan, *My son, give glory to the Lord God of Israel, and confess and tell me what thou hast done, hide it not* (Jos. vii. 19). Therefore it is a mortal sin to lie in order to cover one's guilt.

*I answer that,* Whoever acts against the due order of justice, sins mortally, as stated above (Q. LIX., A. 4). Now it belongs to the order of justice that a man should obey his superior in those matters to which the rights of his authority extend. Again, the judge, as stated above (Q. LXVII., A. 1), is the superior in relation to the person whom he judges. Therefore the accused is in duty bound to tell the judge the truth which the latter exacts from him according to the form of law. Hence if he refuse to tell the truth which he is under obligation to tell, or if he mendaciously deny it, he sins mortally. If, on the other hand, the judge asks of him that which he cannot ask in accordance with the order of justice, the accused is not bound to satisfy him, and he may lawfully escape by appealing or otherwise: but it is not lawful for him to lie.

*Reply Obj.* 1. When a man is examined by the judge according to the order of justice, he does not lay bare his own guilt, but his guilt is unmasked by another, since the obligation of answering is imposed on him by one whom he is bound to obey.

*Reply Obj.* 2. To lie, with injury to another person, in

order to rescue a man from death is not a purely officious
lie, for it has an admixture of the pernicious lie: and when
a man lies in court in order to exculpate himself, he does an
injury to one whom he is bound to obey, since he refuses
him his due, namely an avowal of the truth.

*Reply Obj.* 3. He who lies in court by denying his guilt,
acts both against the love of God to Whom judgment belongs,
and against the love of his neighbour, and this not only as
regards the judge, to whom he refuses his due, but also as
regards his accuser, who is punished if he fail to prove his
accusation. Hence it is written (Ps. cxl. 4): *Incline not
my heart to evil words, to make excuses in sins :* on which
words a gloss says: *Shameless men are wont by lying to deny
their guilt when they have been found out.* And Gregory,
in expounding Job xxxi. 33, *If as a man I have hid my sin,*
says (*Moral.* xxii. 15): *It is a common vice of mankind to sin
in secret, by lying to hide the sin that has been committed,
and when convicted to aggravate the sin by defending oneself.*

## SECOND ARTICLE.

### WHETHER IT IS LAWFUL FOR THE ACCUSED TO DEFEND HIMSELF WITH CALUMNIES ?

*We proceed thus to the Second Article :—*

*Objection* 1. It would seem lawful for the accused to defend
himself with calumnies. Because, according to civil law
(Cod. II., iv., *De transact.* 18), when a man is on trial for
his life it is lawful for him to bribe his adversary. Now
this is done chiefly by defending oneself with calumnies.
Therefore the accused who is on trial for his life does not sin
if he defend himself with calumnies.

*Obj.* 2. Further, An accuser who is guilty of collusion with
the accused, is punishable by law (Decret. II., qu. iii.,
can. *Si quem pœnit*). Yet no punishment is imposed on
the accused for collusion with the accuser. Therefore it
would seem lawful for the accused to defend himself with
calumnies.

*Obj.* 3. Further, It is written (Prov. xiv. 16): *A wise
man feareth and declineth from evil, the fool leapeth over and*

*is confident.* Now what is done wisely is no sin. Therefore no matter how a man declines from evil, he does not sin.

*On the contrary,* In criminal cases an oath has to be taken against calumnious allegations (Extra, *De juramento calumniæ,* cap. *Inhærentes*): and this would not be the case if it were lawful to defend oneself with calumnies. Therefore it is not lawful for the accused to defend himself with calumnies.

*I answer that,* It is one thing to withhold the truth, and another to utter a falsehood. The former is lawful sometimes, for a man is not bound to divulge all truth, but only such as the judge can and must require of him according to the order of justice; as, for instance, when the accused is already disgraced through the commission of some crime, or certain indications of his guilt have already been discovered, or again when his guilt is already more or less proven. On the other hand it is never lawful to make a false declaration.

As regards what he may do lawfully, a man can employ either lawful means, and such as are adapted to the end in view, which belongs to prudence; or he can use unlawful means, unsuitable to the proposed end, and this belongs to craftiness, which is exercised by fraud and guile, as shown above (Q. LV., AA. 3, *seqq.*). His conduct in the former case is praiseworthy, in the latter sinful. Accordingly it is lawful for the accused to defend himself by withholding the truth that he is not bound to avow, by suitable means, for instance by not answering such questions as he is not bound to answer. This is not to defend himself with calumnies, but to escape prudently. But it is unlawful for him, either to utter a falsehood, or to withhold a truth that he is bound to avow, or to employ guile or fraud, because fraud and guile have the force of a lie, and so to use them would be to defend oneself with calumnies.

*Reply Obj.* 1. Human laws leave many things unpunished, which according to the Divine judgment are sins, as, for example, simple fornication; because human law does not exact perfect virtue from man, for such virtue belongs to few and cannot be found in so great a number of people as human law has to direct. That a man is sometimes unwilling to commit a sin in order to escape from the death of the body, the danger of which threatens the accused who is on trial for his life, is an act of perfect virtue, since *death is the most fearful of all temporal things* (*Ethic.* iii. 6). Wherefore if the accused, who is on trial for his life, bribes his adversary, he sins indeed by inducing him to do what is unlawful, yet the civil law does not punish this sin, and in this sense it is said to be lawful.

*Reply Obj.* 2. If the accuser is guilty of collusion with the accused and the latter is guilty, he incurs punishment, and so it is evident that he sins. Wherefore, since it is a sin to induce a man to sin, or to take part in a sin in any way—for the Apostle says (Rom. i. 32,) that *they . . . are worthy of death . . . that consent* to those who sin—it is evident that the accused also sins if he is guilty of collusion with his adversary. Nevertheless according to human laws no punishment is inflicted on him, for the reason given above.

*Reply Obj.* 3. The wise man hides himself not by slandering others but by exercising prudence.

### Third Article.

#### WHETHER IT IS LAWFUL FOR THE ACCUSED TO ESCAPE JUDGMENT BY APPEALING ?

*We proceed thus to the Third Article :—*

*Objection* 1. It would seem unlawful for the accused to escape judgment by appealing. The Apostle says (Rom. xiii. 1): *Let every soul be subject to the higher powers.* Now the accused by appealing refuses to be subject to a higher power, viz. the judge. Therefore he commits a sin.

*Obj.* 2. Further, Ordinary authority is more binding than that which we choose for ourselves. Now according to the Decretals (II., qu. vi., cap. *A judicibus*) *it is unlawful to appeal from the judges chosen by common consent.* Much less therefore is it lawful to appeal from ordinary judges.

*Obj.* 3. Further, Whatever is lawful once is always lawful.

But it is not lawful to appeal after the tenth day,* nor a third time on the same point.† Therefore it would seem that an appeal is unlawful in itself.

*On the contrary,* Paul appealed to Cæsar (Acts xxv.).

*I answer that,* There are two motives for which a man appeals. First through confidence in the justice of his cause, seeing that he is unjustly oppressed by the judge, and then it is lawful for him to appeal, because this is a prudent means of escape. Hence it is laid down (Decret. II., qu. vi., can. *Omnis oppressus*): *All those who are oppressed are free, if they so wish, to appeal to the judgment of the priests, and no man may stand in their way.* Secondly, a man appeals in order to cause a delay, lest a just sentence be pronounced against him. This is to defend oneself calumniously, and is unlawful as stated above (A. 2). For he inflicts an injury both on the judge, whom he hinders in the exercise of his office, and on his adversary, whose justice he disturbs as far as he is able. Hence it is laid down (II., qu. vi., can. *Omnino puniendus*): *Without doubt a man should be punished if his appeal be declared unjust.*

*Reply Obj.* 1. A man should submit to the lower authority in so far as the latter observes the order of the higher authority. If the lower authority departs from the order of the higher, we ought not to submit to it, for instance *if the proconsul order one thing and the emperor another,* according to a gloss on Rom. xiii. 2. Now when a judge oppresses anyone unjustly, in this respect he departs from the order of the higher authority, whereby he is obliged to judge justly. Hence it is lawful for a man who is oppressed unjustly, to have recourse to the authority of the higher power, by appealing either before or after sentence has been pronounced. And since it is to be presumed that there is no rectitude where true faith is lacking, it is unlawful for a catholic to appeal to an unbelieving judge, according to Decret. II., qu. vi., can. *Catholicus : The catholic who appeals to the decision of a judge of another faith shall be excommunicated, whether his case be just or unjust.* Hence the Apostle

* Can. *Anteriorum*, caus. ii., qu. 6.
† Can. *Si autem*, caus. ii., qu. 6.

also rebuked those who went to law before unbelievers (I Cor. vi. 6).

*Reply Obj.* 2. It is due to a man's own fault or neglect that, of his own accord, he submits to the judgment of one in whose justice he has no confidence. Moreover it would seem to point to levity of mind for a man not to abide by what he has once approved of. Hence it is with reason that the law refuses us the faculty of appealing from the decision of judges of our own choice, who have no power save by virtue of the consent of the litigants. On the other hand the authority of an ordinary judge depends, not on the consent of those who are subject to his judgment, but on the authority of the king or prince who appointed him. Hence, as a remedy against his unjust oppression, the law allows one to have recourse to appeal, so that even if the judge be at the same time ordinary and chosen by the litigants, it is lawful to appeal from his decision, since seemingly his ordinary authority occasioned his being chosen as arbitrator. Nor is it to be imputed as a fault to the man who consented to his being arbitrator, without adverting to the fact that he was appointed ordinary judge by the prince.

*Reply Obj.* 3. The equity of the law so guards the interests of the one party that the other is not oppressed. Thus it allows ten days for appeal to be made, this being considered sufficient time for deliberating on the expediency of an appeal. If on the other hand there were no fixed time limit for appealing, the certainty of judgment would ever be in suspense, so that the other party would suffer an injury. The reason why it is not allowed to appeal a third time on the same point, is that it is not probable that the judges would fail to judge justly so many times.

## FOURTH ARTICLE.

### WHETHER A MAN WHO IS CONDEMNED TO DEATH MAY LAWFULLY DEFEND HIMSELF IF HE CAN?

*We proceed thus to the Fourth Article :—*

*Objection* 1. It would seem that a man who is condemned to death may lawfully defend himself if he can. For it is always lawful to do that to which nature inclines us, as being of natural right, so to speak. Now, to resist corruption is an inclination of nature not only in men and animals but also in things devoid of sense. Therefore if he can do so, the accused, after condemnation, may lawfully resist being put to death.

*Obj.* 2. Further, Just as a man, by resistance, escapes the death to which he has been condemned, so does he by flight. Now it is lawful seemingly to escape death by flight, according to Ecclus. ix. 18, *Keep thee far from the man that hath power to kill [and not to quicken].** Therefore it is also lawful for the accused to resist.

*Obj.* 3. Further, It is written (Prov. xxiv. 11): *Deliver them that are led to death: and those that are drawn to death frobear not to deliver.* Now a man is under greater obligation to himself than to another. Therefore it is lawful for a condemned man to defend himself from being put to death.

*On the contrary,* The Apostle says (Rom. xiii. 2): *He that resisteth the power, resisteth the ordinance of God: and they that resist, purchase to themselves damnation.* Now a condemned man, by defending himself, resists the power in the point of its being ordained by God *for the punishment of evil-doers, and for the praise of the good.*† Therefore he sins in defending himself.

*I answer that,* A man may be condemned to death in two ways. First justly, and then it is not lawful for the condemned to defend himself, because it is lawful for the judge to combat his resistance by force, so that on his part the fight is unjust, and consequently without any doubt he sins.

Secondly a man is condemned unjustly: and such a sentence is like the violence of robbers, according to Ezech. xxii. 27, *Her princes in the midst of her are like wolves ravening the prey to shed blood.* Wherefore even as it is lawful to resist robbers, so is it lawful, in a like case, to resist wicked princes; except perhaps in order to avoid scandal, whence some grave disturbance might be feared to arise.

* The words in brackets are not in the Vulgate.   † 1 Pet. ii. 14.

*Reply Obj.* 1. Reason was given to man that he might ensue those things to which his nature inclines, not in all cases, but in accordance with the order of reason. Hence not all self-defence is lawful, but only such as is accomplished with due moderation.

*Reply Obj.* 2. When a man is condemned to death, he has not to kill himself, but to suffer death: wherefore he is not bound to do anything from which death would result, such as to stay in the place whence he would be led to execution. But he may not resist those who lead him to death, in order that he may not suffer what is just for him to suffer. Even so, if a man were condemned to die of hunger, he does not sin if he partakes of food brought to him secretly, because to refrain from taking it would be to kill himself.

*Reply Obj.* 3. This saying of the wise man does not direct that one should deliver a man from death in opposition to the order of justice: wherefore neither should a man deliver himself from death by resisting against justice.

# QUESTION LXX.

## OF INJUSTICE WITH REGARD TO THE PERSON OF THE WITNESS.

### (*In Four Articles.*)

WE must now consider injustice with regard to the person of the witness. Under this head there are four points of inquiry: (1) Whether a man is bound to give evidence? (2) Whether the evidence of two or three witnesses suffices? (3) Whether a man's evidence may be rejected without any fault on his part? (4) Whether it is a mortal sin to bear false witness?

### FIRST ARTICLE.

#### WHETHER A MAN IS BOUND TO GIVE EVIDENCE?

*We proceed thus to the First Article :—*

*Objection* 1. It would seem that a man is not bound to give evidence. Augustine says (*QQ. Genes.* i. 26),* that when Abraham said of his wife (Gen. xx. 2), *She is my sister,* he wished the truth to be concealed and not a lie to be told. Now, by hiding the truth a man abstains from giving evidence. Therefore a man is not bound to give evidence.

*Obj.* 2. Further, No man is bound to act deceitfully. Now it is written (Prov. xi. 13): *He that walketh deceitfully revealeth secrets, but he that is faithful concealeth the thing committed to him by his friend.* Therefore a man is not always bound to give evidence, especially on matters committed to him as a secret by a friend.

*Obj.* 3. Further, Clerics and priests, more than others, are bound to those things that are necessary for salvation. Yet clerics and priests are forbidden to give evidence when a man is on trial for his life. Therefore it is not necessary for salvation to give evidence.

* Cf. *Contra Faust.* xxii. 33, 34.

*On the contrary,* Augustine* says: *Both he who conceals the truth and he who tells a lie are guilty, the former because he is unwilling to do good, the latter because he desires to hurt.*

*I answer that,* We must make a distinction in the matter of giving evidence: because sometimes a certain man's evidence is necessary, and sometimes not. If the necessary evidence is that of a man subject to a superior whom, in matters pertaining to justice, he is bound to obey, without doubt he is bound to give evidence on those points which are required of him in accordance with the order of justice, for instance on manifest things or when ill-report has preceded. If however he is required to give evidence on other points, for instance secret matters, and those of which no ill-report has preceded, he is not bound to give evidence. On the other hand, if his evidence be required by one who has not the authority of a superior whom he is bound to obey, we must make a distinction: because if his evidence is required in order to deliver a man from an unjust death or any other penalty, or from false defamation, or some loss, in such cases he is bound to give evidence. Even if his evidence is not demanded, he is bound to do what he can to declare the truth to someone who may profit thereby. For it is written (Ps. lxxxi. 4): *Rescue the poor, and deliver the needy from the hand of the sinner ;* and (Prov. xxiv. 11): *Deliver them that are led to death ;* and (Rom. i. 32): *They are worthy of death, not only they that do them, but they also that consent to them that do them,* on which words a gloss says: *To be silent when one can disprove is to consent.* In matters pertaining to a man's condemnation, one is not bound to give evidence, except when one is constrained by a superior in accordance with the order of justice; since if the truth of such a matter be concealed, no particular injury is inflicted on anyone. Or, if some danger threatens the accuser, it matters not since he risked the danger of his own accord: whereas it is different with the accused, who incurs the danger against his will.

* Can. *Quisquis,* caus. xi., qu. 3, cap. *Falsidicus ;* cf. Isidor. *Sentent.* iii. 55.

*Reply Obj.* 1. Augustine is speaking of concealment of the truth in a case when a man is not compelled by his superior's authority to declare the truth, and when such concealment is not specially injurious to any person.

*Reply Obj.* 2. A man should by no means give evidence on matters secretly committed to him in confession, because he knows such things, not as man but as God's minister: and the sacrament is more binding than any human precept. But as regards matters committed to man in some other way under secrecy, we must make a distinction. Sometimes they are of such a nature that one is bound to make them known as soon as they come to our knowledge, for instance if they conduce to the spiritual or corporal corruption of the community, or to some grave personal injury, in short any like matter that a man is bound to make known either by giving evidence or by denouncing it. Against such a duty a man cannot be obliged to act on the plea that the matter is committed to him under secrecy, for he would break the faith he owes to another.—On the other hand sometimes they are such as one is not bound to make known, so that one may be under obligation not to do so on account of their being committed to one under secrecy. In such a case one is by no means bound to make them known, even if the superior should command; because to keep faith is of natural right, and a man cannot be commanded to do what is contrary to natural right.

*Reply Obj.* 3. It is unbecoming for ministers of the altar to slay a man or to co-operate in his slaying, as stated above (Q. LXIV., A. 4); hence according to the order of justice they cannot be compelled to give evidence when a man is on trial for his life.

## SECOND ARTICLE.

### WHETHER THE EVIDENCE OF TWO OR THREE PERSONS SUFFICES ?

*We proceed thus to the Second Article :—*

*Objection* 1. It would seem that the evidence of two or three persons is not sufficient. For judgment requires certitude.

Now certitude of the truth is not obtained by the assertions of two or three witnesses, for we read that Naboth was unjustly condemned on the evidence of two witnesses (3 Kings xxi.). Therefore the evidence of two or three witnesses does not suffice.

*Obj.* 2. Further, In order for evidence to be credible it must agree. But frequently the evidence of two or three disagrees in some point. Therefore it is of no use for proving the truth in court.

*Obj.* 3. Further, It is laid down (Decret. II., qu. iv., can. *Præsul*): *A bishop shall not be condemned save on the evidence of seventy-two witnesses; nor a cardinal priest of the Roman Church, unless there be sixty-four witnesses; nor a cardinal deacon of the Roman Church, unless there be twenty-seven witnesses; nor a subdeacon, an acolyte, an exorcist, a reader or a door-keeper without seven witnesses.* Now the sin of one who is of higher dignity is more grievous, and consequently should be treated more severely. Therefore neither is the evidence of two or three witnesses sufficient for the condemnation of other persons.

*On the contrary,* It is written (Deut. xvii. 6): *By the mouth of two or three witnesses shall he die that is to be slain,* and further on (xix. 15): *In the mouth of two or three witnesses every word shall stand.*

*I answer that,* According to the Philosopher (*Ethic.* i. 3), *we must not expect to find certitude equally in every matter.* For in human acts, on which judgments are passed and evidence required, it is impossible to have demonstrative certitude, because they are about things contingent and variable. Hence the certitude of probability suffices, such as may reach the truth in the greater number of cases, although it fail in the minority. Now it is probable that the assertion of several witnesses contains the truth rather than the assertion of one: and since the accused is the only one who denies, while several witnesses affirm the same as the prosecutor, it is reasonably established both by Divine and by human law, that the assertion of several witnesses should be upheld. Now all multitude is comprised of three elements, the beginning, the middle and the end. Wherefore, according to the Philosopher (*De Cælo* i. 1), *we reckon ' all ' and ' whole ' to consist of three parts.* Now we have a triple voucher when two agree with the prosecutor: hence two witnesses are required; or for the sake of greater certitude, three, which is the perfect number. Wherefore it is written (Eccles. iv. 12): *A threefold cord is not easily broken :* and Augustine, commenting on Jo. viii. 17, *The testimony of two men is true,* says (*Tract.* xxxvi.) that *there is here a mystery by which we are given to understand that Trinity wherein is perpetual stability of truth.*

*Reply Obj.* 1. No matter how great a number of witnesses may be determined, their evidence might sometimes be unjust, since it is written (Exod. xxiii. 2): *Thou shalt not follow the multitude to do evil.* And yet the fact that in so many it is not possible to have certitude without fear of error, is no reason why we should reject the certitude which can probably be had through two or three witnesses, as stated above.

*Reply Obj.* 2. If the witnesses disagree in certain principal circumstances which change the substance of the fact, for instance in time, place, or persons, which are chiefly in question, their evidence is of no weight, because if they disagree in such things, each one would seem to be giving distinct evidence and to be speaking of different facts. For instance, if one say that a certain thing happened at such and such a time or place, while another says it happened at another time or place, they seem not to be speaking of the same event. The evidence is not weakened if one witness says that he does not remember, while the other attests to a determinate time or place. And if on such points as these the witnesses for prosecution and defence disagree altogether, and if they be equal in number on either side, and of equal standing, the accused should have the benefit of the doubt, because the judge ought to be more inclined to acquit than to condemn, except perhaps in favourable suits, such as a pleading for liberty and the like. If, however, the witnesses for the same side disagree, the judge ought to use his own discretion in discerning which side to favour, by considering either the number of witnesses, or their standing, or the favourableness of the suit, or the nature of the business and of the evidence.

Much more ought the evidence of one witness to be rejected if he contradict himself when questioned about what he has seen and about what he knows; not, however, if he contradict himself when questioned about matters of opinion and report, since he may be moved to answer differently according to the different things he has seen and heard.

On the other hand if there be discrepancy of evidence in circumstances not touching the substance of the fact, for instance, whether the weather were cloudy or fine, whether the house were painted or not, or suchlike matters, such discrepancy does not weaken the evidence, because men are not wont to take much notice of such things, wherefore they easily forget them. Indeed, a discrepancy of this kind renders the evidence more credible, as Chrysostom states (*Hom.* i. *in Matth.*), because if the witnesses agreed in every point, even in the minutest details, they would seem to have conspired together to say the same thing: but this must be left to the prudent discernment of the judge.

*Reply Obj.* 3. This passage refers specially to the bishops, priests, deacons and clerics of the Roman Church, on account of its dignity: and this for three reasons. First because in that Church those men ought to be promoted whose sanctity makes their evidence of more weight than that of many witnesses. Secondly, because those who have to judge other men, often have many opponents on account of their justice, wherefore those who give evidence against them should not be believed indiscriminately, unless they be very numerous. Thirdly, because the condemnation of any one of them would detract in public opinion from the dignity and authority of that Church, a result which would be more fraught with danger than if one were to tolerate a sinner in that same Church, unless he were very notorious and manifest, so that a grave scandal would arise if he were tolerated.

## Third Article.

### WHETHER A MAN'S EVIDENCE CAN BE REJECTED WITHOUT ANY FAULT OF HIS?

*We proceed thus to the Third Article :—*

*Objection* 1. It would seem that a man's evidence ought not to be rejected except on account of some fault. For it is inflicted as a penalty on some that their evidence is inadmissible, as in the case of those who are branded with infamy. Now a penalty must not be inflicted save for a fault. Therefore it would seem that no man's evidence ought to be rejected save on account of a fault.

*Obj.* 2. Further, *Good is to be presumed of every one, unless the contrary appear.*\* Now it pertains to a man's goodness that he should give true evidence. Since therefore there can be no proof of the contrary, unless there be some fault of his, it would seem that no man's evidence should be rejected save for some fault.

*Obj.* 3. Further, No man is rendered unfit for things necessary for salvation except by some sin. But it is necessary for salvation to give true evidence, as stated above (A. 1). Therefore no man should be excluded from giving evidence save for some fault.

*On the contrary,* Gregory says (*Regist.* xiii. 44). *As to the bishop who is said to have been accused by his servants, you are to know that they should by no means have been heard:* which words are embodied in the Decretals (II., qu. 1, can. *Imprimis*).

*I answer that,* As stated above (A. 2), the authority of evidence is not infallible but probable; and consequently the evidence for one side is weakened by whatever strengthens the probability of the other. Now the reliability of a person's evidence is weakened, sometimes indeed on account of some fault of his, as in the case of unbelievers and persons of evil repute, as well as those who are guilty of a public crime and who are not allowed even to accuse; sometimes, without any fault on his part, and this owing either to a defect in the reason, as in the case of children, imbeciles and women, or to personal feeling, as in the case of enemies,

\* Cap. *Dudum, de Præsumpt.*

or persons united by family or household ties, or again owing to some external condition, as in the case of poor people, slaves, and those who are under authority, concerning whom it is to be presumed that they might easily be induced to give evidence against the truth.

Thus it is manifest that a person's evidence may be rejected either with or without some fault of his.

*Reply Obj.* 1. If a person is disqualified from giving evidence this is done as a precaution against false evidence rather than as a punishment. Hence the argument does not prove.

*Reply Obj.* 2. Good is to be presumed of everyone unless the contrary appear, provided this does not threaten injury to another: because, in that case, one ought to be careful not to believe everyone readily, according to 1 Jo. iv. 1: *Believe not every spirit.*

*Reply Obj.* 3. To give evidence is necessary for salvation, provided the witness be competent, and the order of justice observed. Hence nothing hinders certain persons being excused from giving evidence, if they be considered unfit according to law.

## Fourth Article.

### WHETHER IT IS ALWAYS A MORTAL SIN TO GIVE FALSE EVIDENCE ?

*We proceed thus to the Fourth Article :—*

*Objection* 1. It would seem that it is not always a mortal sin to give false evidence. For a person may happen to give false evidence, through ignorance of fact. Now such ignorance excuses from mortal sin. Therefore the giving of false evidence is not always a mortal sin.

*Obj.* 2. Further, A lie that benefits someone and hurts no man is officious, and this is not a mortal sin. Now sometimes a lie of this kind occurs in false evidence, as when a person gives false evidence in order to save a man from death, or from an unjust sentence which threatens him through other false witnesses or a perverse judge. Therefore in such cases it is not a mortal sin to give false evidence.

*Obj.* 3. Further, A witness is required to take an oath in

order that he may fear to commit a mortal sin of perjury. But this would not be necessary, if it were already a mortal sin to give false evidence. Therefore the giving of false evidence is not always mortal sin.

*On the contrary,* It is written (Prov. xix. 5): *A false witness shall not be unpunished.*

*I answer that,* False evidence has a threefold deformity. The first is owing to perjury, since witnesses are admitted only on oath, and on this count it is always a mortal sin. Secondly, owing to the violation of justice, and on this account it is a mortal sin generically, even as any kind of injustice. Hence the prohibition of false evidence by the precept of the decalogue is expressed in this form, when it is said (Exod. xx. 16), *Thou shalt not bear false witness against thy neighbour.* For one does nothing against a man by preventing him from doing someone an injury, but only by taking away his justice. Thirdly, owing to the falsehood itself, by reason of which every lie is a sin: on this account, the giving of false evidence is not always a mortal sin.

*Reply Obj.* 1. In giving evidence a man ought not to affirm as certain, as though he knew it, that about which he is not certain: and he should confess his doubt in doubtful terms, and that which he is certain about, in terms of certainty. Owing however to the frailty of the human memory, a man sometimes thinks he is certain about something that is not true; and then if after thinking over the matter with due care he deems himself certain about that false thing, he does not sin mortally if he asserts it, because the evidence which he gives is not directly and intentionally, but accidentally contrary to what he intends.

*Reply Obj.* 2. An unjust judgment is not a judgment, wherefore the false evidence given in an unjust judgment, in order to prevent injustice is not a mortal sin by virtue of the judgment, but only by reason of the oath violated.

*Reply Obj.* 3. Men abhor chiefly those sins that are against God, as being most grievous; and among them is perjury: whereas they do not abhor so much sins against their neighbour. Consequently, for the greater certitude of evidence, the witness is required to take an oath.

# QUESTION LXXI.

## OF INJUSTICE IN JUDGMENT ON THE PART OF COUNSEL.

### (*In Four Articles.*)

WE must now consider the injustice which takes place in judgment on the part of counsel, and under this head there are four points of inquiry: (1) Whether an advocate is bound to defend the suits of the poor? (2) Whether certain persons should be prohibited from exercising the office of advocate? (3) Whether an advocate sins by defending an unjust cause? (4) Whether he sins if he accept a fee for defending a suit?

## FIRST ARTICLE

### WHETHER AN ADVOCATE IS BOUND TO DEFEND THE SUITS OF THE POOR?

*We proceed thus to the First Article :—*

*Objection* 1. It would seem that an advocate is bound to defend the suits of the poor. For it is written (Exod. xxiii. 5): *If thou see the ass of him that hateth thee lie underneath his burden, thou shalt not pass by, but shall lift him up with him.* Now no less a danger threatens the poor man whose suit is being unjustly prejudiced, than if his ass were to lie underneath its burden. Therefore an advocate is bound to defend the suits of the poor.

*Obj.* 2. Further, Gregory says in a homily (ix. *in Ev.*): *Let him that hath understanding beware lest he withhold his knowledge ; let him that hath abundance of wealth watch lest he slacken his merciful bounty ; let him who is a servant to art share his skill with his neighbour ; let him who has an oppor-*

*tunity of speaking with the wealthy plead the cause of the poor :
for the slightest gift you have received will be reputed a talent.*
Now every man is bound, not to hide but faithfully to dispense the talent committed to him; as evidenced by the
punishment inflicted on the servant who hid his talent
(Matth. xxv. 30).   Therefore an advocate is bound to plead
for the poor.

*Obj.* 3. Further, The precept about performing works of
mercy, being affirmative, is binding according to time and
place, and this is chiefly in cases of need.   Now it seems to be
a case of need when the suit of a poor man is being prejudiced.
Therefore it seems that in such a case an advocate is bound to
defend the poor man's suit.

*On the contrary,* He that lacks food is no less in need than
he that lacks an advocate.   Yet he that is able to give food
is not always bound to feed the needy.   Therefore neither
is an advocate always bound to defend the suits of the poor.

*I answer that,* Since defence of the poor man's suit belongs
to the works of mercy, the answer to this inquiry is the same
as the one given above with regard to the other works of
mercy (Q. XXXII., AA. 5, 9).   Now no man is sufficient to
bestow a work of mercy on all those who need it.   Wherefore, as Augustine says (*De Doct. Christ.* i. 28), *since one cannot
do good to all, we ought to consider those chiefly who by reason
of place, time, or any other circumstance, by a kind of chance
are more closely united to us.*   He says *by reason of place,*
because one is not bound to search throughout the world
for the needy that one may succour them; and it suffices
to do works of mercy to those one meets with.   Hence it is
written (Exod. xxiii. 4): *If thou meet thy enemy's ass going
astray, bring it back to him.*   He says also *by reason of time,*
because one is not bound to provide for the future needs of
others, and it suffices to succour present needs.   Hence it is
written (1 Jo. iii. 17): *He that . . . shall see his brother in
need, and shall put up his bowels from him, how doth the
charity of God abide in him ?*   Lastly he says, *or any other
circumstance,* because one ought to show kindness to those
especially who are by any tie whatever united to us, accord-

ing to 1 Tim. v. 8, *If any man have not care of his own, and especially of those of his house, he hath denied the faith and is worse than an infidel.*

It may happen however that these circumstances concur, and then we have to consider whether this particular man stands in such a need that it is not easy to see how he can be succoured otherwise, and then one is bound to bestow the work of mercy on him. If, however, it is easy to see how he can be otherwise succoured, either by himself, or by some other person still more closely united to him, or in a better position to help him, one is not bound so strictly to help the one in need that it would be a sin not to do so: although it would be praiseworthy to do so where one is not bound to. Therefore an advocate is not always bound to defend the suits of the poor, but only when the aforesaid circumstances concur, else he would have to put aside all other business, and occupy himself entirely in defending the suits of poor people. The same applies to a physician with regard to attendance on the sick.

*Reply Obj.* 1. So long as the ass lies under the burden, there is no means of help in this case, unless those who are passing along come to the man's aid, and therefore they are bound to help. But they would not be so bound if help were possible from another quarter.

*Reply Obj.* 2. A man is bound to make good use of the talent bestowed on him, according to the opportunities afforded by time, place, and other circumstances, as stated above.

*Reply Obj.* 3. Not every need is such that it is one's duty to remedy it, but only such as we have stated above.

## SECOND ARTICLE.

### WHETHER IT IS FITTING THAT THE LAW SHOULD DEBAR CERTAIN PERSONS FROM THE OFFICE OF ADVOCATE?

*We proceed thus to the Second Article :—*

*Objection* 1. It would seem unfitting for the law to debar certain persons from the office of advocate. For no man should be debarred from doing works of mercy. Now it belongs to the works of mercy to defend a man's suit, as stated above (A. 1). Therefore no man should be debarred from this office.

*Obj.* 2. Further, Contrary causes have not, seemingly, the same effect. Now to be busy with Divine things and to be busy about sin are contrary to one another. Therefore it is unfitting that some should be debarred from the office of advocate, on account of religion, as monks and clerics, while others are debarred on account of sin, as persons of ill repute and heretics.

*Obj.* 3. Further, A man should love his neighbour as himself. Now it is a duty of love for an advocate to plead a person's cause. Therefore it is unfitting that certain persons should be debarred from pleading the cause of others, while they are allowed to advocate their own cause.

*On the contrary,* According to Decret. III., qu. vii., can. *Infames*, many persons are debarred from the office of advocate.

*I answer that,* In two ways a person is debarred from performing a certain act: first because it is impossible to him, secondly because it is unbecoming to him: but, whereas the man to whom a certain act is impossible, is absolutely debarred from performing it, he to whom an act is unbecoming is not debarred altogether, since necessity may do away with its unbecomingness. Accordingly some are debarred from the office of advocate because it is impossible to them through lack of sense,—either interior, as in the case of madmen and minors,—or exterior, as in the case of the deaf and dumb. For an advocate needs to have both interior skill so that he may be able to prove the justice of the cause he defends, and also speech and hearing, that he may speak and hear what is said to him. Consequently those who are defective in these points, are altogether debarred from being advocates either in their own or in another's cause. The becomingness of exercising this office is removed in two ways. First, through a man being engaged in higher things. Wherefore it is unfitting that monks or priests should be advocates in any cause whatever, or that clerics should plead in a secular court, because such persons are engaged in Divine things.  Secondly, on account of some personal defect, either of body (for instance a blind man whose attendance in a court of justice would be unbecoming) or of soul, for it ill becomes one who has disdained to be just himself, to plead for the justice of another.  Wherefore it is unbecoming that persons of ill repute, unbelievers, and those who have been convicted of grievous crimes should be advocates.  Nevertheless this unbecomingness is outweighed by necessity: and for this reason such persons can plead either their own cause or that of persons closely connected with them.  Moreover, clerics can be advocates in the cause of their own church, and monks in the cause of their own monastery, if the abbot direct them to do so.

*Reply Obj.* 1. Certain persons are sometimes debarred by unbecomingness, and others by inability from performing works of mercy: for not all the works of mercy are becoming to all persons: thus it ill becomes a fool to give counsel, or the ignorant to teach.

*Reply Obj.* 2. Just as virtue is destroyed by *too much* and *too little*, so does a person become incompetent by *more* and *less*.  For this reason some, like religious and clerics, are debarred from pleading in causes, because they are above such an office; and others because they are less than competent to exercise it, such as persons of ill repute and unbelievers.

*Reply Obj.* 3. The necessity of pleading the causes of others is not so pressing as the necessity of pleading one's own cause, because others are able to help themselves otherwise: hence the comparison fails.

## THIRD ARTICLE.

### WHETHER AN ADVOCATE SINS BY DEFENDING AN UNJUST CAUSE ?

*We proceed thus to the Third Article :—*

*Objection* 1. It would seem that an advocate does not sin by defending an unjust cause.  For just as a physician proves his skill by healing a desperate disease, so does an advocate prove his skill, if he can defend an unjust cause. Now a physician is praised if he heals a desperate malady. Therefore an advocate also commits no sin, but ought to be praised, if he defends an unjust cause.

*Obj.* 2. Further, It is always lawful to desist from committing a sin. Yet an advocate is punished if he throws up his brief (Decret. II., qu. iii., can. *Si quem pœnit.*). Therefore an advocate does not sin by defending an unjust cause, when once he has undertaken its defence.

*Obj.* 3. Further, It would seem to be a greater sin for an advocate to use unjust means in defence of a just cause (e.g. by producing false witnesses, or alleging false laws), than to defend an unjust cause, since the former is a sin against the form, the latter against the matter of justice. Yet it is seemingly lawful for an advocate to make use of such underhand means, even as it is lawful for a soldier to lay ambushes in a battle. Therefore it would seem that an advocate does not sin by defending an unjust cause.

*On the contrary*, It is said (2 Paralip. xix. 2): *Thou helpesı the ungodly . . . and therefore thou didst deserve . . . the wrath of the Lord.* Now an advocate by defending an unjust cause, helps the ungodly. Therefore he sins and deserves the wrath of the Lord.

*I answer that*, It is unlawful to co-operate in an evil deed, by counselling, helping, or in any way consenting, because to counsel or assist an action is, in a way, to do it, and the Apostle says (Rom. i. 32) that *they . . . are worthy of death, not only they that do* a sin, *but they also that consent to them that do* it. Hence it was stated above (Q. LXII., A. 7), that all such are bound to restitution. Now it is evident that an advocate provides both assistance and counsel to the party for whom he pleads. Wherefore, if knowingly he defends an unjust cause, without doubt he sins grievously, and is bound to restitution of the loss unjustly incurred by the other party by reason of the assistance he has provided. If, however, he defends an unjust cause unknowingly, thinking it just, he is to be excused according to the measure in which ignorance is excusable.

*Reply Obj.* 1. The physician injures no man by undertaking to heal a desperate malady, whereas the advocate who accepts service in an unjust cause, unjustly injures the party against whom he pleads unjustly. Hence the comparison fails. For though he may seem to deserve praise for showing skill in his art, nevertheless he sins by reason of injustice in his will, since he abuses his art for an evil end.

*Reply Obj.* 2. If an advocate believes from the outset that the cause is just, and discovers afterwards while the case is proceeding that it is unjust, he ought not to throw up his brief in such a way as to help the other side, or so as to reveal the secrets of his client to the other party. But he can and must give up the case, or induce his client to give way, or make some compromise without prejudice to the opposing party.

*Reply Obj.* 3. As stated above (Q. XL., A. 3), it is lawful for a soldier, or a general to lay ambushes in a just war, by prudently concealing what he has a mind to do, but not by means of fraudulent falsehoods, since we should keep faith even with a foe, as Tully says (*De Offic.* iii. 29). Hence it is lawful for an advocate, in defending his case, prudently to conceal whatever might hinder its happy issue, but it is unlawful for him to employ any kind of falsehood.

### Fourth Article.

#### WHETHER IT IS LAWFUL FOR AN ADVOCATE TO TAKE A FEE FOR PLEADING?

*We proceed thus to the Fourth Article :—*

*Objection* 1. It would seem unlawful for an advocate to take a fee for pleading. Works of mercy should not be done with a view to human remuneration, according to Luke xiv. 12, *When thou makest a dinner or a supper, call not thy friends, . . . nor thy neighbours who are rich: lest perhaps they also invite thee again, and a recompense be made to thee.* Now it is a work of mercy to plead another's cause, as stated above (A. 1). Therefore it is not lawful for an advocate to take payment in money for pleading.

*Obj.* 2. Further, Spiritual things are not to be bartered with temporal things. But pleading a person's cause seems to be a spiritual good since it consists in using one's knowledge of law. Therefore it is not lawful for an advocate to take a fee for pleading.

*Obj.* 3. Further, Just as the person of the advocate concurs towards the pronouncement of the verdict, so do the persons of the judge and of the witness. Now, according to Augustine (*Ep.* cliii. *ad Macedon.*), *the judge should not sell a just sentence, nor the witness true evidence.* Therefore neither can an advocate sell a just pleading.

*On the contrary,* Augustine says (*ibid.*) that *an advocate may lawfully sell his pleading, and a lawyer his advice.*

*I answer that,* A man may justly receive payment for granting what he is not bound to grant. Now it is evident that an advocate is not always bound to consent to plead, or to give advice in other people's causes. Wherefore, if he sell his pleading or advice, he does not act against justice. The same applies to the physician who attends on a sick person to heal him, and to all like persons; provided, however, they take a moderate fee, with due consideration for persons, for the matter in hand, for the labour entailed, and for the custom of the country. If, however, they wickedly extort an immoderate fee, they sin against justice. Hence Augustine says (*ibid.*) that *it is customary to demand from them restitution of what they have extorted by a wicked excess, but not what has been given to them in accordance with a commendable custom.*

*Reply Obj.* 1. Man is not bound to do gratuitously whatever he can do from motives of mercy: else no man could lawfully sell anything, since anything may be given from motives of mercy. But when a man does give a thing out of mercy, he should seek, not a human, but a Divine reward. In like manner an advocate, when he mercifully pleads the cause of a poor man, should have in view not a human but a Divine meed; and yet he is not always bound to give his services gratuitously.

*Reply Obj.* 2. Though knowledge of law is something

spiritual, the use of that knowledge is accomplished by the work of the body: hence it is lawful to take money in payment of that use, else no craftsman would be allowed to make profit by his art.

*Reply Obj.* 3. The judge and witnesses are common to either party, since the judge is bound to pronounce a just verdict, and the witness to give true evidence.   Now justice and truth do not incline to one side rather than to the other: and consequently judges receive out of the public funds a fixed pay for their labour; and witnesses receive their expenses (not as payment for giving evidence, but as a fee for their labour) either from both parties or from the party by whom they are adduced, because no man *serveth as a soldier at any time at his own charge* (1 Cor. ix. 7).*   On the other hand an advocate defends one party only, and so he may lawfully accept a fee from the party he assists.

* Vulg.,—*Who serveth as a soldier*, etc.?

# QUESTION LXXII.

## OF REVILING.

### (*In Four Articles.*)

WE must now consider injuries inflicted by words uttered extrajudicially. We shall consider (1) reviling, (2) back-biting, (3) tale bearing, (4) derision, (5) cursing.

Under the first head there are four points of inquiry: (1) What is reviling? (2) Whether every reviling is a mortal sin? (3) Whether one ought to check revilers? (4) Of the origin of reviling.

## FIRST ARTICLE.

### WHETHER REVILING CONSISTS IN WORDS?

*We proceed thus to the First Article :—*

*Objection* 1. It would seem that reviling does not consist in words. Reviling implies some injury inflicted on one's neighbour, since it is a kind of injustice. But words seem to inflict no injury on one's neighbour, neither in his person, nor in his belongings. Therefore reviling does not consist in words.

*Obj.* 2. Further, Reviling seems to imply dishonour. But a man can be dishonoured or slighted by deeds more than by words. Therefore it seems that reviling consists, not in words but in deeds.

*Obj.* 3. Further, A dishonour inflicted by words is called a railing or a taunt. But reviling seems to differ from railing or taunt. Therefore reviling does not consist in words.

*On the contrary*, Nothing, save words, is perceived by the

hearing.   Now reviling is perceived by the hearing according to Jerem. xx. 10, *I heard reviling* (Douay,—*contumelies*) *on every side.*   Therefore reviling consists in words.

*I answer that,* Reviling denotes the dishonouring of a person, and this happens in two ways: for since honour results from excellence, one person dishonours another, first, by depriving him of the excellence for which he is honoured. This is done by sins of deed, whereof we have spoken above (QQ. LXIV., *seqq.*).   Secondly, when a man publishes something against another's honour, thus bringing it to the knowledge of the latter and of other men. This is reviling properly so called, and is done by some kind of signs.   Now, according to Augustine (*De Doctr. Christ.* ii. 3), *compared with words all other signs are very few, for words have obtained the chief place among men for the purpose of expressing whatever the mind conceives.*   Hence reviling, properly speaking, consists in words: wherefore, Isidore says (*Etym.* x.) that a reviler (*contumeliosus*) *is hasty and bursts out* (*tumet*) *in injurious words.*   Since, however, things are also signified by deeds, which on this account have the same significance as words, it follows that reviling in a wider sense extends also to deeds. Wherefore a gloss on Rom. i. 30, *contumelious, proud,* says: *The contumelious are those who by word or deed revile and shame others.*

*Reply Obj.* 1. Our words, if we consider them in their essence, i.e. as audible sounds, injure no man, except perhaps by jarring on the ear, as when a person speaks too loud. But, considered as signs conveying something to the knowledge of others, they may do many kinds of harm.   Such is the harm done to a man to the detriment of his honour, or of the respect due to him from others.   Hence the reviling is greater if one man reproach another in the presence of many: and yet there may still be reviling if he reproach him by himself, in so far as the speaker acts unjustly against the respect due to the hearer.

*Reply Obj.* 2. One man slights another by deeds in so far as such deeds cause or signify that which is against that

other man's honour.   In the former case it is not a matter of
reviling but of some other kind of injustice, of which we have
spoken above (QQ. LXIV., LXV., LXVI.): whereas in the
latter case there is reviling, in so far as deeds have the
significant force of words.

*Reply Obj.* 3.  Railing and taunts consist in words, even as
reviling, because by all of them a man's faults are exposed
to the detriment of his honour.  Such faults are of three
kinds.  First, there is the fault of guilt, which is exposed by
*reviling* words.  Secondly, there is the fault of both guilt
and punishment, which is exposed by *taunts* (*convicium*),
because *vice* is commonly spoken of in connection with not
only the soul but also the body.  Hence if one man says
spitefully to another that he is blind, he taunts but does not
revile him: whereas if one man calls another a thief, he not
only taunts but also reviles him.  Thirdly, a man reproaches
another for his inferiority or indigence, so as to lessen the
honour due to him for any kind of excellence.  This is done
by *upbraiding* words, and properly speaking, occurs when
one spitefully reminds a man that one has succoured him
when he was in need.  Hence it is written (Ecclus. xx. 15):
*He will give a few things and upbraid much.*  Nevertheless
these terms are sometimes employed one for the other.

## SECOND ARTICLE.

### WHETHER REVILING OR RAILING IS A MORTAL SIN?

*We proceed thus to the Second Article :—*

*Objection* 1.  It would seem that reviling or railing is not a
mortal sin.  For no mortal sin is an act of virtue.  Now
railing is the act of a virtue, viz. of wittiness ($\epsilon\dot{v}\tau\rho\alpha\pi\epsilon\lambda\acute{\iota}a$),*
to which it pertains to rail well, according to the Philosopher
(*Ethic.* iv. 8).  Therefore railing or reviling is not a mortal sin.

*Obj.* 2.  Further, Mortal sin is not to be found in perfect
men; and yet these sometimes give utterance to railing or
reviling.  Thus the Apostle says (Gal. iii. 1): *O senseless
Galatians!*, and Our Lord said (Luke xxiv. 25): *O foolish,*

* Cf. I.-II., Q. LX., A. 5.

*and slow of heart to believe!* Therefore railing or reviling is not a mortal sin.

*Obj.* 3. Further, Although that which is a venial sin by reason of its genus may become mortal, that which is mortal by reason of its genus cannot become venial, as stated above (I.-II., Q. LXXXVIII., AA. 4, 6). Hence if by reason of its genus it were a mortal sin to give utterance to railing or reviling, it would follow that it is always a mortal sin. But this is apparently untrue, as may be seen in the case of one who utters a reviling word indeliberately or through slight anger. Therefore reviling or railing is not a mortal sin, by reason of its genus.

*On the contrary*, Nothing but mortal sin deserves the eternal punishment of hell. Now railing or reviling deserves the punishment of hell, according to Matth. v. 22, *Whosoever shall say to his brother . . . Thou fool, shall be in danger of hell fire.* Therefore railing or reviling is a mortal sin.

*I answer that,* As stated above (A. 1), words are injurious to other persons, not as sounds, but as signs, and this signification depends on the speaker's inward intention. Hence, in sins of word, it seems that we ought to consider with what intention the words are uttered. Since then railing or reviling essentially denotes a dishonouring, if the intention of the utterer is to dishonour the other man, this is properly and essentially to give utterance to railing or reviling: and this is a mortal sin no less than theft or robbery, since a man loves his honour no less than his possessions. If, on the other hand, a man says to another a railing or reviling word, yet with the intention, not of dishonouring him, but rather perhaps of correcting him or with some like purpose, he utters a railing or reviling not formally and essentially, but accidentally and materially, in so far to wit as he says that which might be a railing or reviling. Hence this may be sometimes a venial sin, and sometimes without any sin at all. Nevertheless there is need of discretion in such matters, and one should use such words with moderation, because the railing might be so grave that being uttered inconsiderately it might dishonour the person against whom it is uttered.   In such a case a man might commit a mortal sin, even though he did not intend to dishonour the other man: just as were a man incautiously to injure grievously another by striking him in fun, he would not be without blame.

*Reply Obj.* 1. It belongs to wittiness to utter some slight mockery, not with intent to dishonour or pain the person who is the object of the mockery, but rather with intent to please and amuse: and this may be without sin, if the due circumstances be observed.   On the other hand if a man does not shrink from inflicting pain on the object of his witty mockery, so long as he makes others laugh, this is sinful, as stated in the passage quoted.

*Reply Obj.* 2. Just as it is lawful to strike a person, or damnify him in his belongings for the purpose of correction, so too, for the purpose of correction, may one say a mocking word to a person whom one has to correct.   It is thus that Our Lord called the disciples *foolish*, and the Apostle called the Galatians *senseless*.   Yet, as Augustine says (*De Serm. Dom. in Monte* ii. 19), *seldom and only when it is very necessary should we have recourse to invectives, and then so as to urge God's service, not our own.*

*Reply Obj.* 3. Since the sin of railing or reviling depends on the intention of the utterer, it may happen to be a venial sin, if it be a slight railing that does not inflict much dishonour on a man, and be uttered through lightness of heart or some slight anger, without the fixed purpose of dishonouring him, for instance when one intends by such a word to give but little pain.

### Third Article.

#### WHETHER ONE OUGHT TO SUFFER ONESELF TO BE REVILED ?

*We proceed thus to the Third Article :—*

*Objection* 1. It would seem that one ought not to suffer oneself to be reviled.   For he that suffers himself to be reviled, encourages the reviler.   But one ought not to do this.

Therefore one ought not to suffer oneself to be reviled, but rather reply to the reviler.

*Obj.* 2. Further, One ought to love oneself more than another.   Now one ought not to suffer another to be reviled, wherefore it is written (Prov. xxvi. 10): *He that putteth a fool to silence appeaseth anger.*   Therefore neither should one suffer oneself to be reviled.

*Obj.* 3. Further, A man is not allowed to revenge himself, for it is said: *Vengeance belongeth to Me, I will repay.** Now by submitting to be reviled a man revenges himself, according to Chrysostom (*Hom.* xxii. *in Ep. ad Rom.*): *If thou wilt be revenged, be silent; thou hast dealt him a fatal blow.* Therefore one ought not by silence to submit to reviling words, but rather answer back.

*On the contrary*, It is written (Ps. xxxvii. 13): *They that sought evils to me spoke vain things*, and afterwards (*verse* 14) he says: *But I as a deaf man, heard not; and as a dumb man not opening his mouth.*

*I answer that*, Just as we need patience in things done against us, so do we need it in those said against us.   Now the precepts of patience in those things done against us refer to the preparedness of the mind, according to Augustine's (*De Serm. Dom. in Monte* i. 19) exposition on Our Lord's precept, *If one strike thee on thy right cheek, turn to him also the other :*† that is to say, a man ought to be prepared to do so if necessary.   But he is not always bound to do this actually: since not even did Our Lord do so, for when He received a blow, He said: *Why strikest thou Me ?* (Jo. xviii. 23).   Consequently the same applies to the reviling words that are said against us.   For we are bound to hold our minds prepared to submit to be reviled, if it should be expedient.   Nevertheless it sometimes behoves us to withstand against being reviled, and this chiefly for two reasons. First, for the good of the reviler; namely, that his daring may be checked, and that he may not repeat the attempt, according to Prov. xxvi. 5, *Answer a fool according to his*

* Heb. x. 30.
† The words as quoted by S. Thomas are a blending of Matth. v. 39 and Luke vi. 29.

*folly, lest he imagine himself to be wise.* Secondly, for the good of many who would be prevented from progressing in virtue on account of our being reviled.  Hence Gregory says (*Hom.* ix. *super Ezech.*): *Those who are so placed that their life should be an example to others, ought, if possible to silence their detracters, lest their preaching be not heard by those who could have heard it, and they continue their evil conduct through contempt of a good life.*

*Reply Obj.* 1. The daring of the railing reviler should be checked with moderation, i.e. as a duty of charity, and not through lust for one's own honour.  Hence it is written (Prov. xxvi. 4): *Answer not a fool according to his folly, lest thou be like him.*

*Reply Obj.* 2. When one man prevents another from being reviled there is not the danger of lust for one's own honour as there is when a man defends himself from being reviled: indeed rather would it seem to proceed from a sense of charity.

*Reply Obj.* 3. It would be an act of revenge to keep silence with the intention of provoking the reviler to anger, but it would be praiseworthy to be silent, in order to give place to anger.  Hence it is written (Ecclus. viii. 4): *Strive not with a man that is full of tongue, and heap not wood upon his fire.*

## FOURTH ARTICLE.

### WHETHER REVILING ARISES FROM ANGER ?

*We proceed thus to the Fourth Article :—*

*Objection* 1. It would seem that reviling does not arise from anger.  For it is written (Prov. xi. 2): *Where pride is, there shall also be reviling* (Douay,—*reproach*).  But anger is a vice distinct from pride.  Therefore reviling does not arise from anger.

*Obj.* 2. Further, It is written (Prov. xx. 3): *All fools are meddling with revilings* (Douay,—*reproaches*).  Now folly is a vice opposed to wisdom, as stated above (Q. XLVI., A. 1); whereas anger is opposed to meekness.  Therefore reviling does not arise from anger.

*Obj.* 3. Further, No sin is diminished by its cause. But the sin of reviling is diminished if one gives vent to it through anger: for it is a more grievous sin to revile out of hatred than out of anger. Therefore reviling does not arise from anger.

*On the contrary,* Gregory says (*Moral.* xxxi. 45) that *anger gives rise to revilings.*

*I answer that,* While one sin may arise from various causes, it is nevertheless said to have its source chiefly in that one from which it is wont to arise most frequently, through being closely connected with its end. Now reviling is closely connected with anger's end, which is revenge: since the easiest way for the angry man to take revenge on another is to revile him. Therefore reviling arises chiefly from anger.

*Reply Obj.* 1. Reviling is not directed to the end of pride which is excellency. Hence reviling does not arise directly from pride. Nevertheless pride disposes a man to revile, in so far as those who think themselves to excel, are more prone to despise others and inflict injuries on them, because they are more easily angered, through deeming it an affront to themselves whenever anything is done against their will.

*Reply Obj.* 2. According to the Philosopher (*Ethic.* vii. 6) *anger listens imperfectly to reason :* wherefore an angry man suffers a defect of reason, and in this he is like the foolish man. Hence reviling arises from folly on account of the latter's kinship with anger.

*Reply Obj.* 3. According to the Philosopher (*Rhet.* ii. 4) *an angry man seeks an open offence, but he who hates does not worry about this.* Hence reviling which denotes a manifest injury belongs to anger rather than to hatred.

# QUESTION LXXIII.

## OF BACKBITING.*

### (*In Four Articles.*)

WE must now consider backbiting, under which head there are four points of inquiry: (1) What is backbiting? (2) Whether it is a mortal sin? (3) Of its comparison with other sins: (4) Whether it is a sin to listen to backbiting?

### FIRST ARTICLE.

#### WHETHER BACKBITING IS SUITABLY DEFINED AS THE BLACKENING OF ANOTHER'S CHARACTER BY SECRET WORDS?

*We proceed thus to the First Article :—*

*Objection* 1. It would seem that backbiting is not as defined by some,† *the blackening of another's good name by words uttered in secret.* For *secretly* and *openly* are circumstances that do not constitute the species of a sin, because it is accidental to a sin that it be known by many or by few. Now that which does not constitute the species of a sin, does not belong to its essence, and should not be included in its definition. Therefore it does not belong to the essence of backbiting that it should be done by secret words.

*Obj.* 2. Further, The notion of a good name implies something known to the public. If, therefore, a person's good name is blackened by backbiting, this cannot be done by secret words, but by words uttered openly.

*Obj.* 3. Further, To detract is to subtract, or to diminish something already existing. But sometimes a man's good name is blackened, even without subtracting from the truth:

---

* Or detraction.          † Albert the Great, *Sum. Theol.*, II., cxvii.

for instance, when one reveals the crimes which a man has in truth committed. Therefore not every blackening of a good name is backbiting.

*On the contrary*, It is written (Eccles. x. 11): *If a serpent bite in silence, he is nothing better that backbiteth.*

*I answer that*, Just as one man injures another by deed in two ways,—openly, as by robbery or by doing him any kind of violence,—and secretly, as by theft, or by a crafty blow, so again one man injures another by words in two ways;—in one way, openly, and this is done by reviling him, as stated above (Q. LXXII., A. 1),—and in another way secretly, and this is done by backbiting. Now from the fact that one man openly utters words against another man, he would appear to think little of him, so that for this very reason he dishonours him, so that reviling is detrimental to the honour of the person reviled. On the other hand, he that speaks against another secretly, seems to respect rather than slight him, so that he injures directly, not his honour but his good name, in so far as by uttering such words secretly, he, for his own part, causes his hearers to have a bad opinion of the person against whom he speaks. For the backbiter apparently intends and aims at being believed. It is therefore evident that backbiting differs from reviling in two points: first, in the way in which the words are uttered, the reviler speaking openly against someone, and the backbiter secretly; secondly, as to the end in view, i.e. as regards the injury inflicted, the reviler injuring a man's honour, the backbiter injuring his good name.

*Reply Obj.* 1. In involuntary commutations, to which are reduced all injuries inflicted on our neighbour, whether by word or by deed, the kind of sin is differentiated by the circumstances *secretly* and *openly*, because involuntariness itself is diversified by violence and by ignorance, as stated above (Q. LXV., A. 4: I.-II., Q. VI., AA. 5, 8).

*Reply Obj.* 2. The words of a backbiter are said to be secret, not altogether, but in relation to the person of whom they are said, because they are uttered in his absence and without his knowledge. On the other hand, the reviler speaks against a man to his face. Wherefore if a man speaks ill of another in the presence of several, it is a case of backbiting if he be absent, but of reviling if he alone be present: although if a man speak ill of an absent person to one man alone, he destroys his good name not altogether but partly.

*Reply Obj.* 3. A man is said to backbite (*detrahere*) another, not because he detracts from the truth, but because he lessens his good name. This is done sometimes directly, sometimes indirectly. Directly, in four ways: first, by saying that which is false about him; secondly, by stating his sin to be greater than it is; thirdly, by revealing something unknown about him; fourthly, by ascribing his good deeds to a bad intention. Indirectly, this is done either by gainsaying his good, or by maliciously concealing it, or by diminishing it.

### SECOND ARTICLE.

#### WHETHER BACKBITING IS A MORTAL SIN?

*We proceed thus to the Second Article :—*

*Objection* 1. It would seem that backbiting is not a mortal sin. For no act of virtue is a mortal sin. Now, to reveal an unknown sin, which pertains to backbiting, as stated above (A. 1, *ad* 3) is an act of the virtue of charity, whereby a man denounces his brother's sin in order that he may amend: or else it is an act of justice, whereby a man accuses his brother. Therefore backbiting is not a mortal sin.

*Obj.* 2. Further, A gloss on Prov. xxiv. 21, *Have nothing to do with detracters*, says: *The whole human race is in peril from this vice*. But no mortal sin is to be found in the whole of mankind, since many refrain from mortal sin: whereas they are venial sins that are found in all. Therefore backbiting is a venial sin.

*Obj.* 3. Further, Augustine in a homily *on the Fire of Purgatory** reckons it a slight sin *to speak ill without hesitation or forethought*. But this pertains to backbiting. Therefore backbiting is a venial sin.

*On the contrary*, It is written (Rom. i. 30): *Backbiters*,

* *Serm.* civ. in the appendix to St. Augustine's works.

*hateful to God*, which epithet, according to a gloss, is inserted, *lest it be deemed a slight sin because it consists in words.*

*I answer that,* As stated above (Q. LXXII., A. 2), sins of word should be judged chiefly from the intention of the speaker. Now backbiting by its very nature aims at blackening a man's good name. Wherefore, properly speaking, to backbite is to speak ill of an absent person in order to blacken his good name. Now it is a very grave matter to blacken a man's good name, because of all temporal things a man's good name seems the most precious, since for lack of it he is hindered from doing many things well. For this reason it is written (Ecclus. xli. 15): *Take care of a good name, for this shall continue with thee, more than a thousand treasures precious and great.* Therefore backbiting, properly speaking, is a mortal sin. Nevertheless it happens sometimes that a man utters words, whereby someone's good name is tarnished, and yet he does not intend this, but something else. This is not backbiting strictly and formally speaking, but only materially and accidentally as it were. And if such defamatory words be uttered for the sake of some necessary good, and with attention to the due circumstances, it is not a sin and cannot be called backbiting. But if they be uttered out of lightness of heart or for some unnecessary motive, it is not a mortal sin, unless perchance the spoken word be of such a grave nature, as to cause a notable injury to a man's good name, especially in matters pertaining to his moral character, because from the very nature of the words this would be a mortal sin. And one is bound to restore a man his good name, no less than any other thing one has taken from him, in the manner stated above (Q. LXII., A. 2) when we were treating of restitution.

*Reply Obj.* 1. As stated above, it is not backbiting to reveal a man's hidden sin in order that he may mend, whether one denounce it, or accuse him for the good of public justice.

*Reply Obj.* 2. This gloss does not assert that backbiting is to be found throughout the whole of mankind, but *almost,* both because *the number of fools is infinite,** and few are they

* Eccles. i. 15.

that walk in the way of salvation,* and because there are few or none at all who do not at times speak from lightness of heart, so as to injure someone's good name at least slightly, for it is written (James iii. 2): *If any man offend not in word, the same is a perfect man.*

*Reply Obj.* 3. Augustine is referring to the case when a man utters a slight evil about someone, not intending to injure him, but through lightness of heart or a slip of the tongue.

### THIRD ARTICLE.

#### WHETHER BACKBITING IS THE GRAVEST OF ALL SINS COMMITTED AGAINST ONE'S NEIGHBOUR?

*We proceed thus to the Third Article :—*

*Objection* 1. It would seem that backbiting is the gravest of all sins committed against one's neighbour. Because a gloss on Ps. cviii. 4, *Instead of making me a return of love they detracted me,* a gloss says: *Those who detract Christ in His members and slay the souls of future believers are more guilty than those who killed the flesh that was soon to rise again.* From this it seems to follow that backbiting is by so much a graver sin than murder, as it is a graver matter to kill the soul than to kill the body. Now murder is the gravest of the other sins that are committed against one's neighbour. Therefore backbiting is absolutely the gravest of all.

*Obj.* 2. Further, Backbiting is apparently a graver sin than reviling, because a man can withstand reviling, but not a secret backbiting. Now backbiting is seemingly a graver sin than adultery, because adultery unites two persons in one flesh, whereas reviling severs utterly those who were united. Therefore backbiting is more grievous than adultery: and yet of all other sins a man commits against his neighbour, adultery is most grave.

*Obj.* 3. Further, Reviling arises from anger, while backbiting arises from envy, according to Gregory (*Moral.* xxxi. 45). But envy is a graver sin than anger. Therefore backbiting is a graver sin than reviling; and so the same conclusion follows as before.

* Cf. Matth. vii. 14.

*Obj.* 4. Further, The gravity of a sin is measured by the gravity of the defect that it causes. Now backbiting causes a most grievous defect, viz. blindness of mind. For Gregory says (*Regist.* xi., Ep. 2): *What else do backbiters but blow on the dust and stir up the dirt into their eyes, so that the more they breathe of detraction, the less they see of the truth ?* Therefore backbiting is the most grievous sin committed against one's neighbour.

*On the contrary*, It is more grievous to sin by deed than by word. But backbiting is a sin of word, while adultery, murder, and theft are sins of deed. Therefore backbiting is not graver than the other sins committed against one's neighbour.

*I answer that*, The essential gravity of sins committed against one's neighbour must be weighed by the injury they inflict on him, since it is thence that they derive their sinful nature. Now the greater the good taken away, the greater the injury. And while man's good is threefold, namely the good of his soul, the good of his body, and the good of external things; the good of the soul, which is the greatest of all, cannot be taken from him by another save as an occasional cause, for instance by an evil persuasion, which does not induce necessity. On the other hand the two latter goods, viz. of the body and of external things, can be taken away by violence. Since however the goods of the body excel the goods of external things, those sins which injure a man's body are more grievous than those which injure his external things. Consequently, among other sins committed against one's neighbour, murder is the most grievous, since it deprives man of the life which he already possesses: after this comes adultery, which is contrary to the right order of human generation, whereby man enters upon life. In the last place come external goods, among which a man's good name takes precedence of wealth because it is more akin to spiritual goods, wherefore it is written (Prov. xxii. 1): *A good name is better than great riches.* Therefore backbiting according to its genus is a more grievous sin than theft, but is less grievous than murder or adultery.

Nevertheless the order may differ by reason of aggravating or extenuating circumstances.

The accidental gravity of a sin is to be considered in relation to the sinner, who sins more grievously, if he sins deliberately than if he sins through weakness or carelessness. In this respect sins of word have a certain levity, in so far as they are apt to occur through a slip of the tongue, and without much forethought.

*Reply Obj.* 1. Those who detract Christ by hindering the faith of His members, disparage His Godhead, which is the foundation of our faith. Wherefore this is not simple backbiting but blasphemy.

*Reply Obj.* 2. Reviling is a more grievous sin than backbiting, in as much as it implies greater contempt of one's neighbour: even as robbery is a graver sin than theft, as stated above (Q. LXVI., A. 9). Yet reviling is not a more grievous sin than adultery. For the gravity of adultery is measured, not from its being a union of bodies, but from being a disorder in human generation. Moreover the reviler is not the sufficient cause of unfriendliness in another man, but is only the occasional cause of division among those who were united, in so far, to wit, as by declaring the evils of another, he for his own part severs that man from the friendship of other men, though they are not forced by his words to do so. Accordingly a backbiter is a murderer *occasionally*, since by his words he gives another man an occasion for hating or despising his neighbour. For this reason it is stated in the Epistle of Clement,* that *backbiters are murderers*, i.e. occasionally; because *he that hateth his brother is a murderer* (1 Jo. iii. 15).

*Reply Obj.* 3. Anger seeks openly to be avenged, as the Philosopher states (*Rhet.* ii. 2): wherefore backbiting which takes place in secret, is not the daughter of anger, as reviling is, but rather of envy, which strives by any means to lessen one's neighbour's glory. Nor does it follow from this that backbiting is more grievous than reviling: since a lesser vice can give rise to a greater sin, just as anger gives birth to murder and blasphemy. For the origin of a sin depends on

* *Ad Jacob.* Ep. i.

its inclination to an end, i.e. on the thing to which the sin turns, whereas the gravity of a sin depends on what it turns away from.

*Reply Obj.* 4. Since *a man rejoiceth in the sentence of his mouth* (Prov. xv. 23), it follows that a backbiter more and more loves and believes what he says, and consequently more and more hates his neighbour, and thus his knowledge of the truth becomes less and less. This effect however may also result from other sins pertaining to hate of one's neighbour.

## FOURTH ARTICLE.

### WHETHER IT IS A GRAVE SIN FOR THE LISTENER TO SUFFER THE BACKBITER?

*We proceed thus to the Fourth Article :—*

*Objection* 1. It would seem that the listener who suffers a backbiter does not sin grievously. For a man is not under greater obligations to others than to himself. But it is praiseworthy for a man to suffer his own backbiters: for Gregory says (*Hom.* ix. *super Ezech.*): *Just as we ought not to incite the tongue of backbiters, lest they perish, so ought we to suffer them with equanimity when they have been incited by their own wickedness, in order that our merit may be the greater.* Therefore a man does not sin if he does not withstand those who backbite others.

*Obj.* 2. Further, It is written (Ecclus. iv. 30): *In no wise speak against the truth.* Now sometimes a person tells the truth while backbiting, as stated above (A. 1, *ad* 3). Therefore it seems that one is not always bound to withstand a backbiter.

*Obj.* 3. Further, No man should hinder what is profitable to others. Now backbiting is often profitable to those who are backbitten: for Pope Pius* says:† *Not unfrequently backbiting is directed against good persons, with the result that those who have been unduly exalted through the flattery of their kindred, or the favour of others, are humbled by backbiting.* Therefore one ought not to withstand backbiters.

* Saint Pius I.    † Append. Grat. ad can. *Oves*, caus. vi., qu. 1.

*On the contrary*, Jerome says (*Ep. ad Nepot.* lii.): *Take care not to have an itching tongue, nor tingling ears, that is, neither detract others nor listen to backbiters.*

*I answer that*, According to the Apostle (Rom. i. 32), they *are worthy of death*, . . . *not only they that* commit sins, *but they also that consent to them that do them.* Now this happens in two ways. First, directly, when, to wit, one man induces another to sin, or when the sin is pleasing to him: secondly, indirectly, that is, if he does not withstand him when he might do so, and this happens sometimes, not because the sin is pleasing to him, but on account of some human fear.

Accordingly we must say that if a man listens to backbiting without resisting it, he seems to consent to the backbiter, so that he becomes a participator in his sin. And if he induces him to backbite, or at least if the detraction be pleasing to him on account of his hatred for the person detracted, he sins no less than the detracter, and sometimes more. Wherefore Bernard says (*De Consid.* ii. 13): *It is difficult to say which is the more to be condemned the backbiter or he that listens to backbiting.* If however the sin is not pleasing to him, and he fails to withstand the backbiter, through fear, negligence, or even shame, he sins indeed, but much less than the backbiter, and, as a rule, venially. Sometimes too this may be a mortal sin, either because it is his official duty to correct the backbiter, or by reason of some consequent danger; or on account of the radical reason for which human fear may sometimes be a mortal sin, as stated above (Q. XIX., A. 3).

*Reply Obj.* 1. No man hears himself backbitten, because when a man is spoken evil of in his hearing, it is not backbiting, properly speaking, but reviling, as stated above (A. 1, *ad* 2). Yet it is possible for the detractions uttered against a person to come to his knowledge through others telling him, and then it is left to his discretion whether he will suffer the detriment to his good name, unless this endanger the good of others, as stated above (Q. LXXII., A. 3). Wherefore his patience may deserve commendation for as much as he suffers patiently being detracted himself.

But it is not left to his discretion to permit an injury to be done to another's good name, hence he is accounted guilty if he fails to resist when he can, for the same reason whereby a man is bound to raise another man's ass lying *underneath his burden,* as commanded in Deut. xxii. 4.*

*Reply Obj.* 2. One ought not always to withstand a backbiter by endeavouring to convince him of falsehood, especially if one knows that he is speaking the truth: rather ought one to reprove him with words, for that he sins in backbiting his brother, or at least by our pained demeanour show him that we are displeased with his backbiting, because according to Prov. xxv. 23, *the north wind driveth away rain, as doth a sad countenance a backbiting tongue.*

*Reply Obj.* 3. The profit one derives from being backbitten is due, not to the intention of the backbiter, but to the ordinance of God Who produces good out of every evil. Hence we should none the less withstand backbiters, just as those who rob or oppress others, even though the oppressed and the robbed may gain merit by patience.

* Exod. xxiii. 5.

# QUESTION LXXIV.

## OF TALE-BEARING.*

### (*In Two Articles.*)

WE must now consider tale-bearing: under which head there are two points of inquiry: (1) Whether tale-bearing is a sin distinct from backbiting? (2) Which of the two is the more grievous?

### FIRST ARTICLE.

#### WHETHER TALE-BEARING IS A SIN DISTINCT FROM BACKBITING?

*We proceed thus to the First Article :—*

*Objection* 1. It would seem that tale-bearing is not a distinct sin from backbiting. Isidore says (*Etym.* x.): The *susurro* (tale-bearer) *takes his name from the sound of his speech, for he speaks disparagingly not to the face but into the ear.* But to speak of another disparagingly belongs to backbiting. Therefore tale-bearing is not a distinct sin from backbiting.

*Obj.* 2. Further, It is written (Levit. xix. 16): *Thou shalt not be an informer* (Douay,—*a detracter*) *nor a tale-bearer* (Douay,—*whisperer*) *among the people.* But an informer is apparently the same as a backbiter. Therefore neither does tale-bearing differ from backbiting.

*Obj.* 3. Further, It is written (Ecclus. xxviii. 15): *The tale-bearer* (Douay,—*whisperer*) *and the double-tongued is accursed.* But a double-tongued man is apparently the same as a backbiter, because a backbiter speaks with a double tongue, with one in your absence, with another in your presence. Therefore a tale-bearer is the same as a backbiter.

* *Susurratio,* i.e. whispering.

*On the contrary*, A gloss on Rom. i. 29, 30, *Tale-bearers, backbiters* (Douay, — *whisperers, detracters*) says: *Tale-bearers sow discord among friends ; backbiters deny or disparage others' good points.*

*I answer that*, The tale-bearer and the backbiter agree in matter, and also in form or mode of speaking, since they both speak evil secretly of their neighbour: and for this reason these terms are sometimes used one for the other. Hence a gloss on Ecclus. v. 16, *Be not called a tale-bearer* (Douay,—*whisperer*) says: *i.e. a backbiter*. They differ however in end, because the backbiter intends to blacken his neighbour's good name, wherefore he brings forward those evils especially about his neighbour which are likely to defame him, or at least to depreciate his good name: whereas a tale-bearer intends to sever friendship, as appears from the gloss quoted above and from the saying of Prov. xxvi. 20, *Where the tale-bearer is taken away, contentions shall cease*. Hence it is that a tale-bearer speaks such ill about his neighbours as may stir his hearer's mind against them, according to Ecclus. xxviii. 11, *A sinful man will trouble his friends, and bring in debate in the midst of them that are at peace.*

*Reply Obj.* 1. A tale-bearer is called a backbiter in so far as he speaks ill of another; yet he differs from a backbiter since he intends, not to speak ill as such, but to say anything that may stir one man against another, though it be good simply, and yet has a semblance of evil through being unpleasant to the hearer.

*Reply Obj.* 2. An informer differs from a tale-bearer and a backbiter, for an informer is one who charges others publicly with crimes, either by accusing or by railing them, which does not apply to a backbiter or tale-bearer.

*Reply Obj.* 3. A double-tongued person is properly speaking a tale-bearer. For since friendship is between two, the tale-bearer strives to sever friendship on both sides. Hence he employs a double tongue towards two persons, by speaking ill of one to the other: wherefore it is written (Ecclus.

xxviii. 15): *The tale-bearer* (Douay,—*whisperer*) *and the double-tongued is accursed,* and then it is added, *for he hath troubled many that were at peace.*

## SECOND ARTICLE.

### WHETHER BACKBITING IS A GRAVER SIN THAN TALE-BEARING ?

*We proceed thus to the Second Article :—*

*Objection* 1. It would seem that backbiting is a graver sin than tale-bearing. For sins of word consist in speaking evil. Now a backbiter speaks of his neighbour things that are evil simply, for such things lead to the loss or depreciation of his good name: whereas a tale-bearer is only intent on saying what is apparently evil, because to wit they are unpleasant to the hearer. Therefore backbiting is a graver sin than tale-bearing.

*Obj.* 2. Further, He that deprives a man of his good name, deprives him not merely of one friend, but of many, because everyone is minded to scorn the friendship of a person with a bad name. Hence it is reproached against a certain individual*(2 Paralip. xix. 2): *Thou art joined in friendship with them that hate the Lord.* But tale-bearing deprives one of only one friend. Therefore backbiting is a graver sin than tale-bearing.

*Obj.* 3. Further, It is written (James iv. 11): *He that backbiteth* (Douay,—*detracteth*) *his brother . . . detracteth the law,* and consequently God the giver of the law. Wherefore the sin of backbiting seems to be a sin against God, which is most grievous, as stated above (Q. XX., A. 3: I.-II., Q. LXXIII., A. 3). On the other hand the sin of tale-bearing is against one's neighbour. Therefore the sin of backbiting is graver than the sin of tale-bearing.

*On the contrary,* It is written (Ecclus. v. 17): *An evil mark of disgrace is upon the double-tongued ; but to the tale-bearer* (Douay,—*whisperer*) *hatred, and enmity, and reproach.*

*I answer that,* As stated above (Q. LXXIII., A. 3: I.-II.,

* King Josaphat.

Q. LXXIII., A. 8), sins against one's neighbour are the more grievous, according as they inflict a greater injury on him: and an injury is so much the greater, according to the greatness of the good which it takes away. Now of all one's external goods a friend takes the first place, since *no man can live without friends*, as the Philosopher declares (*Ethic.* viii. 1). Hence it is written (Ecclus. vi. 15): *Nothing can be compared to a faithful friend.* Again, a man's good name whereof backbiting deprives him, is most necessary to him that he may be fitted for friendship. Therefore tale-bearing is a greater sin than backbiting or even reviling, because a friend is better than honour, and to be loved is better than to be honoured, according to the Philosopher (*Ethic.* viii.).

*Reply Obj.* 1. The species and gravity of a sin depend on the end rather than on the material object, wherefore, by reason of its end, tale-bearing is worse than backbiting, although sometimes the backbiter says worse things.

*Reply Obj.* 2. A good name is a disposition for friendship, and a bad name is a disposition for enmity. But a disposition falls short of the thing for which it disposes. Hence to do anything that leads to a disposition for enmity is a less grievous sin than to do what conduces directly to enmity.

*Reply Obj.* 3. He that backbites his brother, seems to detract the law, in so far as he despises the precept of love for one's neighbour: while he that strives to sever friendship seems to act more directly against this precept. Hence the latter sin is more specially against God, because *God is charity* (1 Jo. iv. 16), and for this reason it is written (Prov. vi. 16): *Six things there are, which the Lord hateth, and the seventh His soul detesteth,* and the seventh is *he* (*verse* 19) *that soweth discord among brethren.*

# QUESTION LXXV.

## OF DERISION.*

### (*In Two Articles.*)

WE must now speak of derision, under which head there are two points of inquiry: (1) Whether derision is a special sin distinct from the other sins whereby one's neighbour is injured by words? (2) Whether derision is a mortal sin?

## FIRST ARTICLE.

### WHETHER DERISION IS A SPECIAL SIN DISTINCT FROM THOSE ALREADY MENTIONED?

*We proceed thus to the First Article :—*

*Objection* 1. It would seem that derision is not a special sin distinct from those mentioned above. For laughing to scorn is apparently the same as derision. But laughing to scorn pertains to reviling. Therefore derision would seem not to differ from reviling.

*Obj.* 2. Further, No man is derided except for something reprehensible which puts him to shame. Now such are sins; and if they be imputed to a person publicly, it is a case of reviling, if privately, it amounts to backbiting or tale-bearing. Therefore derision is not distinct from the foregoing vices.

*Obj.* 3. Further, Sins of this kind are distinguished by the injury they inflict on one's neighbour. Now the injury inflicted on a man by derision affects either his honour, or his good name, or is detrimental to his friendship. Therefore derision is not a sin distinct from the foregoing.

*On the contrary,* Derision is done in jest, wherefore it is

* Or mockery.

304

described as *making fun.* Now all the foregoing are done seriously and not in jest. Therefore derision differs from all of them.

*I answer that,* As stated above (Q. LXXII., A. 2), sins of word should be weighed chiefly by the intention of the speaker, wherefore these sins are differentiated according to the various intentions of those who speak against another. Now just as the railer intends to injure the honour of the person he rails, the backbiter to depreciate a good name, and the tale-bearer to destroy friendship, so too the derider intends to shame the person he derides. And since this end is distinct from the others, it follows that the sin of derision is distinct from the foregoing sins.

*Reply Obj.* 1. Laughing to scorn and derision agree as to the end but differ in mode, because derision is done with the *mouth,* i.e. by words and laughter, while laughing to scorn is done by wrinkling the nose, as a gloss says on Ps. ii. 4, *He that dwelleth in heaven shall laugh at them :* and such a distinction does not differentiate the species. Yet they both differ from reviling, as being shamed differs from being dishonoured: for to be ashamed is *to fear dishonour,* as Damascene states (*De Fide Orthod.* ii. 15).

*Reply Obj.* 2. For doing a virtuous deed a man deserves both respect and a good name in the eyes of others, and in his own eyes the glory of a good conscience, according to 2 Cor. i. 12, *Our glory is this, the testimony of our conscience.* Hence, on the other hand, for doing a reprehensible, i.e. a vicious action, a man forfeits his honour and good name in the eyes of others,—and for this purpose the reviler and the backbiter speak of another person;—while in his own eyes, he loses the glory of his conscience through being confused and ashamed at reprehensible deeds being imputed to him,—and for this purpose the derider speaks ill of him. It is accordingly evident that derision agrees with the foregoing vices as to the matter but differs as to the end.

*Reply Obj.* 3. A secure and calm conscience is a great good, according to Prov. xv. 15, *A secure mind is like a continual feast.* Wherefore he that disturbs another's conscience by confounding him inflicts a special injury on him: hence derision is a special kind of sin.

## SECOND ARTICLE.

### WHETHER DERISION CAN BE A MORTAL SIN?

*We proceed thus to the Second Article :—*

*Objection* 1. It would seem that derision cannot be a mortal sin. Every mortal sin is contrary to charity. But derision does not seem contrary to charity, for sometimes it takes place in jest among friends, wherefore it is known as *making fun.* Therefore derision cannot be a mortal sin.

*Obj.* 2. Further, The greatest derision would appear to be that which is done as an injury to God. But derision is not always a mortal sin when it tends to the injury of God: else it would be a mortal sin to relapse into a venial sin of which one has repented. For Isidore says (*De Sum. Bon.* ii. 16) that *he who continues to do what he has repented of, is a derider and not a penitent.* It would likewise follow that all hypocrisy is a mortal sin, because, according to Gregory (*Moral.* xxxi. 15) *the ostrich signifies the hypocrite, who derides the horse, i.e. the just man, and his rider, i.e. God.* Therefore derision is not a mortal sin.

*Obj.* 3. Further, Reviling and backbiting seem to be graver sins than derision, because it is more to do a thing seriously than in jest. But not all backbiting or reviling is a mortal sin. Much less therefore is derision a mortal sin.

*On the contrary,* It is written (Prov. iii. 34): *He derideth* (Vulg.,—*shall scorn*) *the scorners.* But God's derision is eternal punishment for mortal sin, as appears from the words of Ps. ii. 4, *He that dwelleth in heaven shall laugh at them.* Therefore derision is a mortal sin.

*I answer that,* The object of derision is always some evil or defect. Now when an evil is great, it is taken, not in jest, but seriously: consequently if it is taken in jest or turned to ridicule (whence the terms *derision* and *jesting*), this is because it is considered to be slight. Now an evil may be considered to be slight in two ways: first, in itself, secondly, in relation to the person. When anyone makes game or fun of another's evil or defect, because it is a slight evil in itself, this is a venial sin by reason of its genus. On the other hand this defect may be considered as a slight evil in relation to the person, just as we are wont to think little of the defects of children and imbeciles: and then to make game or fun of a person, is to scorn him altogether, and to think him so despicable that his misfortune troubles us not one whit, but is held as an object of derision. In this way derision is a mortal sin, and more grievous than reviling, which is also done openly: because the reviler would seem to take another's evil seriously; whereas the derider does so in fun, and so would seem the more to despise and dishonour the other man. Wherefore, in this sense, derision is a grievous sin, and all the more grievous according as a greater respect is due to the person derided.

Consequently it is an exceedingly grievous sin to deride God and the things of God, according to Isa. xxxvii. 23, *Whom hast thou reproached, and whom hast thou blasphemed, and against whom hast thou exalted thy voice?* and he replies: *Against the Holy One of Israel.* In the second place comes derision of one's parents, wherefore it is written (Prov. xxx. 17): *The eye that mocketh at his father, and that despiseth the labour of his mother in bearing him, let the ravens of the brooks pick it out, and the young eagles eat it.* Further, the derision of good persons is grievous, because honour is the reward of virtue, and against this it is written (Job xii. 4): *The simplicity of the just man is laughed to scorn.* Suchlike derision does very much harm: because it turns men away from good deeds, according to Gregory (*Moral.* xx. 14), *Who when they perceive any good points appearing in the acts of others, directly pluck them up with the hand of a mischievous reviling.*

*Reply Obj.* 1. Jesting implies nothing contrary to charity in relation to the person with whom one jests, but it may imply something against charity in relation to the person who is the object of the jest, on account of contempt, as stated above.

*Reply Obj.* 2. Neither he that relapses into a sin of which he has repented, nor a hypocrite, derides God explicitly, but implicitly, in so far as either's behaviour is like a derider's. Nor is it true that to commit a venial sin is to relapse or dissimulate altogether, but only dispositively and imperfectly.

*Reply Obj.* 3. Derision considered in itself is less grievous than backbiting or reviling, because it does not imply contempt, but jest. Sometimes however it includes greater contempt than reviling does, as stated above, and then it is a grave sin.

# QUESTION LXXVI.

## OF CURSING.

### (*In Four Articles.*)

WE must now consider cursing. Under this head there are four points of inquiry: (1) Whether one may lawfully curse another? (2) Whether one may lawfully curse an irrational creature? (3) Whether cursing is a mortal sin? (4) Of its comparison with other sins.

## FIRST ARTICLE.

### WHETHER IT IS LAWFUL TO CURSE ANYONE?

*We proceed thus to the First Article :—*

*Objection* 1. It would seem unlawful to curse anyone. For it is unlawful to disregard the command of the Apostle in whom Christ spoke, according to 2 Cor. xiii. 3. Now he commanded (Rom. xii. 14), *Bless and curse not.* Therefore it is not lawful to curse anyone.

*Obj.* 2. Further, All are bound to bless God, according to Dan. iii. 82, *O ye sons of men, bless the Lord.* Now the same mouth cannot both bless God and curse man, as proved in the third chapter of James. Therefore no man may lawfully curse another man.

*Obj.* 3. Further, He that curses another would seem to wish him some evil either of fault or of punishment, since a curse appears to be a kind of imprecation. But it is not lawful to wish ill to anyone, indeed we are bound to pray that all may be delivered from evil. Therefore it is unlawful for any man to curse.

*Obj.* 4. Further, The devil exceeds all in malice on account of his obstinacy. But it is not lawful to curse the devil, as neither is it lawful to curse oneself; for it is written (Ecclus. xxi. 30): *While the ungodly curseth the devil, he curseth his own soul.* Much less therefore is it lawful to curse a man.

*Obj.* 5. Further, A gloss on Num. xxiii. 8, *How shall I curse whom God hath not cursed ?* says: *There cannot be a just cause for cursing a sinner if one be ignorant of his sentiments.* Now one man cannot know another man's sentiments, nor whether he is cursed by God. Therefore no man may lawfully curse another.

*On the contrary,* It is written (Deut. xxvii. 26): *Cursed be he that abideth not in the words of this law.* Moreover Eliseus cursed the little boys who mocked him (4 Kings ii. 24).

*I answer that,* To curse (*maledicere*) is the same as to speak ill (*malum dicere*). Now *speaking* has a threefold relation to the thing spoken. First, by way of assertion, as when a thing is expressed in the indicative mood: in this way *maledicere* signifies simply to tell someone of another's evil, and this pertains to backbiting, wherefore tellers of evil (*maledici*) are sometimes called backbiters. Secondly, speaking is related to the thing spoken, by way of cause, and this belongs to God first and foremost, since He made all things by His word, according to Ps. xxxii. 9, *He spoke, and they were made ;* while secondarily it belongs to man, who, by his word, commands others and thus moves them to do something: it is for this purpose that we employ verbs in the imperative mood. Thirdly, *speaking* is related to the thing spoken by expressing the sentiments of one who desires that which is expressed in words; and for this purpose we employ the verb in the optative mood.

Accordingly we may omit the first kind of evil speaking which is by way of simple assertion of evil, and consider the other two kinds. And here we must observe that to do something and to will it are consequent on one another in the matter of goodness and wickedness, as shown above (I.-II., Q. XX., A. 3). Hence in these two ways of evil speaking, by way of command and by way of desire, there is the same aspect of lawfulness and unlawfulness, for if a man commands or desires another's evil, as evil, being intent on the evil itself, then evil speaking will be unlawful in both ways, and this is what is meant by cursing. On the other hand if a man commands or desires another's evil under the aspect of good, it is lawful; and it may be called cursing, not strictly speaking, but accidentally, because the chief intention of the speaker is directed not to evil but to good.

Now evil may be spoken, by commanding or desiring it, under the aspect of a twofold good. Sometimes under the aspect of just, and thus a judge lawfully curses a man whom he condemns to a just penalty: thus too the Church curses by pronouncing anathema. In the same way the prophets in the Scriptures sometimes call down evils on sinners, as though conforming their will to Divine justice, although suchlike imprecation may be taken by way of foretelling. Sometimes evil is spoken under the aspect of useful, as when one wishes a sinner to suffer sickness or hindrance of some kind, either that he may himself reform, or at least that he may cease from harming others.

*Reply Obj.* 1. The Apostle forbids cursing strictly so called with an evil intent: and the same answer applies to the *Second Objection*.

*Reply Obj.* 3. To wish another man evil under the aspect of good, is not opposed to the sentiment whereby one wishes him good simply, in fact rather is it in conformity therewith.

*Reply Obj.* 4. In the devil both nature and guilt must be considered. His nature indeed is good and is from God, nor is it lawful to curse it. On the other hand his guilt is deserving of being cursed, according to Job iii. 8, *Let them curse it who curse the day*. Yet when a sinner curses the devil on account of his guilt, for the same reason he judges himself worthy of being cursed; and in this sense he is said to curse his own soul.

*Reply Obj.* 5. Although the sinner's sentiments cannot be perceived in themselves, they can be perceived through some manifest sin, which has to be punished. Likewise although it is not possible to know whom God curses in respect of final reprobation, it is possible to know who is accursed of God in respect of being guilty of present sin.

## SECOND ARTICLE.
### WHETHER IT IS LAWFUL TO CURSE AN IRRATIONAL CREATURE ?

*We proceed thus to the Second Article :—*

*Objection* 1. It would seem that it is unlawful to curse an irrational creature. Cursing would seem to be lawful chiefly in its relation to punishment. Now irrational creatures are not competent subjects either of guilt or of punishment. Therefore it is unlawful to curse them.

*Obj.* 2. Further, In an irrational creature there is nothing but the nature which God made. But it is unlawful to curse this even in the devil, as stated above (A. 1). Therefore it is nowise lawful to curse an irrational creature.

*Obj.* 3. Further, Irrational creatures are either stable, as bodies, or transient, as the seasons. Now, according to Gregory (*Moral.* iv. 2), *it is useless to curse what does not exist, and wicked to curse what exists.* Therefore it is nowise lawful to curse an irrational creature.

*On the contrary*, Our Lord cursed the fig-tree, as related in Matth. xxi. 19; and Job cursed his day, according to Job iii. 1.

*I answer that*, Benediction and malediction, properly speaking, regard things to which good or evil may happen, viz. rational creatures: while good and evil are said to happen to irrational creatures in relation to the rational creature for whose sake they are. Now they are related to the rational creature in several ways. First by way of ministration, in so far as irrational creatures minister to the needs of man. In this sense the Lord said to man (Gen. iii. 17): *Cursed is the earth in thy work*, so that its barrenness would be a punishment to man. Thus also David cursed the mountains of Gelboe, according to Gregory's expounding (*Moral.* iv. 3). Again the irrational

creature is related to the rational creature by way of signification: and thus Our Lord cursed the fig-tree in signification of Judea. Thirdly, the irrational creature is related
to rational creatures as something containing them, namely
by way of time or place: and thus Job cursed the day of his
birth, on account of the original sin which he contracted
in birth, and on account of the consequent penalties. In
this sense also we may understand David to have cursed
the mountains of Gelboe, as we read in 2 Kings i. 21,
namely, on account of the people slaughtered there.

But to curse irrational beings, considered as creatures of
God, is a sin of blasphemy; while to curse them considered
in themselves is idle and vain and consequently unlawful.

From this the *Replies* to the *Objections* may easily be
gathered.

### THIRD ARTICLE.

#### WHETHER CURSING IS A MORTAL SIN ?

*We proceed thus to the Third Article :—*

*Objection* 1. It would seem that cursing is not a mortal sin.
For Augustine in a homily *on the Fire of Purgatory*\* reckons
cursing among slight sins. But such sins are venial. Therefore cursing is not a mortal but a venial sin.

*Obj.* 2. Further, That which proceeds from a slight movement of the mind does not seem to be generically a mortal
sin. But cursing sometimes arises from a slight movement.
Therefore cursing is not a mortal sin.

*Obj.* 3. Further, Evil deeds are worse than evil words.
But evil deeds are not always mortal sins. Much less therefore is cursing a mortal sin.

*On the contrary*, Nothing save mortal sin excludes one from
the kingdom of God. But cursing excludes from the kingdom of God, according to 1 Cor. vi. 10, *Nor cursers* (Douay,—
*railers*), *nor extortioners shall possess the kingdom of God.*
Therefore cursing is a mortal sin.

*I answer that*, The evil words of which we are speaking
now are those whereby evil is uttered against someone by
way of command or desire. Now to wish evil to another

---

\* See footnote, p. 292.

man, or to conduce to that evil by commanding it, is, of its very nature, contrary to charity whereby we love our neighbour by desiring his good. Consequently it is a mortal sin, according to its genus, and so much the graver, as the person whom we curse has a greater claim on our love and respect. Hence it is written (Levit. xx. 9): *He that curseth his father, or mother, dying let him die.*

It may happen however that the word uttered in cursing is a venial sin either through the slightness of the evil invoked on another in cursing him, or on account of the sentiments of the person who utters the curse; because he may say such words through some slight movement, or in jest, or without deliberation, and sins of word should be weighed chiefly with regard to the speaker's intention, as stated above (Q. LXXII., A. 2).

From this the *Replies* to the *Objections* may be easily gathered.

## Fourth Article.

### Whether Cursing is a Graver Sin than Backbiting?

*We proceed thus to the Fourth Article :—*

*Objection* 1. It would seem that cursing is a graver sin than backbiting. Cursing would seem to be a kind of blasphemy, as implied in the canonical epistle of Jude (*verse* 9) where it is said that *when Michael the archangel, disputing with the devil, contended about the body of Moses, he durst not bring against him the judgment of blasphemy* (Douay,— *railing speech*), where blasphemy stands for cursing, according to a gloss. Now blasphemy is a graver sin than backbiting. Therefore cursing is a graver sin than backbiting.

*Obj.* 2. Further, Murder is more grievous than backbiting, as stated above (Q. LXXIII., A. 3). But cursing is on a par with the sin of murder; for Chrysostom says (*Hom.* xix. *super Matth.*): *When thou sayest: ' Curse him, down with his house, away with everything,' you are no better than a murderer.* Therefore cursing is graver than backbiting.

*Obj.* 3. Further, To cause a thing is more than to signify it. But the curser causes evil by commanding it, whereas the backbiter merely signifies an evil already existing. Therefore the curser sins more grievously than the backbiter.

*On the contrary,* It is impossible to do well in backbiting, whereas cursing may be either a good or an evil deed, as appears from what has been said (A. 1). Therefore backbiting is graver than cursing.

*I answer that,* As stated in the First Part (Q. XLVIII., A. 5), evil is twofold, evil of fault, and evil of punishment; and of the two, evil of fault is the worse (*ibid.,* A. 6). Hence to speak evil of fault is worse than to speak evil of punishment, provided the mode of speaking be the same. Accordingly it belongs to the reviler, the tale-bearer, the backbiter and the derider to speak evil of fault, whereas it belongs to the evil-speaker, as we understand it here, to speak evil of punishment, and not evil of fault except under the aspect of punishment. But the mode of speaking is not the same, for in the case of the four vices mentioned above, evil of fault is spoken by way of assertion, whereas in the case of cursing evil of punishment is spoken, either by causing it in the form of a command, or by wishing it. Now the utterance itself of a person's fault is a sin, in as much as it inflicts an injury on one's neighbour, and it is more grievous to inflict an injury, than to wish to inflict it, other things being equal.

Hence backbiting considered in its generic aspect is a graver sin than the cursing which expresses a mere desire; while the cursing which is expressed by way of command, since it has the aspect of a cause, will be more or less grievous than backbiting, according as it inflicts an injury more or less grave than the blackening of a man's good name. Moreover this must be taken as applying to these vices considered in their essential aspects: for other accidental points might be taken into consideration, which would aggravate or extenuate the aforesaid vices.

*Reply Obj.* 1. To curse a creature, as such, reflects on God, and thus accidentally it has the character of blasphemy; not so if one curse a creature on account of its fault: and the same applies to backbiting.

*Reply Obj.* 2. As stated above (A. 3), cursing, in one way, includes the desire for evil, where if the curser desire the evil of another's violent death, he does not differ, in desire, from a murderer, but he differs from him in so far as the external act adds something to the act of the will.

*Reply Obj.* 3. This argument considers cursing by way of command.

# QUESTION LXXVII.

## OF CHEATING, WHICH IS COMMITTED IN BUYING AND SELLING.

### (*In Four Articles.*)

WE must now consider those sins which relate to voluntary commutations. First, we shall consider cheating, which is committed in buying and selling: secondly, we shall consider usury, which occurs in loans. In connection with the other voluntary commutations no special kind of sin is to be found distinct from rapine and theft.

Under the first head there are four points of inquiry: (1) Of unjust sales as regards the price; namely, whether it is lawful to sell a thing for more than its worth? (2) Of unjust sales on the part of the thing sold. (3) Whether the seller is bound to reveal a fault in the thing sold? (4) Whether it is lawful in trading to sell a thing at a higher price than was paid for it?

### FIRST ARTICLE.

#### WHETHER IT IS LAWFUL TO SELL A THING FOR MORE THAN ITS WORTH?

*We proceed thus to the First Article :—*

*Objection* 1. It would seem that it is lawful to sell a thing for more than its worth. In the commutations of human life, civil laws determine that which is just. Now according to these laws it is just for buyer and seller to deceive one another (Cod., IV., xliv., *De Rescind. Vend.* 8, 15): and this occurs by the seller selling a thing for more than its worth, and the buyer buying a thing for less than its worth. Therefore it is lawful to sell a thing for more than its worth.

*Obj.* 2. Further, That which is common to all would seem to be natural and not sinful. Now Augustine relates that the saying of a certain jester was accepted by all, *You wish to buy for a song and to sell at a premium*, which agrees with the saying of Prov. xx. 14, *It is naught, it is naught, saith every buyer : and when he is gone away, then he will boast.* Therefore it is lawful to sell a thing for more than its worth.

*Obj.* 3. Further, It does not seem unlawful if that which honesty demands be done by mutual agreement. Now, according to the Philosopher (*Ethic.* viii. 13), in the friendship which is based on utility, the amount of the recompense for a favour received should depend on the utility accruing to the receiver: and this utility sometimes is worth more than the thing given, for instance if the receiver be in great need of that thing, whether for the purpose of avoiding a danger, or of deriving some particular benefit. Therefore, in contracts of buying and selling, it is lawful to give a thing in return for more than its worth.

*On the contrary*, It is written (Matth. vii. 12): *All things . . . whatsoever you would that men should do to you, do you also to them.* But no man wishes to buy a thing for more than its worth. Therefore no man should sell a thing to another man for more than its worth.

*I answer that*, It is altogether sinful to have recourse to deceit in order to sell a thing for more than its just price, because this is to deceive one's neighbour so as to injure him. Hence Tully says (*De Offic.* iii. 15): *Contracts should be entirely free from double-dealing ; the seller must not impose upon the bidder, nor the buyer upon one that bids against him.*

But, apart from fraud, we may speak of buying and selling in two ways. First, as considered in themselves, and from this point of view, buying and selling seem to be established for the common advantage of both parties, one of whom requires that which belongs to the other, and vice versa, as the Philosopher states (*Polit.* i. 3). Now whatever is established for the common advantage, should not be more of a burden to one party than to another, and consequently all contracts between them should observe equality of thing and thing. Again, the quality of a thing that comes into human use is measured by the price given for it, for which purpose money was invented, as stated in *Ethic*. v. 5. Therefore if either the price exceed the quantity of the thing's worth, or, conversely, the thing exceed the price, there is no longer the equality of justice: and consequently, to sell a thing for more than its worth, or to buy it for less than its worth, is in itself unjust and unlawful.

Secondly we may speak of buying and selling, considered as accidentally tending to the advantage of one party, and to the disadvantage of the other: for instance, when a man has great need of a certain thing, while another man will suffer if he be without it. In such a case the just price will depend not only on the thing sold, but on the loss which the sale brings on the seller. And thus it will be lawful to sell a thing for more than it is worth in itself, though the price paid be not more than it is worth to the owner. Yet if the one man derive a great advantage by becoming possessed of the other man's property, and the seller be not at a loss through being without that thing, the latter ought not to raise the price, because the advantage accruing to the buyer, is not due to the seller, but to a circumstance affecting the buyer. Now no man should sell what is not his, though he may charge for the loss he suffers.

On the other hand if a man find that he derives great advantage from something he has bought, he may, of his own accord, pay the seller something over and above: and this pertains to his honesty.

*Reply Obj.* 1. As stated above (I.-II., Q. XCVI., A. 2) human law is given to the people among whom there are many lacking virtue, and it is not given to the virtuous alone. Hence human law was unable to forbid all that is contrary to virtue; and it suffices for it to prohibit whatever is destructive of human intercourse, while it treats other matters as though they were lawful, not by approving of them, but by not punishing them. Accordingly, if without employing deceit the seller disposes of his goods for more than their worth, or the buyer obtain them for less than their worth, the law looks upon this as licit, and provides no punishment for so doing, unless the excess be too great, because then even human law demands restitution to be made, for instance if a man be deceived in regard of more than half the amount of the just price of a thing.*

On the other hand the Divine law leaves nothing unpunished that is contrary to virtue. Hence, according to the Divine law, it is reckoned unlawful if the equality of justice be not observed in buying and selling: and he who has received more than he ought must make compensation to him that has suffered loss, if the loss be considerable. I add this condition, because the just price of things is not fixed with mathematical precision, but depends on a kind of estimate, so that a slight addition or subtraction would not seem to destroy the equality of justice.

*Reply Obj.* 2. As Augustine says (*ibid.*) *this jester, either by looking into himself or by his experience of others, thought that all men are inclined to wish to buy for a song and sell at a premium. But since in reality this is wicked, it is in every man's power to acquire that justice whereby he may resist and overcome this inclination.* And then he gives the example of a man who gave the just price for a book to a man who through ignorance asked a low price for it. Hence it is evident that this common desire is not from nature but from vice, wherefore it is common to many who walk along the broad road of sin.

*Reply Obj.* 3. In commutative justice we consider chiefly real equality. On the other hand, in friendship based on utility we consider equality of usefulness, so that the recompense should depend on the usefulness accruing, whereas in buying it should be equal to the thing bought.

## SECOND ARTICLE.

### WHETHER A SALE IS RENDERED UNLAWFUL THROUGH A FAULT IN THE THING SOLD?

*We proceed thus to the Second Article :—*

*Objection* 1. It would seem that a sale is not rendered unjust and unlawful through a fault in the thing sold. For less

* Cod., *loc. cit.*, 2, 8.

account should be taken of the other parts of a thing than of what belongs to its substance. Yet the sale of a thing does not seem to be rendered unlawful through a fault in its substance: for instance, if a man sell instead of the real metal, silver or gold produced by some chemical process, which is adapted to all the human uses for which silver and gold are necessary, for instance in the making of vessels and the like. Much less therefore will it be an unlawful sale if the thing be defective in other ways.

*Obj.* 2. Further, Any fault in the thing, affecting the quantity, would seem chiefly to be opposed to justice which consists in equality. Now quantity is known by being measured: and the measures of things that come into human use are not fixed, but in some places are greater, in others less, as the Philosopher states (*Ethic*. v. 7). Therefore just as it is impossible to avoid defects on the part of the thing sold, it seems that a sale is not rendered unlawful through the thing sold being defective.

*Obj.* 3. Further, the thing sold is rendered defective by lacking a fitting quality. But in order to know the quality of a thing, much knowledge is required that is lacking in most buyers. Therefore a sale is not rendered unlawful by a fault (in the thing sold).

*On the contrary,* Ambrose says (*De Offic*. iii. 11): *It is manifestly a rule of justice that a good man should not depart from the truth, nor inflict an unjust injury on anyone, nor have any connection with fraud.*

*I answer that,* A threefold fault may be found pertaining to the thing which is sold. One, in respect of the thing's substance: and if the seller be aware of a fault in the thing he is selling, he is guilty of a fraudulent sale, so that the sale is rendered unlawful. Hence we find it written against certain people (Isa. i. 22), *Thy silver is turned into dross, thy wine is mingled with water :* because that which is mixed is defective in its substance.

Another defect is in respect of quantity which is known by being measured: wherefore if anyone knowingly make use of a faulty measure in selling, he is guilty of fraud, and the sale is illicit. Hence it is written (Deut. xxv. 13, 14): *Thou shalt not have divers weights in thy bag, a greater and a less : neither shall there be in thy house a greater bushel and a less,* and further on (*verse* 16): *For the Lord . . . abhorreth him that doth these things, and He hateth all injustice.*

A third defect is on the part of the quality, for instance, if a man sell an unhealthy animal as being a healthy one: and if anyone do this knowingly he is guilty of a fraudulent sale, and the sale, in consequence, is illicit.

In all these cases not only is the man guilty of a fraudulent sale, but he is also bound to restitution. But if any of the foregoing defects be in the thing sold, and he knows nothing about this, the seller does not sin, because he does that which is unjust materially, nor is his deed unjust, as shown above (Q. LIX., A. 2). Nevertheless he is bound to compensate the buyer, when the defect comes to his knowledge. Moreover what has been said of the seller applies equally to the buyer. For sometimes it happens that the seller thinks his goods to be specifically of lower value, as when a man sells gold instead of copper, and then if the buyer be aware of this, he buys it unjustly and is bound to restitution: and the same applies to a defect in quantity as to a defect in quality.

*Reply Obj.* 1. Gold and silver are costly not only on account of the usefulness of the vessels and other like things made from them, but also on account of the excellence and purity of their substance. Hence if the gold or silver produced by alchemists has not the true specific nature of gold and silver, the sale thereof is fraudulent and unjust, especially as real gold and silver can produce certain results by their natural action, which the counterfeit gold and silver of alchemists cannot produce. Thus the true metal has the property of making people joyful, and is helpful medicinally against certain maladies. Moreover real gold can be employed more frequently, and lasts longer in its condition of purity than counterfeit gold. If however real gold were to be produced by alchemy, it would not be unlawful to sell it for the genuine article, for nothing prevents art from employing certain natural causes for the production of natural and true effects, as Augustine says (*De Trin.* iii. 8) of things produced by the art of the demons.

*Reply Obj.* 2. The measures of saleable commodities must needs be different in different places, on account of the difference of supply: because where there is greater abundance, the measures are wont to be larger. However in each place those who govern the state must determine the just measures of things saleable, with due consideration for the conditions of place and time. Hence it is not lawful to disregard such measures as are established by public authority or custom.

*Reply Obj.* 3. As Augustine says (*De Civ. Dei* xi. 16) the price of things saleable does not depend on their degree of nature, since at times a horse fetches a higher price than a slave; but it depends on their usefulness to man. Hence it is not necessary for the seller or buyer to be cognizant of the hidden qualities of the thing sold, but only of such as render the thing adapted to man's use, for instance, that the horse be strong, run well and so forth. Such qualities the seller and buyer can easily discover.

## THIRD ARTICLE.

### WHETHER THE SELLER IS BOUND TO STATE THE DEFECTS OF THE THING SOLD?

*We proceed thus to the Third Article :—*

*Objection* 1. It would seem that the seller is not bound to state the defects of the thing sold. Since the seller does not bind the buyer to buy, he would seem to leave it to him to judge of the goods offered for sale. Now judgment about a thing and knowledge of that thing belong to the same person. Therefore it does not seem imputable to the seller if the buyer be deceived in his judgment, and be hurried into buying a thing without carefully inquiring into its condition.

*Obj.* 2. Further, It seems foolish for anyone to do what prevents him carrying out his work. But if a man states the defects of the goods he has for sale, he prevents their sale: wherefore Tully (*De Offic.* iii. 13) pictures a man as saying: *Could anything be more absurd than for a public crier, instructed by the owner, to cry*: ' *I offer this unhealthy house for sale*'? Therefore the seller is not bound to state the defects of the thing sold.

*Obj.* 3. Further, Man needs more to know the road of virtue than to know the faults of things offered for sale. Now one is not bound to offer advice to all or to tell them the truth about matters pertaining to virtue, though one should not tell anyone what is false. Much less therefore is a seller bound to tell the faults of what he offers for sale, as though he were counselling the buyer.

*Obj.* 4. Further, If one were bound to tell the faults of what one offers for sale, this would only be in order to lower the price. Now sometimes the price would be lowered for some other reason, without any defect in the thing sold: for instance, if the seller carry wheat to a place where wheat fetches a high price, knowing that many will come after him carrying wheat; because if the buyers knew this they would give a lower price. But apparently the seller need not give the buyer this information. Therefore, in like manner, neither need he tell him the faults of the goods he is selling.

*On the contrary*, Ambrose says (*De Offic.* iii. 10): *In all contracts the defects of the saleable commodity must be stated ; and unless the seller make them known, although the buyer has already acquired a right to them, the contract is voided on account of the fraudulent action.*

*I answer that*, It is always unlawful to give anyone an occasion of danger or loss, although a man need not always give another the help or counsel which would be for his advantage in any way; but only in certain fixed cases, for instance when someone is subject to him, or when he is the only one who can assist him. Now the seller who offers goods for sale, gives the buyer an occasion of loss or danger, by the very fact that he offers him defective goods, if such defect may occasion loss or danger to the buyer:—loss, if, by reason of this defect, the goods are of less value, and he takes nothing off the price on that account:—danger, if this defect either hinder the use of the goods or render it hurtful, for instance, if a man sells a lame for a fleet horse, a tottering house for a safe one, rotten or poisonous food for wholesome. Wherefore if suchlike defects be hidden, and the seller does not make them known, the sale will be illicit and fraudulent, and the seller will be bound to compensation for the loss incurred.

On the other hand, if the defect be manifest, for instance if a horse have but one eye, or if the goods though useless to the buyer, be useful to someone else, provided the seller take as much as he ought from the price, he is not bound to state the defect of the goods, since perhaps on account of that defect the buyer might want him to allow a greater rebate than he need. Wherefore the seller may look to his own indemnity, by withholding the defect of the goods.

*Reply Obj.* 1. Judgment cannot be pronounced save on what is manifest: for *a man judges of what he knows* (*Ethic.* i. 3). Hence if the defects of the goods offered for sale be hidden, judgment of them is not sufficiently left with the buyer unless such defects be made known to him. The case would be different if the defects were manifest.

*Reply Obj.* 2. There is no need to publish beforehand by the public crier the defects of the goods one is offering for sale, because if he were to begin by announcing its defects, the bidders would be frightened to buy, through ignorance of other qualities that might render the thing good and serviceable. Such defect ought to be stated to each individual that offers to buy: and then he will be able to compare the various points one with the other, the good with the bad: for nothing prevents that which is defective in one respect being useful in many others.

*Reply Obj.* 3. Although a man is not bound strictly speaking to tell everyone the truth about matters pertaining to virtue, yet he is so bound in a case when, unless he tells the truth, his conduct would endanger another man in detriment to virtue: and so it is in this case.

*Reply Obj.* 4. The defect in a thing makes it of less value now than it seems to be: but in the case cited, the goods are expected to be of less value at a future time, on account of the arrival of other merchants, which was not foreseen by the buyers. Wherefore the seller, since he sells his goods at the price actually offered him, does not seem to act contrary to justice through not stating what is going to happen. If however he were to do so, or if he lowered his price, it would be exceedingly virtuous on his part: although he does not seem to be bound to do this as a debt of justice.

## FOURTH ARTICLE.

### WHETHER, IN TRADING, IT IS LAWFUL TO SELL A THING AT A HIGHER PRICE THAN WHAT WAS PAID FOR IT?

*We proceed thus to the Fourth Article :—*

*Objection* 1. It would seem that it is not lawful, in trading, to sell a thing for a higher price than we paid for it. For Chrysostom* says on Matth. xxi. 12: *He that buys a thing in order that he may sell it, entire and unchanged, at a profit, is the trader who is cast out of God's temple.* Cassiodorus speaks in the same sense in his commentary on Ps. lxx. 15, *Because I have not known learning,* or *trading* according to another version:† *What is trade,* says he, *but buying at a cheap price with the purpose of retailing at a higher price?* and he adds: *Such were the tradesmen whom Our Lord cast out of the temple.* Now no man is cast out of the temple except for a sin. Therefore suchlike trading is sinful.

*Obj.* 2. Further, It is contrary to justice to sell goods at a higher price than their worth, or to buy them for less than their value, as shown above (A. 1). Now if you sell a thing for a higher price than you paid for it, you must either have bought it for less than its value, or sell it for more than its value. Therefore this cannot be done without sin.

*Obj.* 3. Further, Jerome says (*Ep. ad Nepot.* lii.): *Shun, as you would the plague, a cleric who from being poor has be-*

---

* *Hom.* xxxviii. in the *Opus Imperfectum*, falsely ascribed to S. John Chrysostom.

† The Septuagint.

*come wealthy, or who, from being a nobody has become a celebrity.* Now trading would not seem to be forbidden to clerics except on account of its sinfulness. Therefore it is a sin in trading, to buy at a low price and to sell at a higher price.

*On the contrary,* Augustine commenting on Ps. lxx. 15, *Because I have not known learning,** says: *The greedy tradesman blasphemes over his losses ; he lies and perjures himself over the price of his wares. But these are vices of the man, not of the craft, which can be exercised without these vices.* Therefore trading is not in itself unlawful.

*I answer that,* A tradesman is one whose business consists in the exchange of things. According to the Philosopher (*Polit.* i. 3), exchange of things is twofold; one, natural as it were, and necessary, whereby one commodity is exchanged for another, or money taken in exchange for a commodity, in order to satisfy the needs of life. Suchlike trading, properly speaking, does not belong to tradesmen, but rather to housekeepers or civil servants who have to provide the household or the state with the necessaries of life. The other kind of exchange is either that of money for money, or of any commodity for money, not on account of the necessities of life, but for profit, and this kind of exchange, properly speaking, regards tradesmen, according to the Philosopher (*Polit.*i. 3). The former kind of exchange is commendable because it supplies a natural need: but the latter is justly deserving of blame, because, considered in itself, it satisfies the greed for gain, which knows no limit and tends to infinity. Hence trading, considered in itself, has a certain debasement attaching thereto, in so far as, by its very nature, it does not imply a virtuous or necessary end. Nevertheless gain which is the end of trading, though not implying, by its nature, anything virtuous or necessary, does not, in itself, connote anything sinful or contrary to virtue: wherefore nothing prevents gain from being directed to some necessary or even virtuous end, and thus trading becomes lawful. Thus, for instance, a man may intend the moderate gain which he seeks to acquire by trading for the upkeep of his household, or for the assistance of the needy: or again, a man

* Cf. *obj.* 1.

may take to trade for some public advantage, for instance, lest his country lack the necessaries of life, and seek gain, not as an end, but as payment for his labour.

*Reply Obj.* 1. The saying of Chrysostom refers to the trading which seeks gain as a last end. This is especially the case where a man sells something at a higher price without its undergoing any change. For if he sells at a higher price something that has changed for the better, he would seem to receive the reward of his labour. Nevertheless the gain itself may be lawfully intended, not as a last end, but for the sake of some other end which is necessary or virtuous, as stated above.

*Reply Obj.* 2. Not everyone that sells at a higher price than he bought is a tradesman, but only he who buys that he may sell at a profit. If, on the contrary, he buys not for sale but for possession, and afterwards, for some reason wishes to sell, it is not a trade transaction even if he sell at a profit. For he may lawfully do this, either because he has bettered the thing, or because the value of the thing has changed with the change of place or time, or on account of the danger he incurs in transferring the thing from one place to another, or again in having it carried by another. In this sense neither buying nor selling is unjust.

*Reply Obj.* 3. Clerics should abstain not only from things that are evil in themselves, but even from those that have an appearance of evil. This happens in trading, both because it is directed to worldly gain, which clerics should despise, and because trading is open to so many vices, since *a merchant is hardly free from sins of the lips** (Ecclus. xxvi. 28). There is also another reason, because trading engages the mind too much with worldly cares, and consequently withdraws it from spiritual cares; wherefore the Apostle says (2 Tim. ii. 4): *No man being a soldier to God entangleth himself with secular businesses.* Nevertheless it is lawful for clerics to engage in the first mentioned kind of exchange, which is directed to supply the necessaries of life, either by buying or by selling.

* *A merchant is hardly free from negligence, and a huckster shall not be justified from the sins of the lips.*

# QUESTION LXXVIII.

## OF THE SIN OF USURY.

### (*In Four Articles.*)

WE must now consider the sin of usury, which is committed in loans: and under this head there are four points of inquiry: (1) Whether it is a sin to take money as a price for money lent, which is to receive usury? (2) Whether it is lawful to lend money for any other kind of consideration, by way of payment for the loan? (3) Whether a man is bound to restore just gains derived from money taken in usury? (4) Whether it is lawful to borrow money under a condition of usury?

## FIRST ARTICLE.

### WHETHER IT IS A SIN TO TAKE USURY FOR MONEY LENT?

*We proceed thus to the First Article :—*

*Objection* 1. It would seem that it is not a sin to take usury for money lent. For no man sins through following the example of Christ. But Our Lord said of Himself (Luke xix. 23): *At My coming I might have exacted it*, i.e. the money lent, *with usury*. Therefore it is not a sin to take usury for lending money.

*Obj.* 2. Further, According to Ps. xviii. 8, *The law of the Lord is unspotted*, because, to wit, it forbids sin. Now usury of a kind is allowed in the Divine law, according to Deut. xxiii. 19, 20 *Thou shalt not fenerate\* to thy brother money, nor corn, nor any other thing, but to the stranger :* nay more, it is even promised as a reward for the observance of the Law, according to Deut. xxviii. 12: *Thou*

*\* See note on following page.*

329

evil simply, because we ought to treat every man as our neighbour and brother, especially in the state of the Gospel, whereto all are called. Hence it is said without any distinction in Ps. xiv. 5: *He that hath not put out his money to usury*, and (Ezech. xviii. 8): *Who hath not taken usury.** They were permitted, however, to take usury from foreigners, not as though it were lawful, but in order to avoid a greater evil, lest, to wit, through avarice to which they were prone according to Is. lvi. 11, they should take usury from the Jews who were worshippers of God.

Where we find it promised to them as a reward, *Thou shalt fenerate to many nations*, etc., fenerating is to be taken in a broad sense for lending, as in Ecclus. xxix. 10, where we read: *Many have refused to fenerate, not out of wickedness*, i.e. they would not lend. Accordingly the Jews are promised in reward an abundance of wealth, so that they would be able to lend to others.

*Reply Obj.* 3. Human laws leave certain things unpunished, on account of the condition of those who are imperfect, and who would be deprived of many advantages, if all sins were strictly forbidden and punishments appointed for them. Wherefore human law has permitted usury, not that it looks upon usury as harmonizing with justice, but lest the advantage of many should be hindered. Hence it is that in civil law† it is stated that *those things according to natural reason and civil law which are consumed by being used, do not admit of usufruct*, and that *the senate did not (nor could it) appoint a usufruct to such things, but established a quasi-usufruct*, namely by permitting usury. Moreover the Philosopher, led by natural reason, says (*Polit.* i. 3) that *to make money by usury is exceedingly unnatural*.

*Reply Obj.* 4. A man is not always bound to lend, and for this reason it is placed among the counsels. Yet it is a matter of precept not to seek profit by lending: although it may be called a matter of counsel in comparison with the

* Vulg.,—*If a man . . . hath not lent upon money, nor taken any increase . . . he is just.*   † Inst., II. iv., *de Usufructu.*

maxims of the Pharisees, who deemed some kinds of usury to be lawful, just as love of one's enemies is a matter of counsel. Or again, He speaks here not of the hope of usurious gain, but of the hope which is put in man. For we ought not to lend or do any good deed through hope in man, but only through hope in God.

*Reply Obj.* 5. He that is not bound to lend, may accept repayment for what he has done, but he must not exact more. Now he is repaid according to equality of justice if he is repaid as much as he lent. Wherefore if he exacts more for the usufruct of a thing which has no other use but the consumption of its substance, he exacts a price of something non-existent: and so his exaction is unjust.

*Reply Obj.* 6. The principal use of a silver vessel is not its consumption, and so one may lawfully sell its use while retaining one's ownership of it. On the other hand the principal use of silver money is sinking it in exchange, so that it is not lawful to sell its use and at the same time expect the restitution of the amount lent. It must be observed, however, that the secondary use of silver vessels may be an exchange, and such use may not be lawfully sold. In like manner there may be some secondary use of silver money; for instance, a man might lend coins for show, or to be used as security.

*Reply Obj.* 7. He who gives usury does not give it voluntarily simply, but under a certain necessity, in so far as he needs to borrow money which the owner is unwilling to lend without usury.

## Second Article.

### WHETHER IT IS LAWFUL TO ASK FOR ANY OTHER KIND OF CONSIDERATION FOR MONEY LENT?

*We proceed thus to the Second Article :—*

*Objection* 1. It would seem that one may ask for some other kind of consideration for money lent. For everyone may lawfully seek to indemnify himself. Now sometimes a man suffers loss through lending money. Therefore he may lawfully ask for or even exact something else besides the money lent.

*Obj.* 2. Further, As stated in *Ethic.* v. 5 one is in duty bound by a point of honour, to repay anyone who has done us a favour. Now to lend money to one who is in straits is to do him a favour for which he should be grateful. Therefore the recipient of a loan, is bound by a natural debt to repay something. Now it does not seem unlawful to bind oneself to an obligation of the natural law. Therefore it is not unlawful, in lending money to anyone, to demand some sort of compensation as a condition of the loan.

*Obj.* 3. Further, Just as there is real remuneration, so is there verbal remuneration, and remuneration by service, as a gloss says on Isa. xxxiii. 15, *Blessed is he that shaketh his hands from all bribes.** Now it is lawful to accept service or praise from one to whom one has lent money. Therefore in like manner it is lawful to accept any other kind of remuneration.

*Obj.* 4. Further, Seemingly the relation of gift to gift is the same as of loan to loan. But it is lawful to accept money for money given. Therefore it is lawful to accept repayment by loan in return for a loan granted.

*Obj.* 5. Further, The lender, by transferring his ownership of a sum of money removes the money further from himself than he who entrusts it to a merchant or craftsman. Now it is lawful to receive interest for money entrusted to a merchant or craftsman. Therefore it is also lawful to receive interest for money lent.

*Obj.* 6. Further, A man may accept a pledge for money lent, the use of which pledge he might sell for a price: as when a man mortgages his land or the house wherein he dwells. Therefore it is lawful to receive interest for money lent.

*Obj.* 7. Further, It sometimes happens that a man raises the price of his goods under guise of loan, or buys another's goods at a low figure; or raises his price through delay in being paid, and lowers his price that he may be paid the sooner. Now in all these cases there seems to be payment for a loan of money: nor does it appear to be manifestly

* Vulg.,—*Which of you shall dwell with everlasting burnings ?* . . . *He that shaketh his hands from all bribes.*

illicit. Therefore it seems to be lawful to expect or exact some consideration for money lent.

*On the contrary*, Among other conditions requisite in a just man it is stated (Ezech. xviii. 17) that he *hath not taken usury and increase.*

*I answer that*, According to the Philosopher (*Ethic.* iv. 1), a thing is reckoned as money *if its value can be measured by money*. Consequently, just as it is a sin against justice, to take money, by tacit or express agreement, in return for lending money or anything else that is consumed by being used, so also is it a like sin, by tacit or express agreement to receive anything whose price can be measured by money. Yet there would be no sin in receiving something of the kind, not as exacting it, nor yet as though it were due on account of some agreement tacit or expressed, but as a gratuity: since, even before lending the money, one could accept a gratuity, nor is one in a worse condition through lending.

On the other hand it is lawful to exact compensation for a loan, in respect of such things as are not appreciated by a measure of money, for instance, benevolence, and love for the lender, and so forth.

*Reply Obj.* 1. A lender may without sin enter an agreement with the borrower for compensation for the loss he incurs of something he ought to have, for this is not to sell the use of money but to avoid a loss. It may also happen that the borrower avoids a greater loss than the lender incurs, wherefore the borrower may repay the lender with what he has gained. But the lender cannot enter an agreement for compensation, through the fact that he makes no profit out of his money: because he must not sell that which he has not yet and may be prevented in many ways from having.

*Reply Obj.* 2. Repayment for a favour may be made in two ways. In one way, as a debt of justice; and to such a debt a man may be bound by a fixed contract: and its amount is measured according to the favour received. Wherefore the borrower of money or any such thing the use of which is its consumption is not bound to repay more than he received in loan: and consequently it is against justice if he be obliged to pay back more.  In another way a man's obligation to repayment for favour received is based on a debt of friendship, and the nature of this debt depends more on the feeling with which the favour was conferred than on the greatness of the favour itself.  This debt does not carry with it a civil obligation, involving a kind of necessity that would exclude the spontaneous nature of such a repayment.

*Reply Obj.* 3. If a man were, in return for money lent, as though there had been an agreement tacit or expressed, to expect or exact repayment in the shape of some remuneration of service or words, it would be the same as if he expected or exacted some real remuneration, because both can be priced at a money value, as may be seen in the case of those who offer for hire the labour which they exercise by work or by tongue.  If on the other hand the remuneration by service or words be given not as an obligation, but as a favour, which is not to be appreciated at a money value, it is lawful to take, exact, and expect it.

*Reply Obj.* 4. Money cannot be sold for a greater sum than the amount lent, which has to be paid back: nor should the loan be made with a demand or expectation of aught else but of a feeling of benevolence which cannot be priced at a pecuniary value, and which can be the basis of a spontaneous loan.  Now the obligation to lend in return at some future time is repugnant to such a feeling, because again an obligation of this kind has its pecuniary value.  Consequently it is lawful for the lender to borrow something else at the same time, but it is unlawful for him to bind the borrower to grant him a loan at some future time.

*Reply Obj.* 5. He who lends money transfers the ownership of the money to the borrower.  Hence the borrower holds the money at his own risk and is bound to pay it all back: wherefore the lender must not exact more.  On the other hand he that entrusts his money to a merchant or craftsman so as to form a kind of society, does not transfer the ownership of his money to them, for it remains his, so that at his risk the merchant speculates with it, or the crafts-man uses it for his craft, and consequently he may lawfully demand as something belonging to him, part of the profits derived from his money.

*Reply Obj.* 6. If a man in return for money lent to him pledges something that can be valued at a price, the lender must allow for the use of that thing towards the repayment of the loan. Else if he wishes the gratuitous use of that thing in addition to repayment, it is the same as if he took money for lending, and that is usury; unless perhaps it were such a thing as friends are wont to lend to one another gratis, as in the case of the loan of a book.

*Reply Obj.* 7. If a man wish to sell his goods at a higher price than that which is just, so that he may wait for the buyer to pay, it is manifestly a case of usury: because this waiting for the payment of the price has the character of a loan, so that whatever he demands beyond the just price in consideration of this delay, is like a price for a loan, which pertains to usury. In like manner if a buyer wishes to buy goods at a lower price than what is just, for the reason that he pays for the goods before they can be delivered, it is a sin of usury; because again this anticipated payment of money has the character of a loan, the price of which is the rebate on the just price of the goods sold. On the other hand if a man wishes to allow a rebate on the just price in order that he may have his money sooner, he is not guilty of the sin of usury.

## Third Article.

### WHETHER A MAN IS BOUND TO RESTORE WHATEVER PROFITS HE HAS MADE OUT OF MONEY GOTTEN BY USURY?

*We proceed thus to the Third Article :—*

*Objection* 1. It would seem that a man is bound to restore whatever profits he has made out of money gotten by usury. For the Apostle says (Rom. xi. 16): *If the root be holy, so are the branches.* Therefore likewise if the root be rotten so are the branches. But the root was infected with usury.

Therefore whatever profit is made therefrom is infected with usury. Therefore he is bound to restore it.

*Obj.* 2. Further, It is laid down (Extra, *De Usuris*, in the Decretal: *Cum tu sicut asseris*): *Property accruing from usury must be sold, and the price repaid to the persons from whom the usury was extorted.* Therefore, likewise, whatever else is acquired from usurious money must be restored.

*Obj.* 3. Further, That which a man buys with the proceeds of usury is due to him by reason of the money he paid for it. Therefore he has no more right to the thing purchased than to the money he paid. But he was bound to restore the money gained through usury. Therefore he is also bound to restore what he acquired with it.

*On the contrary,* A man may lawfully hold what he has lawfully acquired. Now that which is acquired by the proceeds of usury is sometimes lawfully acquired. Therefore it may be lawfully retained.

*I answer that,* As stated above (A. 1), there are certain things whose use is their consumption, and which do not admit of usufruct, according to law (*ibid.*, *ad* 3). Wherefore if suchlike things be extorted by means of usury, for instance money, wheat, wine and so forth, the lender is not bound to restore more than he received (since what is acquired by such things is the fruit not of the thing but of human industry), unless indeed the other party by losing some of his own goods be injured through the lender retaining them: for then he is bound to make good the loss.

On the other hand there are certain things whose use is not their consumption: such things admit of usufruct, for instance house or land property and so forth. Wherefore if a man has by usury extorted from another his house or land, he is bound to restore not only the house or land but also the fruits accruing to him therefrom, since they are the fruits of things owned by another man and consequently are due to him.

*Reply Obj.* 1. The root has not only the character of matter, as money made by usury has; but has also somewhat the character of an active cause, in so far as it administers nourishment. Hence the comparison fails.

*Reply Obj.* 2. Further, Property acquired from usury does not belong to the person who paid usury, but to the person who bought it. Yet he that paid usury has a certain claim on that property just as he has on the other goods of the usurer. Hence it is not prescribed that such property should be assigned to the persons who paid usury, since the property is perhaps worth more than what they paid in usury, but it is commanded that the property be sold, and the price be restored, of course according to the amount taken in usury

*Reply Obj.* 3. The proceeds of money taken in usury are due to the person who acquired them not by reason of the usurious money as instrumental cause, but on account of his own industry as principal cause. Wherefore he has more right to the goods acquired with usurious money than to the usurious money itself.

## FOURTH ARTICLE

### WHETHER IT IS LAWFUL TO BORROW MONEY UNDER A CONDITION OF USURY ?

*We proceed thus to the Fourth Article :—*

*Objection* 1. It would seem that it is not lawful to borrow money under a condition of usury. For the Apostle says (Rom. i. 32) that they *are worthy of death* . . . *not only they that do* these sins, *but they also that consent to them that do them.* Now he that borrows money under a condition of usury consents in the sin of the usurer, and gives him an occasion of sin. Therefore he sins also.

*Obj.* 2. Further, For no temporal advantage ought one to give another an occasion of committing a sin: for this pertains to active scandal, which is always sinful, as stated above (Q. XLIII., A. 2). Now he that seeks to borrow from a usurer gives him an occasion of sin. Therefore he is not to be excused on account of any temporal advantage.

*Obj.* 3. Further, It seems no less necessary sometimes to

deposit one's money with a usurer than to borrow from him. Now it seems altogether unlawful to deposit one's money with a usurer, even as it would be unlawful to deposit one's sword with a madman, a maiden with a libertine, or food with a glutton. Neither therefore is it lawful to borrow from a usurer.

*On the contrary*, He that suffers injury does not sin, according to the Philosopher (*Ethic.* v. 11), wherefore justice is not a mean between two vices, as stated in the same book (ch. 5). Now a usurer sins by doing an injury to the person who borrows from him under a condition of usury. Therefore he that accepts a loan under a condition of usury does not sin.

*I answer that*, It is by no means lawful to induce a man to sin, yet it is lawful to make use of another's sin for a good end, since even God uses all sin for some good, since He draws some good from every evil as stated in the *Enchiridion* (xi.). Hence when Publicola asked whether it were lawful to make use of an oath taken by a man swearing by false gods (which is a manifest sin, for he gives Divine honour to them) Augustine (*Ep.* xlvii.) answered that he who uses, not for a bad but for a good purpose, the oath of a man that swears by false gods, is a party, not to his sin of swearing by demons, but to his good compact whereby he kept his word. If however he were to induce him to swear by false gods, he would sin.

Accordingly we must also answer to the question in point that it is by no means lawful to induce a man to lend under a condition of usury: yet it is lawful to borrow for usury from a man who is ready to do so and is a usurer by profession; provided the borrower have a good end in view, such as the relief of his own or another's need. Thus too it is lawful for a man who has fallen among thieves to point out his property to them (which they sin in taking) in order to save his life, after the example of the ten men who said to Ismahel (Jerem. xli. 8): *Kill us not : for we have stores in the field.*

*Reply Obj.* 1. He who borrows for usury does not consent to the usurer's sin but makes use of it. Nor is it the usurer's

acceptance of usury that pleases him, but his lending, which
is good.

*Reply Obj.* 2. He who borrows for usury gives the usurer
an occasion, not for taking usury, but for lending; it is the
usurer who finds an occasion of sin in the malice of his heart.
Hence there is passive scandal on his part, while there is no
active scandal on the part of the person who seeks to borrow.
Nor is this passive scandal a reason why the other person
should desist from borrowing if he is in need, since this passive
scandal arises not from weakness or ignorance but from
malice.

*Reply Obj.* 3. If one were to entrust one's money to a
usurer lacking other means of practising usury; or with the
intention of making a greater profit from his money by
reason of the usury, one would be giving a sinner matter for
sin, so that one would be a participator in his guilt.   If, on
the other hand, the usurer to whom one entrusts one's money
has other means of practising usury, there is no sin in en-
trusting it to him that it may be in safer keeping, since this
is to use a sinner for a good purpose.

# QUESTION LXXIX.

## OF THE QUASI-INTEGRAL PARTS OF JUSTICE.

### (*In Four Articles.*)

WE must now consider the quasi-integral parts of justice, which are *to do good*, and *to decline from evil*, and the opposite vices. Under this head there are four points of inquiry: (1) Whether these two are parts of justice? (2) Whether transgression is a special sin? (3) Whether omission is a special sin? (4) Of the comparison between omission and transgression.

### First Article.

#### WHETHER TO DECLINE FROM EVIL AND TO DO GOOD ARE PARTS OF JUSTICE?

*We proceed thus to the First Article :—*

*Objection* 1. It would seem that to decline from evil and to do good are not parts of justice. For it belongs to every virtue to perform a good deed and to avoid an evil one. But parts do not exceed the whole. Therefore to decline from evil and to do good should not be reckoned parts of justice, which is a special kind of virtue.

*Obj.* 2. Further, A gloss on Ps. xxxiii. 15, *Turn away from evil and do good*, says: *The former*, i.e. to turn away from evil, *avoids sin, the latter*, i.e. to do good, *deserves the life and the palm*. But any part of a virtue deserves the life and the palm. Therefore to decline from evil is not a part of justice.

*Obj.* 3. Further, Things that are so related that one implies the other, are not mutually distinct as parts of a whole. Now declining from evil is implied in doing good: since no one does evil and good at the same time. Therefore declining from evil and doing good are not parts of justice.

*On the contrary*, Augustine (*De Correp. et Grat.* i.) declares that *declining from evil and doing good* belong to the justice of the law.

*I answer that,* If we speak of good and evil in general, it belongs to every virtue to do good and to avoid evil: and in this sense they cannot be reckoned parts of justice, except justice be taken in the sense of *all virtue*.* And yet even if justice be taken in this sense it regards a certain special aspect of good; namely, the good as due in respect of Divine or human law.

On the other hand justice considered as a special virtue regards good as due to one's neighbour. And in this sense it belongs to special justice to do good considered as due to one's neighbour, and to avoid the opposite evil, that, namely, which is hurtful to one's neighbour; while it belongs to general justice to do good in relation to the community or in relation to God, and to avoid the opposite evil.

Now these two are said to be quasi-integral parts of general or of special justice, because each is required for the perfect act of justice. For it belongs to justice to establish equality in our relations with others, as shown above (Q. LVIII., A. 2): and it pertains to the same cause to establish and to preserve that which it has established. Now a person establishes the equality of justice by doing good, i.e. by rendering to another his due: and he preserves the already established equality of justice by declining from evil, that is by inflicting no injury on his neighbour.

*Reply Obj.* 1. Good and evil are here considered under a special aspect, by which they are appropriated to justice. The reason why these two are reckoned parts of justice under a special aspect of good and evil, while they are not reckoned parts of any other moral virtue, is that the other moral virtues are concerned with the passions wherein to do good is to observe the mean, which is the same as to

* *Cf.* Q. LVIII., A. 5.

avoid the extremes as evils: so that doing good and avoiding evil come to the same, with regard to the other virtues. On the other hand justice is concerned with operations and external things, wherein to establish equality is one thing, and not to disturb the equality established is another.

*Reply Obj.* 2. To decline from evil, considered as a part of justice, does not denote a pure negation, viz. *not to do evil*; for this does not deserve the palm, but only avoids the punishment. But it implies a movement of the will in repudiating evil, as the very term *decline* shows. This is meritorious; especially when a person resists against an instigation to do evil.

*Reply Obj.* 3. Doing good is the completive act of justice, and the principal part, so to speak, thereof. Declining from evil is a more imperfect act, and a secondary part of that virtue. Hence it is a material part, so to speak, thereof, and a necessary condition of the formal and completive part.

## SECOND ARTICLE.

### WHETHER TRANSGRESSION IS A SPECIAL SIN ?

*We proceed thus to the Second Article :—*

*Objection* 1. It would seem that transgression is not a special sin. For no species is included in the definition of its genus. Now transgression is included in the definition of sin; because Ambrose says (*De Parad.* viii.) that sin is *a transgression of the Divine law*. Therefore transgression is not a species of sin.

*Obj.* 2. Further, No species is more comprehensive than its genus. But transgression is more comprehensive than sin, because sin is a *word, deed or desire against the law of God*, according to Augustine (*Contra Faust.* xxii. 27), while transgression is also against nature, or custom. Therefore transgression is not a species of sin.

*Obj.* 3. Further, No species contains all the parts into which its genus is divided. Now the sin of transgression extends to all the capital vices, as well as to sins of thought, word and deed. Therefore transgression is not a special sin.

*On the contrary,* It is opposed to a special virtue, namely justice.

*I answer that,* The term transgression is derived from bodily movement and applied to moral actions. Now a person is said to transgress in bodily movement, when he steps (*graditur*) beyond (*trans*) a fixed boundary:—and it is a negative precept that fixes the boundary that man must not exceed in his moral actions. Wherefore to transgress, properly speaking, is to act against a negative precept.

Now materially considered this may be common to all the species of sin, because man transgresses a Divine precept by any species of mortal sin. But if we consider it formally, namely under its special aspect of an act against a negative precept, it is a special sin in two ways. First, in so far as it is opposed to those kinds of sin that are opposed to the other virtues: for just as it belongs properly to legal justice to consider a precept as binding, so it belongs properly to a transgression to consider a precept as an object of contempt. Secondly, in so far as it is distinct from omission which is opposed to an affirmative precept.

*Reply Obj.* 1. Even as legal justice is *all virtue* (Q. LVIII., A. 5) as regards its subject and matter, so legal injustice is materially *all sin*. It is in this way that Ambrose defined sin, considering it from the point of view of legal injustice.

*Reply Obj.* 2. The natural inclination concerns the precepts of the natural law. Again, a laudable custom has the force of a precept, since as Augustine says in an epistle *on the Fast of the Sabbath* (*Ep.* xxxvi.), *a custom of God's people should be looked upon as law.* Hence both sin and transgression may be against a laudable custom and against a natural inclination.

*Reply Obj.* 3. All these species of sin may include transgression, if we consider them not under their proper aspects, but under a special aspect, as stated above. The sin of omission, however, is altogether distinct from the sin of transgression.

## THIRD ARTICLE.

### WHETHER OMISSION IS A SPECIAL SIN?

*We proceed thus to the Third Article :—*

*Objection* 1. It would seem that omission is not a special sin. For every sin is either original or actual. Now omission is not original sin, for it is not contracted through origin; nor is it actual sin, for it may be altogether without act, as stated above (I.-II., Q. LXXI., A. 5), when we were treating of sins in general. Therefore omission is not a special sin.

*Obj.* 2. Further, Every sin is voluntary. Now omission sometimes is not voluntary but necessary, as when a woman is violated after taking a vow of virginity, or when one loses that which one is under an obligation to restore, or when a priest is bound to say mass, and is prevented from doing so. Therefore omission is not always a sin.

*Obj.* 3. Further, It is possible to fix the time when any special sin begins. But this is not possible in the case of omission, since one is not altered by not doing a thing, no matter when the omission occurs, and yet the omission is not always sinful. Therefore omission is not a special sin.

*Obj.* 4. Further, Every special sin is opposed to a special virtue. But it is not possible to assign any special virtue to which omission is opposed, both because the good of any virtue can be omitted, and because justice, to which it would seem more particularly opposed, always requires an act, even in declining from evil, as stated above (A. 1, *ad* 2), while omission may be altogether without act. Therefore omission is not a special sin.

*On the contrary,* It is written (James iv. 17): *To him . . . who knoweth to do good, and doth it not, to him it is sin.*

*I answer that,* Omission signifies the non-fulfilment of a good, not indeed of any good, but of a good that is due. Now good under the aspect of due belongs properly to justice; to legal justice, if the thing due depends on Divine or human law; to special justice, if the due is something in relation

to one's neighbour.    Wherefore, in the same way as justice
is a special virtue, as stated above (Q. LVIII., AA. 6, 7),
omission is a special sin distinct from the sins which are
opposed to the other virtues; and just as doing good,
which is the opposite of omitting it, is a special part of justice,
distinct from avoiding evil, to which transgression is
opposed, so too is omission distinct from transgression.

*Reply Obj.* 1. Omission is not original but actual sin,
not as though it had some act essential to it, but for as much
as the negation of an act is reduced to the genus of act, and
in this sense non-action is a kind of action, as stated above
(I.-II., Q. LXXI., A. 6, *ad* 1).

*Reply Obj.* 2. Omission, as stated above, is only of such
good as is due and to which one is bound.    Now no man
is bound to the impossible: wherefore no man sins by omission, if he does not do what he cannot.    Accordingly she
who is violated after vowing virginity, is guilty of an omission, not through not having virginity, but through not re-
penting of her past sin, or through not doing what she can
to fulfil her vow by observing continence.    Again a priest
is not bound to say mass, except he have a suitable opportunity, and if this be lacking, there is no omission.    And in
like manner, a person is bound to restitution, supposing
he has the wherewithal; if he has not and cannot have it,
he is not guilty of an omission, provided he does what he
can.    The same applies to other similar cases.

*Reply Obj.* 3. Just as the sin of transgression is opposed
to negative precepts which regard the avoidance of evil,
so the sin of omission is opposed to affirmative precepts,
which regard the doing of good.    Now affirmative precepts
bind not for always, but for a fixed time, and at that time
the sin of omission begins.    But it may happen that then
one is unable to do what one ought, and if this inability is
without any fault on his part, he does not omit his duty, as
stated above (*ad* 2: I.-II., Q. LXXI., A. 5)    On the other
hand if this inability is due to some previous fault of his (for
instance, if a man gets drunk at night, and cannot get up
for matins, as he ought to), some say that the sin of omission

begins when he engages in an action that is illicit and incompatible with the act to which he is bound.  But this does not seem to be true, for supposing one were to rouse him by violence and that he went to matins, he would not omit to go, so that, evidently, the previous drunkenness was not an omission, but the cause of an omission.  Consequently, we must say that the omission begins to be imputed to him as a sin, when the time comes for the action; and yet this is on account of a preceding cause by reason of which the subsequent omission becomes voluntary.

*Reply Obj.* 4. Omission is directly opposed to justice, as stated above; because it is a non-fulfilment of a good of virtue, but only under the aspect of due, which pertains to justice.  Now more is required for an act to be virtuous and meritorious than for it to be sinful and demeritorious, because *good results from an entire cause, whereas evil arises from each single defect.*\* Wherefore the merit of justice requires an act, whereas an omission does not.

## FOURTH ARTICLE.

### WHETHER A SIN OF OMISSION IS MORE GRIEVOUS THAN A SIN OF TRANSGRESSION ?

*We proceed thus to the Fourth Article :—*

*Objection* 1. It would seem that a sin of omission is more grievous than a sin of transgression.  For *delictum* would seem to signify the same as *derelictum,*† and therefore is seemingly the same as an omission.  But *delictum* denotes a more grievous offence than transgression, because it deserves more expiation as appears from Lev. v.  Therefore the sin of omission is more grievous than the sin of transgression.

*Obj.* 2. Further, The greater evil is opposed to the greater good, as the Philosopher declares (*Ethic.* viii. 10).  Now to do good is a more excellent part of justice, than to decline from evil, to which transgression is opposed, as stated above (A. 1, *ad* 3).  Therefore omission is a graver sin than transgression.

*Obj.* 3. Further, Sins of transgression may be either venial

---

\* Dionysius, *De Div. Nom.* iv.   † Augustine, *QQ. in Levit.*, qu. xx.

or mortal.   But sins of omission seem to be always mortal, since they are opposed to an affirmative precept.   Therefore omission would seem to be a graver sin than transgression.

*Obj.* 4. Further, The pain of loss which consists in being deprived of seeing God and is inflicted for the sin of omission, is a greater punishment than the pain of sense, which is inflicted for the sin of transgression, as Chrysostom states (*Hom.* xxiii. *super Matth.*).   Now punishment is proportionate to fault.   Therefore the sin of omission is graver than the sin of transgression.

*On the contrary,* It is easier to refrain from evil deeds than to accomplish good deeds.   Therefore it is a graver sin not to refrain from an evil deed, i.e. *to transgress,* than not to accomplish a good deed, which is *to omit.*

*I answer that,* The gravity of a sin depends on its remoteness from virtue.   Now contrariety is the greatest remoteness, according to *Metaph.* x.*   Wherefore a thing is further removed from its contrary than from its simple negation; thus black is further removed from white than not-white is, since every black is not-white, but not conversely.   Now it is evident that transgression is contrary to an act of virtue while omission denotes the negation thereof: for instance it is a sin of omission, if one fail to give one's parents due reverence, while it is a sin of transgression to revile them or injure them in any way.   Hence it is evident that, simply and absolutely speaking, transgression is a graver sin than omission, although a particular omission may be graver than a particular transgression.

*Reply Obj.* 1. *Delictum* in its widest sense denotes any kind of omission; but sometimes it is taken strictly for the omission of something concerning God, or for a man's intentional and as it were contemptuous dereliction of duty: and then it has a certain gravity, for which reason it demands a greater expiation.

*Reply Obj.* 2. The opposite of *doing good* is both *not doing good,* which is an omission, and *doing evil,* which is a transgression: but the first is opposed by contradiction, the

* Didot ed. ix. 4.

second by contrariety, which implies greater remoteness: wherefore transgression is the more grievous sin.

*Reply Obj.* 3. Just as omission is opposed to affirmative precepts, so is transgression opposed to negative precepts: wherefore both, strictly speaking, have the character of mortal sin. Transgression and omission, however, may be taken broadly for any infringement of an affirmative or negative precept, disposing to the opposite of such precept: and so taking both in a broad sense they may be venial sins.

*Reply Obj.* 4. To the sin of transgression there correspond both the pain of loss on account of the aversion from God, and the pain of sense, on account of the inordinate conversion to a mutable good. In like manner omission deserves not only the pain of loss, but also the pain of sense, according to Matth. vii. 19, *Every tree that bringeth not forth good fruit shall be cut down, and shall be cast into the fire ;* and this on account of the root from which it grows, although it does not necessarily imply conversion to any mutable good.